MW01715873

J.B. HIXSON

The Great Last Days Apostasy

How the American Church Is Falling Away

NBW
ministries
with Dr. J.B. Hixson

First published by Not By Works, Inc. 2025

Copyright © 2025 by J.B. Hixson

All rights reserved. No part of this publication may be reproduced, stored or transmitted in any form or by any means, electronic, mechanical, photocopying, recording, scanning, or otherwise without written permission from the publisher. It is illegal to copy this book, post it to a website, or distribute it by any other means without permission.

Designations used by companies to distinguish their products are often claimed as trademarks. All brand names and product names used in this book and on its cover are trade names, service marks, trademarks and registered trademarks of their respective owners. The publishers and the book are not associated with any product or vendor mentioned in this book. None of the companies referenced within the book have endorsed the book.

All Scripture quotations taken from the New King James Version unless otherwise indicated.

Cover artwork and design by Brooke Hixson

Portions of this book have been adapted from the author's previously published works including books, articles, sermons, and interviews.

First edition

ISBN: 979-8-9858535-6-8

This book was professionally typeset on Reedsy.
Find out more at reedsy.com

To Billy J. Crosby, who taught me to believe the Bible is the Word of God.

"The church is so subnormal that if it ever got back to the New Testament normal it would seem to people to be abnormal."

~ Vance Havner

Contents

Preface

... and on this rock I will build My church, and the gates of Hades shall not prevail against it. (Matthew 16:18)

* * *

A lot has changed in the world since I first trusted in Jesus Christ as my personal Savior more than fifty years ago. It was a simpler time back then with fewer distractions. At least, that is the way I remember it. There was no Internet. There was very little on television. The allure of video games, which invaded mainstream culture when I was in my teens, thankfully never ensnared me. Being raised in a conservative Christian family, it was the church that occupied my time and played a central role in my everyday life as a young boy. If the doors were open, we were there.

I have fond memories of sitting in church singing beautiful hymns and listening to powerful sermons by solid, Bible-preaching pastors like Billy J. Crosby, to whom this book is dedicated. Brother Billy, as we called him, in typical Southern Baptist vernacular, was our pastor during my high school years and the man who licensed me to the ministry on June 2, 1985. This year marks my fortieth year in ministry. Brother Billy began every sermon with the words, "I believe the Bible is the Word of God." His conviction as he preached, and his passion for God's Word, left an impression that still resonates deep inside me today. He once said, "The Bible says it. I believe it. And that settles it." He later made this revision: "The Bible says it. And that settles it, whether I believe it or not!" As I heard those sermons as a young man, it was as if the Holy Spirit was talking directly to me.

My parents did not have to drag me to church. I *wanted* to go. I listened attentively. I took notes. I sang loudly, even harmonizing when I could. Over the years, the church's impact on my life has continued. Some of my closest friends have been in the church. The Lord called me into full-time ministry through the church. I met my amazing wife, Wendy, in church. The church remains a vital part of my life. I *love* the church. That is why it grieves me to see how far the church in America has drifted from its biblical and historical moorings. The church today looks nothing like the church of my youth, and call me nostalgic, but I miss Mayberry.

Ironically, it seems the closer we get to the return of the Lord, the further the church gets from Him. This should come as no surprise, since the Bible warns, "Now the Spirit expressly says that in latter times some will depart from the faith, giving heed to deceiving spirits and doctrines of demons" (1 Timothy 4:1). The term for this moral and spiritual decline within the church is *apostasy.* The American church today resembles the first-century church in Laodicea, to whom Jesus issued a stern rebuke. "I know your works, that you are neither cold nor hot. I could wish you were cold or hot. So then, because you are lukewarm, and neither cold nor hot, I will vomit you out of My mouth" (Revelation 3:15–16).

Jesus' reprimand of the lukewarm Laodiceans should not be construed to mean He was threatening them with the loss of eternal life. After all, *eternal* life, by definition, can never be lost. The believer's eternal salvation is secure from the moment he places his faith in Jesus Christ alone for eternal life. Christians are "sealed with the Holy Spirit of promise, who is the guarantee of our inheritance until the redemption of the purchased possession, to the praise of His glory" (Ephesians 1:13-14). Jesus promised, "And I give them eternal life, and they shall never perish; neither shall anyone snatch them out of My hand. My Father, who has given them to Me, is greater than all; and no one is able to snatch them out of My Father's hand" (John 10:28–29).

Rather, Jesus was reminding the Laodiceans of His discipline toward those Christians who fall away and become unuseful in the body of Christ. He used a metaphor that would have been clear to those in the Lycos Valley region (modern western Turkey), where Laodicea was located. The ancient city of Hierapolis, about 7.5 miles north of Laodicea, was known for its hot spring water. It was common for hot water from those springs to be brought south to Laodicea either in containers carried by horses or via an aqueduct. By the time it arrived, however, it was often lukewarm and had lost much of its medicinal value. Another city, Colossae, was 10.5 miles southeast of Laodicea. Colossae was known for its cold, refreshing drinking water.

The Christians in Laodicea were neither hot nor cold; they were like lukewarm water. Dr. Tom Constable explains, "Both the hot and the cold water were useful and effective. But lukewarm water was neither useful nor effective. Such was the condition of the Laodiceans." Jesus exhorted these believers who had fallen away, "As many as I love, I rebuke and chasten. Therefore be zealous and repent" (Revelation 3:19). Christians who fall away are missing out on the intimate fellowship and abundant joy that accompany a close walk with the Lord (Revelation 3:20; 1 John 1:4).

The American church today is following in the footsteps of the Laodiceans, and we too deserve the Lord's discipline. The Bible reminds us, "My son, do not despise the chastening of the Lord, nor detest His correction; for whom the Lord loves He corrects, just as a father the son in whom he delights" (Proverbs 3:11–12). The United States has done more than perhaps any other nation in world history to advance the Gospel. The fingerprints of the Lord are all over the founding and nearly 250-year history of this great country. Yet, the church is falling away, and we are reaping the consequences of our apostasy.

Not only is the sad situation in the American church today inviting God's discipline, but it also serves as yet another prophetic sign of the times. The church, which should be pointing to the nearness of Christ's return and sounding an alarm about the urgency of the hour, has itself become one of the biggest signs of the times. To paraphrase my friend and colleague, J.D. Farag, the church has become a victim of an exceedingly powerful *pull from the world* and an exceedingly great *love for the world*, both of which point to the soon coming *end of the world*. These days not only is the whole world under the sway of the wicked one (1 John 5:19), but the church is as well.

The church, which is called to shine like lights amid a crooked and perverse world (Philippians 2:15), has become virtually indistinguishable from the world. When Christians love the things of the world more than we love the Lord, we are no longer reflecting God's love to a world in desperate need of it. "Do not love the world or the things in the world. If anyone loves the world, the love of the Father is not in him. For all that is in the world—the lust of the flesh, the lust of the eyes, and the pride of life—is not of the Father but is of the world" (1 John 2:15–16).

When John wrote, "the love of the Father is not in" those who love the world, he was not suggesting that lovers of the world are not Christians. After all, anytime Christians sin we are evidencing a love for the world—and we all sin. Nothing can separate us from God's love positionally (Romans 8:37-39). We are in Christ, and our identity as a child of God is permanent (John 1:12; 1 Peter 1:3-5). Yet, if we are not abiding in Christ (Gk. *menō*, remaining in close fellowship), we are not reflecting God's love. "But whoever has this world's goods, and sees his brother in need, and shuts up his heart from him, how does the love of God abide in him" (1 John 3:17)?

On the very night Jesus was betrayed and arrested, He instructed the disciples to abide in Him by keeping His commandments. He said,

> *Abide in Me, and I in you. As the branch cannot bear fruit of itself, unless it abides in the vine, neither can you, unless you abide in Me. I am the vine, you are the branches. He who abides in Me, and I in him, bears much fruit; for without Me you can do nothing. ...If you keep My commandments, you will abide in My love, just as I have kept My Father's commandments and abide in His love (John 15:4-5, 10).*

Sadly, two thousand years later, the church in America is not abiding in Christ; we are abandoning Him.

It is nearly impossible to miss the cavalcade of signs pointing to the end of the world as we know it. Even the secular world, with little or no knowledge of the Bible, is taking notice. The *Bulletin of the Atomic Scientists*, by no means a bastion of biblical truth, warns we are living in "a moment of historic danger." Their Doomsday Clock is a metaphor that advises the public about how close we are to destroying our world with dangerous technologies and unchecked scientific "advancements." Midnight on the clock represents doomsday.

The farthest the clock has been from midnight is seventeen minutes in 1991, reflecting the global optimism spawned by the end of the Cold War. As recently as 2012, the Doomsday Clock was set to five minutes before midnight. By 2015, it had advanced to three minutes before midnight, and in 2023 it moved to ninety seconds before midnight. On January 28, 2025, the clock was moved to *eighty-nine seconds before midnight*, the closest it has ever been to doomsday. A rekindled cold war, a global pandemic, deep-rooted division, populist uprisings, unprecedented natural disasters, a flailing world economy, a rising technocracy with its corresponding depopulation agenda, terrorist attacks (both real and manufactured), and other portentous developments foretell ominous days on the horizon.

In my previous three books, I examined a litany of signs setting the stage for the coming Great Satanic Reset and the Luciferian New World Order. The Bible refers to these signs as the "spirit of the Antichrist" (1 John 4:3). The three-volume series, *Spirit of the Antichrist Volumes One* and *Two* and *Spirit of the False Prophet*, focused on the activities of Satan and his earthly accomplices as they seek to establish global dominance politically, economically, and religiously. In this present work, we shift our attention to the church. Are there indications within the church, particularly the church in the United States, that we are getting ever so close to the return of the Lord?

Just as the Bible predicts evil forces within the global elite will conspire to take over the world (cf. Psalm 2), preparing the way for the Antichrist, it also foresees a time when the church will grow cold and become more and more like the world the closer we get to the end of the age. "For the time will come when they will not endure sound doctrine, but according to their own desires, because they have itching ears, they will heap up for themselves teachers; and they will turn their ears away from the truth, and be turned aside to fables" (2 Timothy 4:3–4). The Lord himself warned, "Many false prophets will rise up and deceive many. And because lawlessness will abound, the love of many will grow cold" (Matthew 24:11–12). Peter foresaw a time when false teachers would infiltrate the church and bring in "destructive heresies" (2 Peter 2:1).

It is evident both biblically and anecdotally that the world is becoming a darker and darker place. Paul stated plainly, "But evil men and impostors will grow worse and worse, deceiving and being deceived" (2 Timothy 3:13). Depravity is, after all, a degenerative disease. It does not get better with time. Satan is the god of this age (Galatians 1:4), and the more time he has to wreak havoc the worse things will get. Even a cursory glance at the world around us indicates evil has cascaded to a magnitude heretofore unseen in the world. Many authors and teachers within the Bible prophecy arena, myself included, have highlighted these external signs of the times through books, conferences, interviews, and more.

My goal in writing *The Great Last Days Apostasy* is to expose one of the most obvious, yet neglected, prophetic signs of the times: apostasy in the church. In our fixation with geopolitical, technological, economic, and other developments that point to the looming New World Order, is it possible we have failed to peer inside our stained-glass windows and steepled buildings to examine the state of the church? As hard as such self-reflection may be, it is vital for such a time as this. Addressing apostasy in the church has at least three worthy benefits.

First, it may lead to repentance on the part of some believers who have drifted away from the Lord in their Christian journey. Remember Jesus' admonition to the lukewarm Laodiceans. "Therefore be zealous and repent" (Revelation 3:19). It is paradoxical to me that so many Christians who have an interest in Bible prophecy are simultaneously neglecting their personal spiritual growth. Can immature Christians ever really be well-grounded in eschatology? It seems like many Christians are leaning over their skis, to use a Colorado metaphor, with their interest in Bible prophecy and disinterest in other spiritual disciplines. God's Word encourages us to "Abide in Him, that when He appears, we may have confidence and not be ashamed before Him at His coming" (1 John 2:28). Before we can look eagerly for the Lord's return, we must first look inwardly at our walk with Him. By examining the state of the church perhaps we will encourage some lukewarm believers to grow in their faith.

Second, focusing on the worsening apostasy in the American church will add to the already considerable catalog of signs pointing to the nearness of Christ's return. This in turn will encourage students of Bible prophecy to "eagerly anticipate" the Rapture, as Scripture exhorts us to do (Romans 8:19, 23, 25; 1 Corinthians 1:7; Galatians 5:5; Philippians 3:20; Hebrews 9:28). There are mixed emotions here, of course. While we are saddened by how far the bride of Christ has drifted from the Bridegroom, we are nevertheless energized by the implications of such apostasy. This is true of all prophetic signs of the times.

For example, we are concerned about the burgeoning global technocracy that I addressed in my previous book, *Spirit of the False Prophet: Rise of the Global Technocracy,* but we know the construction of a planetary control and surveillance grid is necessary for the Antichrist's regime, which means Christ's return is nearer than ever before. We cringe at the drumbeats of war that portend end times battles like the one in Ezekiel 38-39, yet we are encouraged that all these things must take place before the arrival of the great and glorious Kingdom of our Lord. As we observe the world, and the church, falling apart, we realize things are coming together precisely as God's Word predicts.

Third, studying the biblical principle of apostasy reminds us that even though many Christians will fall away, the church will prevail in the end. It is, after all, the Lord's church, and there is always a remnant. (I will have more to say about the remnant principle in Chapter Two.) Jesus told Peter, "And I also say to you that you are Peter, and on this rock I will build My church, and the gates of Hades shall not prevail against it" (Matthew 16:18). Peter failed miserably the night Jesus was betrayed and arrested, and yet he later became a powerful witness for Christ in the early church. Likewise, the church itself, notwithstanding its current apostate condition, will one day play a prominent role in the glorious earthly Kingdom when Christ returns to take the throne.

As always, I encourage you to read this book with a critical eye and analyze everything through the lens of Scripture. If you have questions or comments along the way, please reach out to us here at the NBW Ministries office. My staff and I would love to hear from you. You can reach us online at *NotByWorks.org*.

Thank you for reading *The Great Last Days Apostasy*. I hope you learn a few things from this book, but mostly I hope you come to know the Lord Jesus as your personal Savior if you do not already know Him. This happens the instant you place your faith in Jesus Christ, the Son of God, Who died and rose again to pay your personal penalty for sin. He alone has the power to forgive sin and give you the free gift of eternal life.

If you are already a Christian, I pray you will recognize afresh the amazing love of our Lord, Who loves the church even in its dire state. May this book alert you to the serious problems within the American church today, call your attention to further signs of the times indicating the nearness of Christ's return, and awaken in you a desire to see the church be found "without spot and blameless at our Lord Jesus Christ's appearing" (1 Timothy 6:14).

J.B.H.

Acknowledgments

I wish to thank the following people:

- Wendy, the love of my life and my best friend, whose fingerprints of excellence are all over this ministry.
- Brooke for her diligence serving NBW Ministries, her amazing creative talent, and her help editing this book.
- Lacey, the quiet servant, for her faithful and gracious service to NBW Ministries.
- Zoe for making me smile no matter how stressed I am.
- My family for their patience with me while I worked on this book and attended to other ministry demands.
- Our NBW supporters whose faithful prayers and generous financial gifts make it possible for us to advance the clear, accurate, and urgent Gospel message every day.
- My church family for their ministry partnership.
- My parents for their steady stream of encouragement and for undergirding this ministry with prayer.
- My readers for your encouraging emails, texts, posts, and calls. You are a blessing to me and my family!
- All the churches I have served over the years for the shared joys and pains alike, that have guided and shaped me in this journey.
- All those who have unknowingly helped frame the discussion in this book through conversations we have had.

1

FALLING AWAY

Now the Spirit expressly says that in latter times some will depart from the faith, giving heed to deceiving spirits and doctrines of demons. (1 Timothy 4:1)

* * *

Stanley Kubrick produced or directed some of Hollywood's most iconic movies before his untimely death in 1999. I have followed his work for years because he, like many insiders in the entertainment industry, was well connected to the dark underworld of the Luciferian elite. Using symbolic or subtle messages, Kubrick's films often expose in veiled (or not-so-veiled) ways what is going on behind the curtain in shadowy, smoke-filled rooms where planetary power brokers, working hand in puppet with Satan, gather to conjure up their wicked schemes. One such movie is *Dr. Strangelove,* which satirically exposes the risks and realities of nuclear war during the Cold War era. Released in 1964, it remains the highest-ranked Kubrick film of all time on Rotten Tomatoes with a 98% rating. The American Film Institute ranks *Dr. Strangelove* third on its list of funniest all-time American movies.

The film stars George C. Scott, Peter Sellers (who plays three separate roles), Slim Pickens, and James Earl Jones, among others. There is a little-known story that comes out of the filming of *Dr. Strangelove.* George C.

Scott plays Buck Turgidson, a brash and paranoid U.S. Army general serving as the Chairman of the Joint Chiefs of Staff. In the War Room, with other assembled brass, he frantically advises the President (played by Sellers) on how best to stop a rogue General from dropping nuclear bombs on the Soviet Union. In one scene, Scott walks backwards as he is talking, trips, rolls seamlessly and athletically back onto his feet, and continues his line.

The fall was completely unscripted; Scott genuinely stumbled. He was a professional, however, so rather than ruin the take, he improvised, creating a moment of authentic physical comedy. Since it fit perfectly with the lampooning genre of the film, Kubrick left it in. Some falls are unscripted yet comical, like Buck Turgidson's in *Dr. Strangelove.* Others are scripted but not humorous at all, like most of Jack Tripper's falls on the sitcom, *Three's Company*. In the last days of the church age, Christians are falling in unprecedented numbers, not physically, but spiritually. They are falling away from the faith. This fall is clearly scripted in the New Testament, and like Jack Tripper clumsily falling out of a hammock, it really is not funny at all. On the contrary, this significant falling away among Christians is serious, and it constitutes a major prophetic sign of the times.

The Departure

The word *apostasy* is used in theological terminology to refer to falling away from the faith. The Bible predicts a great apostasy near the end of the church age. "Now the Spirit expressly says that in latter times some will depart from the faith, giving heed to deceiving spirits and doctrines of demons" (1 Timothy 4:1). "But know this, that in the last days perilous times will come. ...For the time will come when they will not endure sound doctrine, but according to their own desires, because they have itching ears, they will heap up for themselves teachers; and they will turn their ears away from the truth, and be turned aside to fables" (2 Timothy 3:1; 4:3–4).

Apostasy comes from the Greek word, *apostasia*. It is used only twice in the New Testament. The first instance is in Acts 21:21 where Paul is accused of teaching the Jews to "forsake" (*apostasia*) the law of Moses. The second instance is in 2 Thessalonians 2:3 where Paul assures the Thessalonian believers they could not be in the prophetic day of the Lord's wrath since the "falling away" (*apostasia*) had not happened yet. Many Bible teachers point to 2 Thessalonians 2:3 as further support for the prophetic last days apostasy in the church. "Let no one deceive you by any means; for that Day will not come unless the falling away comes first, and the man of sin is revealed, the son of perdition" (2 Thessalonians 2:3). However, I do not believe that is what Paul means in this instance.

The word *apostasia* means simply "departure." As with all words, context must determine the precise meaning. Departure from what? In some cases, *apostasia* means spiritual departure (i.e., falling away or departing from the faith). And in other cases, *apostasia* means physical departure (i.e., moving from point A to point B). In the first century, we see *apostasia* used by the historian, Josephus, in a political sense to signify a rebellion against civil authority. However, the term was also used during this time to describe a fever departing from an ill person, a boat departing from a dock, etc.

The term *apostasia* is used in the Greek translation of the Old Testament mostly for departing from the Law of Moses (cf. 2 Chron 29:19; 33:19; Jer 2:19). In the New Testament, the noun is used only twice, as I mentioned above. But the verb form of the word, *aphístēmi,* is used fifteen times. There is no difference between the basic meaning of the noun and the verb. They both mean *departure* (or *depart* in the verb form). Sometimes it refers to a spiritual departure from religious teachings or a philosophical rebellion against civil authority (cf. *aphístēmi* in Acts 5:37-38). Other times it refers to a physical departure. The verb form *aphístēmi* is used most often for physical departure. For example, in Acts 12:10, after an angel had freed Peter from prison and led him past the guard posts, Luke tells us, "immediately the angel departed (*aphístēmi*) from him." And in Acts 15:38, Paul told Barnabas he did not want to take John Mark with them on their second missionary journey because Mark had "departed (*aphístēmi*) from them" during the first journey.

Getting back to 2 Thessalonians 2:3, the context indicates Paul is referring to a physical departure; namely, the Rapture. Paul makes several references to physical movement within the passage. For instance, in 2 Thessalonians 2:1 the Lord *comes* in the sky (cf. 1 Thessalonians 4:13-18) and believers are *gathered together to Him*. Further, Paul refers to the restrainer being *taken out of the way* (2:7). He also speaks of the *coming* (or arrival) of the Antichrist on the world scene (2:9). So, there is a lot of *physical movement* going on in this passage. Moreover, in light of Paul's teaching about the Rapture in his first letter to the Thessalonians, and his insistence twice in that letter that the Thessalonian Christians would not be left on earth during the outpouring of God's prophetic wrath (1 Thessalonians 1:10; 5:9), it seems natural to conclude that in his second letter he would remind them again they could not be in the Day of the Lord yet because the *apostasia* (i.e., the departure from earth to heaven—the Rapture!) had not happened yet.

Here is how I would paraphrase Paul's teaching in 2 Thessalonians 2:1-12.

> *My Thessalonian brethren... concerning the Lord's coming to rescue us from the Day of the Lord's wrath, which I have already told you about in my first letter, I ask you not to be worried or shaken in your faith. I realize that some false teachers are suggesting that the Day of the Lord has already begun and that you are about to face the full force of God's wrath on earth. But don't believe it! Don't be deceived. Remember, as I said before, the Day of the Lord will not begin until after you depart from this earth! And not only that, but before the Day of the Lord can begin, the man of sin—the Antichrist—must be unveiled first.*
>
> *Since neither of these things has happened—the departure and the revelation of the Antichrist—you cannot possibly be in the Day of the Lord. So, fear not! And be aware that when the Antichrist does come, after you have all been rescued from this present evil age (Galatians 1:4), he will bring terrible deception and lying wonders on the earth and many will perish because they never believed the Gospel.*

Considering all the evidence: exegetical, lexical, contextual, and theological, I think it is best to take the word *apostasia* in 2 Thessalonians 2:3 as a reference to a physical departure, namely the Rapture. This view is shared by other scholars such as J. Dwight Pentecost, Andy Woods, Kenneth Wuest, Allan MacRae, E. Schuyler English, Stanley Ellison, H. Wayne House, and others.

Apostasy in the Last Days

Nevertheless, even though 2 Thessalonians 2:3 does not refer to a spiritual apostasy in the last days, it is clear from other passages there will indeed be a great last days apostasy near the end of the church age. I cited some of these passages earlier. "Now the Spirit expressly says that in latter times some will depart from the faith, giving heed to deceiving spirits and doctrines of demons" (1 Timothy 4:1). "But know this, that in the last days perilous times will come. ...For the time will come when they will not endure sound doctrine, but according to their own desires, because they have itching ears, they will heap up for themselves teachers; and they will turn their ears away from the truth, and be turned aside to fables" (2 Timothy 3:1; 4:3–4).

The phrase "last days" (or sometimes "last hour") refers to the present church age. The church age, which we will discuss in greater detail in the next chapter, constitutes the final age before the coming Kingdom [See Figure 1]. In that sense, these are indeed the last days.

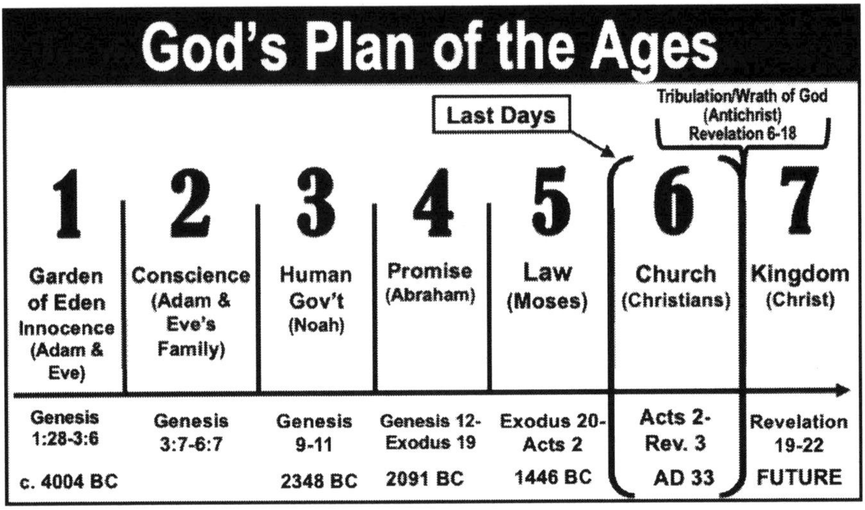

Figure 1

The writer of Hebrews confirms this. He wrote, "God, who at various times and in various ways spoke in time past to the fathers by the prophets, has in these *last days* spoken to us by His Son, whom He has appointed heir of all things, through whom also He made the worlds" (Hebrews 1:1–2, italics added). The Apostle John explained, "Little children, it is the *last hour*; and as you have heard that the Antichrist is coming, even now many antichrists have come, by which we know that it is the *last hour*" (1 John 2:18, italics added).

The Lord himself taught, "Many false prophets will rise up and deceive many. And because lawlessness will abound, the love of many will grow cold" (Matthew 24:11–12). Jesus gave this prophecy as part of His larger Olivet Discourse, which is addressed to the future generation of unbelieving Jews left behind on earth after the Rapture. In this sermon, Jesus warns them not to be deceived by the coming Antichrist. Although Jesus is not referring directly to the church age here, it is worth noting the events Jesus discusses in the Olivet Discourse, such as the rise of false prophets in their midst, will not begin instantly, like the flipping of a switch. They will be the culmination of a gradual and increasing onslaught of apostasy that begins during the church age and reaches a crescendo just prior to the Rapture.

Peter predicted false teachers would infiltrate the church and bring in "destructive heresies" (2 Peter 2:1). This has been happening since the earliest days of the church. Paul's first letter was written to address apostates who had crept into the Galatian churches in AD 48-49. He told these young believers, "I marvel that you are turning away so soon from Him who called you in the grace of Christ, to a different gospel, which is not another; but *there are some who trouble you and want to pervert the gospel of Christ*" (Galatians 1:6–7, italics added). In other words, these false teachers had departed from the pure Gospel. Later Paul warned Timothy, "But evil men and impostors will grow worse and worse, deceiving and being deceived. But you must continue in the things which you have learned and been assured of... [i.e., you must not *depart* from them]" (2 Timothy 3:13–14).

Shipwrecked in the Faith

It is always a serious thing when a Christian drifts away from the Lord, or worse, intentionally walks away from the faith. The Apostle Paul refers to those who do so as "suffering shipwreck" concerning the faith (1 Timothy 1:19). Hymenaeus and Alexander are examples of early Christians who did this, and consequently, they experienced serious discipline from the Lord (1 Timothy 1:20). Hymenaeus is singled out a second time by Paul, along with another early believer, Philetus, for having "strayed concerning the truth" (2 Timothy 2:17-18).

Another example of Christians straying from the faith comes from the Book of Hebrews. In the late 60s AD, a group of Jewish Christians were facing intensifying persecution under Roman Emperor Nero. Christians were being blamed for upsetting the *Pax Romana*—Roman Peace. At the time, the unbelieving Jewish community was still largely in good standing with Rome; it was the Christians who were the primary scapegoats. Thus, many Christian Jews were contemplating abandoning their association with Christianity, or, as it was called in that day, "The Way," and reverting to their Jewish customs. They were "forsaking the assembly" with the church and disavowing any connection with the Christian faith (Hebrews 10:25).

The author of Hebrews presents a lengthy and compelling treatise to convince these early Christians to "hold fast their confession" (Hebrews 10:23). He pointed out there are great blessings associated with standing firm for the faith, even amid painful persecution. "Therefore do not cast away your confidence, which has great reward," he pleaded (Hebrews 10:35). Christians who persevere in the faith until the end of their lives will be rewarded with special positions of authority in the Kingdom one day, and they will hear their Savior say, "Well done, good and faithful servant" (Luke 19:11-27; Hebrews 11:6).

The warning passages throughout Hebrews, though stern, should not be interpreted as threatening the loss of salvation. Rather, they express the reality of God's discipline in the life of a believer. The writer concludes his letter with this reminder, "For the Lord disciplines the one he loves, and chastises every son whom he receives" (Hebrews 12:6, ESV). And he adds, "Now no chastening seems to be joyful for the present, but painful; nevertheless, afterward it yields the peaceable fruit of righteousness to those who have been trained by it" (Hebrews 12:11).

Hebrews is about discipline, not punishment. The Lord will never punish His children with hellfire, even if they fall away from Him. Jesus promised the believer "shall never come into judgment" (John 5:24) and Paul said, "There is therefore now no condemnation to those who are in Christ Jesus..." (Romans 8:1). Figure 2 below explains the difference between God's discipline and God's punishment.

GOD'S PUNISHMENT	GOD'S DISCIPLINE
For UNBELIEVERS	For BELIEVERS
Exercised in JUSTICE	Exercised in GRACE
Because they REJECTED CHRIST	Because we DISOBEYED.
Involves God's WRATH	Involves God's LOVE
NOT for their GOOD	FOR our GOOD
For their CONDEMNATION	For our CORRECTION
NOW and in ETERNITY	Only on EARTH

Figure 2

Apostasy and Eternal Salvation

Unfortunately, some Bible teachers have suggested the writer of Hebrews is threatening believers with the loss of their salvation if they fail to stand firm in the faith. Not only is this idea foreign to the Book of Hebrews, but it also flies in the face of the clear teaching of the Bible as a whole. Our eternal salvation is in no way contingent upon our behavior or our ability to persevere. It is "not by works or righteousness which we have done, but according to His mercy He saved us" (Titus 3:5). "For by grace you have been saved through faith, and that not of yourselves; it is the gift of God, not of works, lest anyone should boast" (Ephesians 2:8–9). If entrance into heaven were gained by perseverance, Christians would have something to boast about. But it is not. We are justified, "freely by His grace" (Romans 3:24). Paul said, "But God forbid that I should boast except in the cross of our Lord Jesus Christ..." (Galatians 6:14).

Our eternal salvation is a free gift of God's grace, and like all gifts, it must be freely offered and freely received. If it is not free, it is not grace. "And if by grace, then it is no longer of works; otherwise grace is no longer grace.

But if it is of works, it is no longer grace; otherwise work is no longer work" (Romans 11:6). We cannot work for our eternal salvation. "Now to him who works, the wages are not counted as grace but as debt. But to him who does not work but believes on Him who justifies the ungodly, his faith is accounted for righteousness" (Romans 4:4-5). A gift that is never received does not become yours. We receive the gift of eternal life simply by faith alone in Christ alone, Who died and rose again to pay our penalty for sin. "Therefore, having been justified by faith, we have peace with God through our Lord Jesus Christ" (Romans 5:1). "But as many as received Him, to them He gave the right to become children of God, to those who believe in His name" (John 1:12).

For many Christians, the thought that a believer who denies the faith at some point in his life will still go to heaven is a bridge too far. They cannot wrap their hands around it because they wrongly assume an action as serious as denying the faith will cause God to go back on His Word. Such an emotional perspective is common, but it is wholly unbiblical and illogical. It evidences a lack of understanding of both God's grace and the believer's eternal salvation. Our eternal salvation is not a bilateral contract between us and God, according to which if we persevere in the faith until the end of our lives we get into heaven. On the contrary, eternal salvation is a unilateral gift. It is free to us, paid for by the blood of our Savior, and received solely by faith. Once we receive eternal life, it can never be lost.

According to Jesus, we get eternal life the very moment we place our faith in Him. "Most assuredly, I say to you, he who believes in Me has everlasting life," He proclaimed (John 6:47). Elsewhere He said, "And I give them eternal life, and they shall never perish; neither shall anyone snatch them out of My hand. My Father, who has given them to Me, is greater than all; and no one is able to snatch them out of My Father's hand" (John 10:28–29). In other words, eternal life is a present possession, not a future possibility. We do not have to wait until we die to receive eternal life; we get it the moment we believe the Gospel! The Bible says, "In Him you also trusted, after you heard the word of truth, the gospel of your salvation; in whom also, having believed, you were sealed with the Holy Spirit of promise, who is the guarantee of our inheritance until the redemption of the purchased possession, to the praise of His glory" (Ephesians 1:13–14). Since eternal life is a present possession, by definition, it can never be lost, or else it was never *eternal* to begin with.

The Seriousness of Apostasy

Although denying the faith can never send a Christian to hell, it is, like all sin, very serious. Denying the faith may seem like an extreme degree of sin, but all sin in the life of a believer is awful. The earthly consequences can be devastating, Sin destroys lives, forfeits blessings, sets a horrible example, and brings the Lord's discipline. It is not as if God is okay with sins like jealousy, anger, or lust, but when it comes to apostasy, He draws the line! God hates *all* sin, and *all* sin breaks fellowship with the Lord. "If we say that we have fellowship with Him, and walk in darkness, we lie and do not practice the truth" (1 John 1:6).

Thankfully, there is no sin that can reach beyond God's grace, even apostasy. "But where sin abounded, grace abounded much more…" (Romans 5:20). God's word directly promises that even Christians who deny the faith are still part of His family, and He will never deny them. "If we are faithless, He remains faithful; He cannot deny Himself" (2 Timothy 2:13). The phrase "are faithless" in Greek is literally "stop believing." Simply put, even if a Christian drifts so far away from the Lord that he stops believing in Him, his identity in Christ is secure. Earlier, I referred to Hymenaeus and Philetus as examples of early Christians who fell away (2 Timothy 2:17-18). In that same context, Paul writes, "Nevertheless the solid foundation of God stands, having this seal: 'The Lord knows those who are His,' and, 'Let everyone who names the name of Christ depart from iniquity'" (2 Timothy 2:19).

What Paul means is that Christians should depart from iniquity, not the Lord. But even if we depart from the Lord and cozy up to iniquity, God knows we belong to Him. We have His seal. "In Him you also trusted, after you heard the word of truth, the gospel of your salvation; in whom also, having believed, you were sealed with the Holy Spirit of promise, who is the guarantee of our inheritance until the redemption of the purchased possession, to the praise of His glory" (Ephesians 1:13–14). In the first century, seals were used to indicate ownership. As the late Gordon Fee, a notable New Testament scholar, explains, "[Paul had in mind] the 'seal' of ownership that the architect or owner would have inscribed on the foundation stone, similar in some ways to our modern cornerstones." Even if a Christian departs from the faith, God's seal remains, and he is eternally secure.

Does Apostasy Mean You Were Never Saved?

There is one more aspect of apostasy that we need to address. Some Bible teachers who agree that our eternal salvation is secure and can never be lost, nevertheless erroneously suggest that apostasy is an indication a person was never really saved to begin with. "Anyone who denies the faith was never a Christian in the first place," the argument goes. According to this view, which emanates from a Calvinist perspective, all "true" Christians will persevere in the faith until the end of their lives. A faith that fails to persevere, they say, cannot rightly be considered *saving* faith. It is *defective* faith. Or in Calvinist jargon, so-called *spurious* faith. This alleged indefectibility of saving faith is commonly referred to by Calvinists as the doctrine of *the perseverance of the saints*. This view is articulated by the famous early 20th-century reformed theologian Louis Berkhof,

> *The doctrine of the perseverance of the saints is to the effect that [Christians] can neither totally nor finally fall away from that state, but shall certainly persevere therein to the end and be eternally saved. ... It should be noted first of all that the doctrine is not merely to the effect that the elect will certainly be saved in the end ...but teaches very specifically that they who have once been regenerated and effectually called by God to a state of grace, can never completely fall from that state...*

Berkhof's explanation of the doctrine of the perseverance of the saints is in keeping with a multitude of Calvinist teachings on this matter. Unfortunately, it is decidedly *not* in keeping with the teaching of Scripture.

As I have discussed above, this view is wrong on its face, since Scripture directly addresses the reality that some believers may in fact fall away from the faith. A natural outgrowth of this false teaching is it invites believers to question the very reality of the saving faith they expressed. It encourages them to look at their actions as the basis for assurance since only those who persevere until the end of their lives are *truly* saved. This false teaching eliminates the possibility of assurance and goads Christians into questioning the validity of their salvation. Since it is impossible to know if one will persevere to the end until the moment of death, Christians under the sway of this teaching spend their lives wondering if their faith is genuine. "Is my faith real? Will it really get me to heaven?" they wonder. "I guess I'll have to wait and see. Fingers crossed!"

To suggest that a person cannot know whether he has really believed the Gospel until the time of his death is not only unbiblical, but it is also illogical. It is a nomological fallacy to suggest we cannot know with certainty whether we have believed something or not. The Bible teaches we can most certainly know we have believed the Gospel. Paul writes, "For this reason I also suffer these things; nevertheless I am not ashamed, for I know whom I have believed and am persuaded that He is able to keep what I have committed to Him until that Day" (2 Timothy 1:12). Notice the strong language here. "I *know* whom I have believed," and I am "*persuaded.*" Notice also it is God who keeps us saved, not our perseverance. Lewis Sperry Chafer resoundingly refutes the ridiculous notion that we cannot know whether we have really believed until the end of our lives.

> *It is quite possible for any intelligent person to know whether he has placed such confidence in the Savior. Saving faith is a matter of personal consciousness. "I know whom I have believed." To have deposited one's eternal welfare in the hands of another is a decision of the mind so definite that it can hardly be confused with anything else. On this*

deposit of oneself into His saving grace depends one's eternal destiny.

For a person to question whether his belief is real is evidence of serious psychological confusion, and it has no place in the Christian life. The only question we need ever ask is, "Have I believed the Gospel?" Not, "Is my faith real?!"

It is hard to overstate the devastating impact of this false teaching on the lives of believers since it first echoed from the Synod of Dort in 17th century Western Netherlands. It leads to an unproductive and defeated Christian life. It causes unfounded fear. It obscures God's amazing grace with works. It is stunning that this false teaching has been so readily adopted. After all, more than 160 times the New Testament unambiguously conditions our eternal life upon faith alone in Christ alone [See Appendix A]. The very moment a person believes the Gospel, he is reborn spiritually, adopted into the family of God, and eternally saved. What is the Gospel? Jesus Christ died and rose again to pay your personal penalty for sin. Only He has the power to forgive sin and give you the free gift of eternal life. If you trust in Him and Him alone for that gift, you are saved! Full stop! Rest in that assurance and stop wondering and waiting to see how you end up. You have no reason to doubt what Jesus said. "Most assuredly, I say to you, he who believes in Me has everlasting life" (John 6:47).

A Sign of the Times

With that foundation about the meaning of apostasy, we turn now in the chapters ahead to a survey of several ways the church in America is falling away from the historical and biblical Christian faith. As we have seen, this large-scale apostasy in the last days is a biblical sign of the times. There has been a slow and steady drift away from orthodoxy that began in earnest in America around the turn of the 20th century with the rise of higher criticism and liberalism in the colleges and seminaries. In the last twenty years, this slow drift has become a precipitous departure that heralds the end of the age.

According to Steve Osunsami and Sean Keane, in an article entitled, *Churches Fight to Stay Open as Attendance Dwindles,* "In 2019, before the COVID-19 pandemic, America was losing as many as 1,000 churches a year." As bad as that sounds, it has only gotten worse. After the Trump administration locked down churches in early 2020, forbidding Christians from worshipping the Lord on Resurrection Sunday for the first time in the history of our country, many churches never recovered. Osunsami and Keane point out,

> *Some former churches are being converted for business or residential use. One old Methodist church in Atlanta, which was down to about 60 members when it closed, was sold to a luxury real estate developer.... Now, it's become a series of 3,000-square-foot condos. Some of the oldest churches in the world have even turned into bars and nightclubs.*

What happened across Western Europe toward the end of the 20th century has made its way to the shores of America. We are witnessing a profound apostasy in the American church.

In the chapters that follow, we will explore seven ways the American church is falling away. These are: biblically, eschatologically, morally, socially, evangelistically, academically, and politically. As discouraging as this is, let us not forget that the more the church falls apart the more Bible prophecy is coming together. In the closing chapter we will discuss where we go from here. Before we get to these seven ways the American church is falling away, we have one more foundational subject to address. To understand apostasy in the church, we must have a clear understanding of what the church is supposed to look like. What is the church? We will answer that in the next chapter.

2

WHAT IS THE CHURCH?

And He put all things under His feet, and gave Him to be head over all things to the church, which is His body, the fullness of Him who fills all in all. (Ephesians 1:22–23)

* * *

In the 1890s, at a small church in Mayfield, Kentucky, two deacons were always bickering with each other. They just simply could not get along. Their quarreling came to a head one Sunday when one of them innocently installed a small wooden peg on the wall at the back of the church. He thought it would be nice for the pastor to have a place to hang his hat. Although it seemed like a benign act done out of love for the pastor, the other deacon was offended that he had not been consulted. When the other deacon discovered what his rival had done, he was furious. "How dare you put a peg in the church wall without checking with me first!" he fumed.

As word got out about this latest disagreement, church members began taking sides. "That's just like old Joe to take matters into his own hands," some grumbled. "Old Bob must not like our pastor if he doesn't want him to have a place to hang his hat," muttered others. Soon factions began to form. Some thought installing the peg was a tribute to the pastor; others thought it desecrated the sanctuary. Eventually, the feud split the congregation, and many people left to start their own church. Legend has it, to this day the residents of Mayfield still refer to the two churches as Peg Baptist Church and Anti-Peg Baptist Church!

I do not know whether that story is rooted in historical fact or myth, but I would not be at all surprised if it were true. With more than thirty-five years of ministry experience, I have witnessed some of the saddest, and funniest, church squabbles you can imagine. On one occasion, a family threatened to leave the church because the communion bread was too crunchy! On another, a family actually did leave the church after the trustees installed a new refrigerator in the church kitchen. Why would a brand-new refrigerator upset anyone, you ask? The door on the new refrigerator opened in the opposite direction from the old refrigerator. It made a lot of sense and seemed logical by any objective evaluation given the layout of the kitchen. Yet, like disgruntled "anti-peg Bob," the family who oversaw fellowship meals in the kitchen was offended that no one consulted them on the decision. "We're outta here!" they said as they stormed off.

I could go on with anecdote after anecdote, and do not get me started on my experience with church business meetings. Oh boy! I think Luke's account of the riot at Ephesus is the perfect description of a typical church business meeting. "Some therefore cried one thing and some another, for the assembly was confused, and most of them did not know why they had come together" (Acts 19:32). That reminds me of another story, and like the one out of Mayfield, Kentucky, I cannot vouch for its historical accuracy, but in my experience it rings true.

As the story goes, the church held a meeting to vote on the purchase of a new chandelier for the sanctuary. During the discussion phase of the meeting, one grumpy fellow took the floor to announce his strong opposition to the purchase. He began, "Why are we wasting time talking about this?" He continued, "I can give you three reasons why this would be a waste of the church's money. First, a chandelier? Why, we haven't got anyone here who can even spell the word. Second, we haven't got anyone here who could even play it if we had one. And lastly, what we really need in this sanctuary is more light!"

Misconceptions about the Church

Over two thousand years of church history, the church has gotten a bad name because of the antics of some Christians. When people hear the word *church*, it invokes a variety of conceptions. For some, the church is a place filled with hypocrites who act one way on Sunday and quite another throughout the week. Some recall trivial disputes that worsened into major conflicts resulting in hurt feelings and deep wounds. Others think of a place of formal worship, with candles, statues, and similar icons associated with high church ceremonialism. Millions of people throughout the world hear the word church and immediately think of Roman Catholicism with its works-based sacramentalism. The church scandals of the 1980s, and again in recent years, have led many to conclude church leaders, pastors, and priests cannot be trusted. They are only in it for the money, fame, power, sex, etc.

Such misconceptions are a sad reflection of how poorly the church has fulfilled its mission of bringing light and hope to a world in desperate need of the Gospel. They also are an indication of just how much the church is falling away. Before we get to the biblical definition of the church, let us examine a few more popular misconceptions about "church." First, the church is not a building. A body of believers renting a school or storefront is just as much a "church" as those worshipping in large, beautiful multi-million-dollar facilities. Indeed, the early church met in homes. "And daily in the temple, and in every house, they did not cease teaching and preaching Jesus as the Christ" (Acts 5:42). When you hear the word church, if the first image that appears in your mind is a *place*, rather than *people*, then you do not understand what a biblical church is.

Second, the church is not a religion. For many in the secular world, church is just a synonym for "religion." To them, Christian, Muslim, Catholic, Jew, etc., all come under the general umbrella of church. The Bible makes clear, however, that religion has nothing to do with the church. "If anyone among you thinks he is religious, and does not bridle his tongue but deceives his own heart, this one's religion is useless. Pure and undefiled religion before God and the Father is this: to visit orphans and widows in their trouble, and to keep oneself unspotted from the world" (James 1:26–27). Religion is a man-made system, whereas the church is a God-ordained institution, as we shall see below.

Third, the church is not a denomination. Baptists, Methodists, Presbyterians, Lutherans, etc., are also man-made organizations, like religion itself. This does not mean they are bad in and of themselves. Organizational structures can be helpful to the extent they further the true mission of the biblical church. But many people worship their denomination rather than Christ. According to Scripture, Christ is the head of the *church,* not a *denomination.* "And He is the head of the body, the church, who is the beginning, the firstborn from the dead, that in all things He may have the preeminence" (Colossians 1:18).

Fourth, the church is not a general term for anyone who believes in God and follows Him. Some people are under the misguided impression that God-fearing Jews in the Old Testament, as well as Christians in the New Testament, are all part of one large group called the church. I will address this more in Chapter Four, but for now, it is enough to know that according to the Bible, the church is a unique, identifiable group of people, distinct from Israel, who serve a specific role in God's plan.

Defining the Church

So, what is the church? The English word church translates the Greek word *ekklesia,* which literally means "a called-out group." *Ekklesia* is derived from *ek,* meaning "out of," and *kaleō,* which means "to call." Hence, the church is "a called-out group." The Greek word appears 114 times in the New Testament. The word can be used in a non-technical sense to refer to any specific group. For instance, in Acts 7:38 it is translated "congregation" and refers to the group of Israelites in the wilderness. In Acts 19:32 it refers to the angry mob at Ephesus, and it is translated "assembly." Most often, however, the word is used to designate a unique group of "called-out believers in Jesus Christ" who form one body that is identified with Christ as its head through the permanent indwelling of the Holy Spirit.

There are two aspects of the church according to Scripture. The *universal church* refers to all those who, since the Day of Pentecost in Acts 2, have been born of the Spirit of God and have by that same Spirit been baptized into the body of Christ. In other words, the universal church is comprised of all those who have placed their faith in Jesus Christ alone for eternal salvation during this present church age. "For by one Spirit we were all baptized into one body—whether Jews or Greeks, whether slaves or free—and have all been made to drink into one Spirit" (1 Corinthians 12:13). The universal church is Christ's church, which He promised to build. "And I also say to you that you are Peter, and on this rock I will build My church, and the gates of Hades shall not prevail against it" (Matthew 16:18).

The *local church* refers to a specific, localized group of believers that meet regularly for worship and mutual edification. The local church is a subset of the universal church. For example, Acts 8:1 refers to "the church at Jerusalem." Romans 16:5 refers to the local church that was meeting in the home of Priscilla and Aquila. Paul's letter to the Galatians is addressed to "the churches of Galatia" (Galatians 1:2), and his letter to the Thessalonian believers is addressed to "the church of the Thessalonians."

The universal church is the *means* of fulfilling the great commission. In other words, every individual Christian is called to make disciples. "And Jesus came and spoke to them, saying, "All authority has been given to Me in heaven and on earth. Go therefore and make disciples of all the nations, baptizing them in the name of the Father and of the Son and of the Holy Spirit, teaching them to observe all things that I have commanded you; and lo, I am with you always, even to the end of the age. Amen" (Matthew 28:18–20).

The local church is the *result* of fulfilling the great commission. Meaning, once a person becomes a Christian by faith alone in Christ alone, he should find a local group of Christians in his area to affiliate with. This is God's divine design. The end of Acts 2 provides some helpful insights into the activities of the local church that formed in Jerusalem.

Then those who gladly received his word were baptized; and that day

> *about three thousand souls were added to them. And they continued steadfastly in the apostles' doctrine and fellowship, in the breaking of bread, and in prayers. Then fear came upon every soul, and many wonders and signs were done through the apostles. Now all who believed were together, and had all things in common, and sold their possessions and goods, and divided them among all, as anyone had need. So continuing daily with one accord in the temple, and breaking bread from house to house, they ate their food with gladness and simplicity of heart, praising God and having favor with all the people. And the Lord added to the church daily those who were being saved.* (Acts 2:41–47)

While this passage is descriptive and not directly prescriptive, we nevertheless may look to the Jerusalem Church as an example of how individual local churches should operate today. Activities of the local church include worship (Acts 2:47); biblical instruction (Acts 2:42); fellowship (Acts 2:42); ministry (Acts 2:44-45); and the ordinances (i.e., the Lord's Supper and baptism; Acts 2:41-42).

When Did the Church Begin?

As a unique, called-out group, the church had a specified beginning. Nowhere in the Old Testament is the church ever mentioned or alluded to. In fact, in Ephesians 3:2-6, Paul specifically tells us the church is a mystery, meaning something previously unknown that is revealed in the New Testament. Paul writes,

> *if indeed you have heard of the dispensation of the grace of God which was given to me for you, how that by revelation He made known to me the mystery (as I have briefly written already, by which, when you read, you may understand my knowledge in the mystery of Christ), which in other ages was not made known to the sons of men, as it has now been revealed by the Spirit to His holy apostles and prophets: that the Gentiles should be fellow heirs, of the same body, and partakers of His*

promise in Christ through the gospel. (Ephesians 3:2–6)

As God's special revelation to mankind unfolds, we learn from His Word that He is temporarily setting aside His people Israel, though not permanently (cf. Romans 9-11), so that He can begin a new work with a group of people called the church. The church began on the Day of Pentecost (Acts 2), and it will end at the Rapture. After the Rapture, God's chosen nation Israel will take center stage in His earthly plan once again.

There are six straightforward steps to proving the church had its definite beginning in Acts 2 on the Day of Pentecost (c. May 24, AD 33). First, in Matthew 16:18, Jesus referred to the church using the future tense. That is, it was not yet in existence as of the days just prior to Christ's crucifixion. "And I also say to you that you are Peter, and on this rock *I will build My church*, and the gates of Hades shall not prevail against it" (Matthew 16:18, italics added).

Second, in Acts 1:5, on the day of His ascension forty days after His resurrection, Jesus promised the baptism of the Holy Spirit would come "not many days from now." Third, ten days later, on the Day of Pentecost, this baptism of the Holy Spirit occurred.

> *When the Day of Pentecost had fully come, they were all with one accord in one place. And suddenly there came a sound from heaven, as of a rushing mighty wind, and it filled the whole house where they were sitting. Then there appeared to them divided tongues, as of fire, and one sat upon each of them. And they were all filled with the Holy Spirit and began to speak with other tongues, as the Spirit gave them utterance. (Acts 2:1–4)*

Fourth, in Acts 11, when Peter was defending the salvation of Cornelius and his family (Gentiles) before the church leaders in Jerusalem, he confirmed that the events of Pentecost described in Acts 2 constituted the baptism of the Holy Spirit Jesus had promised, and he referred to that baptism as a *beginning*. Peter said, "And as I began to speak, the Holy Spirit fell upon them, as upon us at the beginning. Then I remembered the word of the Lord, how He said, 'John indeed baptized with water, but you shall be baptized with the Holy Spirit'" (Acts 11:15–16). This begs the question, the beginning of what?

Fifth, the Bible tells us the baptism of the Holy Spirit formed (i.e., created) one *body*. "For as the body is one and has many members, but all the members of that one body, being many, are one body, so also is Christ. For by one Spirit we were all baptized into one body—whether Jews or Greeks, whether slaves or free—and have all been made to drink into one Spirit" (1 Corinthians 12:12–13). And finally, according to Ephesians 1:22-23 and Colossians 1:18, this *body* is called the *church*. "And He put all things under His feet, and gave Him to be head over all things to the church, *which is His body,* the fullness of Him who fills all in all" (Ephesians 1:22–23, italics added). "And He is the head of *the body, the church,* who is the beginning, the firstborn from the dead, that in all things He may have the preeminence" (Colossians 1:18, italics added).

To review, the baptism of the Holy Spirit which Jesus promised, and which occurred on the Day of Pentecost in Acts 2, formed the body of Christ, which is called the church. Everyone from that day forward who puts his faith in Jesus Christ alone as his Savior is immediately baptized into (i.e., identified with) the body of Christ. There are many kinds of baptism in the Old and New Testaments. "Baptism" just means "identification." Those who experienced Moses' baptism were identifying with his message. Those who experienced John the Baptist's baptism were identifying with his message. Jesus' baptism identified Him with the Father. Holy Spirit baptism occurs the moment we place our faith in Christ and identifies us with Christ.

Christian water baptism, like all types of baptism, has an identifying purpose. It identifies believers with the church by announcing they are now part of the family. Water baptism does not save anyone from hell. If water baptism were necessary for eternal salvation, why did Paul say, "For Christ did not send me to baptize, but to preach the gospel..." (1 Corinthians 1:17)? Water baptism is merely an outward expression of an inward experience. Only faith alone in Christ alone can save anyone.

Biblical Symbols of the Church

Ephesians presents a glorious picture of the church. Tom Constable puts it well.

> *The Book of Ephesians enables us to view God's creation from an alpine altitude. When we study this book, it is as though we have climbed a high mountain peak, because the book gives us that kind of perspective on what God has created. Recall the opening scenes in "The Sound of Music" movie, where Maria Von Trapp is standing in a high meadow looking out over the valleys and mountains beyond. Yet the "creation" that Ephesians opens up to our vision is not the physical creation, but the church and its position and importance in the panorama of God's program for humankind.*

The Apostle Paul wrote this letter during his first Roman imprisonment in the fall of AD 60. In it, he explains many crucial elements of ecclesiology (the doctrine of the church). These can be summarized using six beautiful representations of the power and majesty of the Lord's church taken from each of the six chapters in Ephesians. I have adapted these symbolic descriptions from the writings of the late Dr. Earl Radmacher, who was a friend of mine and wrote the foreword to my first book many years ago. Over the years, I have referred often to these six depictions of the church.

In Ephesians chapter one, the church is described as a *body that can never die*. As we have been discussing, the church is the body of Christ. "And He put all things under His feet, and gave Him to be head over all things to the church, which is His body, the fullness of Him who fills all in all" (Ephesians 1:22–23). Just as Christ defeated death when He rose from the grave, the church likewise has shared in His resurrection and will never die. "But God, who is rich in mercy, because of His great love with which He loved us, even when we were dead in trespasses, made us alive together with Christ (by grace you have been saved), and raised us up together, and made us sit together in the heavenly places in Christ Jesus" (Ephesians 2:4–6). When the church is Raptured at the end of this age, death's defeat will be sealed once and for all. "So when this corruptible has put on incorruption, and this mortal has put on immortality, then shall be brought to pass the saying that is written: 'Death is swallowed up in victory'" (1 Corinthians 15:54).

In chapter two of Ephesians, the church is depicted as a *building that can never be destroyed.*

> *Now, therefore, you are no longer strangers and foreigners, but fellow citizens with the saints and members of the household of God, having been built on the foundation of the apostles and prophets, Jesus Christ Himself being the chief cornerstone, in whom the whole building, being fitted together, grows into a holy temple in the Lord, in whom you also are being built together for a dwelling place of God in the Spirit. (Ephesians 2:19–22)*

When we give Jesus His rightful place as our chief cornerstone, we never need to fear the enemy. This is *His* church, after all. Yet, as we will be discussing over the next seven chapters, if we take our eyes off Christ, and deny Him his place of centrality in the church, we are in danger of falling away.

This brings to mind the account of Jesus' transfiguration on the mountain from Matthew 17. Jesus calls Peter, James, and John, to the top of a mountain. "Now after six days Jesus took Peter, James, and John his brother, led them up on a high mountain by themselves" (Matthew 17:1). This was an intentional, teachable moment. Jesus was the guide, and He led them high up on this mountain for a reason. Jesus knew the disciples had the wrong focus. He wanted to prepare them adequately for His departure and what was to follow in the weeks to come.

These three disciples had been with Jesus for three and a half years. But they had gotten so close to Him that they had forgotten who He really is. They needed to be reminded that Jesus was more than a friend or leader. He is the King of Kings and Lord of Lords. So, the Lord gets their attention during a hiking trip. Here in Colorado, where my family and I live, God often gets people's attention during hiking trips in the mountains.

Just prior to this encounter Jesus had asked His disciples, "Who do men say that I am?" In other words, what do people think about me? The answers varied: John the Baptist, Elijah, Jeremiah. Then Jesus asked, "But what about you? What do you think?" Peter famously replied, "You are the Christ, the Son of the Living God" (Matthew 16:16). Jesus responded (paraphrasing), "You're right! And the church will be built on this Rock—Me!" It is all about Christ. And then, as if to punctuate and authenticate His point, Jesus goes on a hike with His three closest friends who end up on top of what we call the Mount of Transfiguration.

At the end of Matthew 16, Jesus says, "Assuredly, I say to you, there are some standing here who shall not taste death till they see the Son of Man coming in His kingdom" (Matthew 16:28). The account of the transfiguration is the fulfillment of this promise. Peter, James, and John got a glimpse of Christ's future Kingdom on the mountain that day. And Jesus gave them that glimpse for a reason. We should not think Jesus meant His Kingdom would be figurative, spiritual, or metaphorical. Far from it! His own teaching later in Matthew makes it clear that a literal, physical, earthly reign is coming. But this special moment with Peter, James, and John foreshadowed the coming Kingdom and reminded these three friends and disciples of Christ of just who their Friend really was.

On the Mount of Transfiguration, God's Word gives us the answer to the question of the proper perspective for the church. If the transfiguration teaches us anything it is this: when all is said and done, only one thing matters and that is Jesus Christ. He is the reason the church is a building that can never be destroyed. Speaking of buildings, Peter was so focused on building a literal tent and telling Jesus what He should do in that moment, that God the Father had to interrupt Peter to get a word in edgewise.

When the glory of God appeared, Peter, James, and John fell on their faces and heard God's voice. "While [Peter] was still speaking, behold, a bright cloud overshadowed them; and suddenly a voice came out of the cloud, saying, 'This is My beloved Son, in whom I am well pleased. Hear Him!' And when the disciples heard it, they fell on their faces and were greatly afraid"

(Matthew 17:5–6). But notice what happened next. "When they had lifted up their eyes, they saw no one but *Jesus only*" (Matthew 17:8, italics added).

Although Peter, James, and John were present with Him, it was only Jesus who was transfigured. Although Moses and Elijah were present for the occasion, it was only Jesus who was glorified. Think about that for a moment. Neither the Old Testament dignitaries nor the future New Testament church leaders were glorified. This demonstrates the preeminence of Christ over the Law and the centrality of Christ within the church today. Christ's church is a building that can never be destroyed.

The third description we see of the church in Ephesians is in chapter three. The church has a *boldness that can never be discouraged.*

> *For this reason I bow my knees to the Father of our Lord Jesus Christ, from whom the whole family in heaven and earth is named, that He would grant you, according to the riches of His glory, to be strengthened with might through His Spirit in the inner man, that Christ may dwell in your hearts through faith; that you, being rooted and grounded in love, may be able to comprehend with all the saints what is the width and length and depth and height—to know the love of Christ which passes knowledge; that you may be filled with all the fullness of God. Now to Him who is able to do exceedingly abundantly above all that we ask or think, according to the power that works in us, to Him be glory in the church by Christ Jesus to all generations, forever and ever. Amen. (Ephesians 3:14–21)*

When we really come to grips with just how much Christ loves the church, and with His power that works in and through us, there is nothing that should ever discourage us.

In chapter four, the church is pictured as a *brotherhood that can never be disrupted.* A unified church terrifies Satan, but a disunified church is his playground.

> *I, therefore, the prisoner of the Lord, beseech you to walk worthy of the*

> *calling with which you were called, with all lowliness and gentleness, with longsuffering, bearing with one another in love, endeavoring to keep the unity of the Spirit in the bond of peace. There is one body and one Spirit, just as you were called in one hope of your calling; one Lord, one faith, one baptism; one God and Father of all, who is above all, and through all, and in you all. (Ephesians 4:1–6)*

The church has a high calling in Christ Jesus. Sadly, in these last days, many Christians are neglecting and forsaking this calling.

Chapter five of Ephesians portrays the church as a *bride that can never be divorced.* "Husbands, love your wives, just as Christ also loved the church and gave Himself for her, that He might sanctify and cleanse her with the washing of water by the word, that He might present her to Himself a glorious church, not having spot or wrinkle or any such thing, but that she should be holy and without blemish" (Ephesians 5:25–27). Although He could point out many flaws in His bride, especially in these great last days of apostasy, Jesus will never divorce His church!

Lastly, the church is represented as a *battalion that can never be defeated* in Ephesians chapter six. Most Christians are familiar with the famous spiritual warfare section of this chapter.

> *Finally, my brethren, be strong in the Lord and in the power of His might. Put on the whole armor of God, that you may be able to stand against the wiles of the devil. For we do not wrestle against flesh and blood, but against principalities, against powers, against the rulers of the darkness of this age, against spiritual hosts of wickedness in the heavenly places. Therefore take up the whole armor of God, that you may be able to withstand in the evil day, and having done all, to stand. (Ephesians 6:10–13)*

As I discussed in my three-volume *Spirit of the Antichrist* series, there are intense battles being waged in the unseen realm, and most Christians are oblivious. The apostate church in these last days is ill-prepared to face the intensifying spiritual warfare that lies ahead.

Elsewhere in the New Testament, the church is symbolized as a royal priesthood. "But you are a chosen generation, a royal priesthood, a holy nation, His own special people, that you may proclaim the praises of Him who called you out of darkness into His marvelous light; who once were not a people but are now the people of God, who had not obtained mercy but now have obtained mercy" (1 Peter 2:9–10). One of the special blessings for Christians in the church age is our unhindered access to the Lord through prayer. Unlike the children of Israel in Old Testament times, we do not have to go through a human priest, since we are all individual priests with Christ as our High Priest. The writer of Hebrews emphasizes this priestly access.

> *Seeing then that we have a great High Priest who has passed through the heavens, Jesus the Son of God, let us hold fast our confession. For we do not have a High Priest who cannot sympathize with our weaknesses, but was in all points tempted as we are, yet without sin. Let us therefore come boldly to the throne of grace, that we may obtain mercy and find grace to help in time of need. (Hebrews 4:14–16)*

> *Therefore, brethren, having boldness to enter the Holiest by the blood of Jesus, by a new and living way which He consecrated for us, through the veil, that is, His flesh, and having a High Priest over the house of God, let us draw near with a true heart in full assurance of faith, having our hearts sprinkled from an evil conscience and our bodies washed with pure water. (Hebrews 10:19–22)*

This world is under the sway of the wicked one, and things are rapidly getting worse (1 John 5:19; 2 Timothy 3:13). Now more than ever the church needs to exhibit confidence and faith as things heat up. Instead, the church is filled with many timid Christians who have forgotten who they are in Christ.

One more symbol of the church is worth mentioning. Scripture speaks of the New Testament church as a flock. Both Peter (1 Peter 5:3) and Paul (Acts 20:28) use this metaphor to refer to Christians. As a flock, we need a shepherd. The Lord Jesus is described in Scripture as the Good Shepherd. Jesus said, "I am the good shepherd. The good shepherd gives His life for the sheep" (John 10:11). According to Peter, the church is "...like sheep going astray, but have now returned to the Shepherd and Overseer of your souls" (1 Peter 2:25). The church, like Israel, is prone to wander. The prophet Isaiah wrote, "All we like sheep have gone astray; we have turned, every one, to his own way; and the Lord has laid on Him the iniquity of us all" (Isaiah 53:6). As things get worse in these last of the last days, we must stay close to the Shepherd. When the enemy attacks, it will not go well for those who have drifted away from the flock. When you are facing enemy attacks, isolation is not your friend (cf. Proverbs 18:1). The further the church falls away from the Lord, the more we endanger ourselves.

The Purpose of the Church

In God's plan of the ages, He always has a primary group of people whom He is using to advance his divine agenda. If you think of human history as a stage, in each act, or dispensation as the Bible calls them (Ephesians 1:10; 3:2), there is a different group at center stage. In Chapter One, I included a diagram entitled, "God's Plan of the Ages," to illustrate why the present church age is referred to in Scripture as the last days. I am including it again here for your reference as I discuss the various groups that have been center stage throughout the ages. See Figure 3 below. In the early days of creation, Adam and Eve were center stage. They were God's primary representatives through whom God communicated His will.

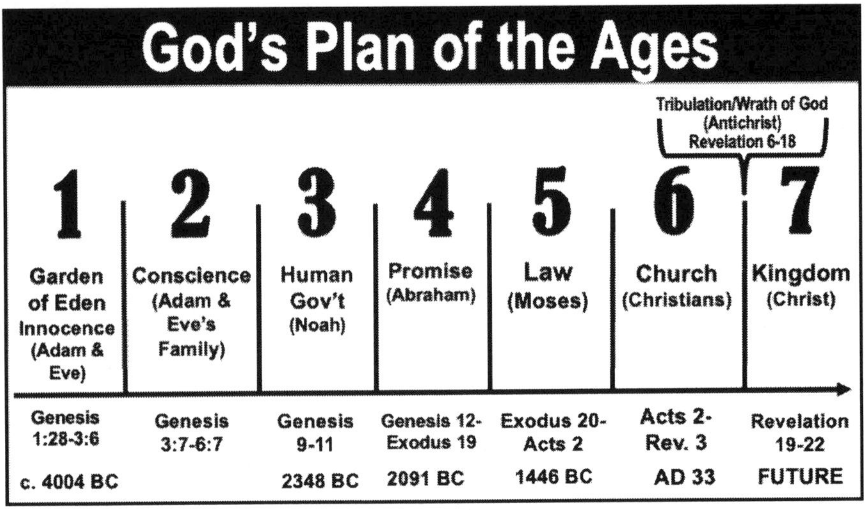

Figure 3

Over time, Noah took center stage. Then it was Abraham. Israel eventually took center stage and became an essential component of God's plan of the ages for roughly two thousand years. God tells us in His Word Israel is His chosen nation. "Blessed is the nation whose God is the Lord, the people He has chosen as His own inheritance" (Psalm 33:12). Israel is the "apple of His eye" (Zechariah 2:6). Based upon the unconditional promise God made to Abraham (Genesis 12:1-3), a global Kingdom of peace, righteousness, and justice will one day proceed from Jerusalem when Jesus Christ returns to take the throne at the end of the seven-year tribulation. "I will bring forth descendants from Jacob, and from Judah an heir of My mountains; My elect [chosen nation] shall inherit it, and My servants shall dwell there" (Isaiah 65:9).

When Israel rejected Christ and crowned Him with thorns, instead of a King's crown, God temporarily set Israel aside. You might say Israel exited the stage and a new act began with the church at center stage (refer to Figure 3). This of course was no surprise to God, but rather, part of His plan all along. Daniel the prophet predicted Israel's Messiah would be cut off and the inauguration of the Messianic Kingdom would be postponed. As the Jews were returning from exile in Babylon, Daniel prayed and asked the Lord to reveal the next phase of His plan for His chosen people. God had previously announced seventy years of captivity through the prophet Jeremiah. "And this whole land shall be a desolation and an astonishment, and these nations shall serve the king of Babylon seventy years" (Jeremiah 25:11). Since the seventy years were almost up, Daniel wanted to know what was next in God's plan.

God answered Daniel's prayer by giving him the now-famous 490-year plan that would lead to everlasting righteousness and the anointing of the King. Dr. John Walvoord, a renowned expert on Bible prophecy, called Daniel's prophecy "the key to prophetic revelation." Here is that prophecy.

> *"Seventy weeks are determined For your people and for your holy city, To finish the transgression, To make an end of sins, To make reconciliation for iniquity, To bring in everlasting righteousness, To seal up vision and prophecy, And to anoint the Most Holy. "Know therefore and understand, That from the going forth of the command To restore and build Jerusalem Until Messiah the Prince, There shall be seven weeks and sixty-two weeks; The street shall be built again, and the wall, Even in troublesome times. "And after the sixty-two weeks Messiah shall be cut off, but not for Himself; And the people of the prince who is to come Shall destroy the city and the sanctuary. The end of it shall be with a flood, And till the end of the war desolations are determined. Then he shall confirm a covenant with many for one week; But in the middle of the week He shall bring an end to sacrifice and offering. And on the wing of abominations shall be one who makes desolate, Even until the consummation, which is determined, Is poured out on the desolate." (Daniel 9:24–27)*

The Hebrew word translated "weeks" is *shabua*, meaning seven years. The word is used four times in Genesis 29 to describe the seven years that Jacob worked for Laban to get Rachel as his wife. If you recall the story, after Jacob had served one *shabua* (seven years), Laban tricked him and gave him Leah instead of Rachel. So, Jacob had to work another *shabua* (seven more years) to get Rachel.

The next phase of the plan God revealed to Daniel would span seventy *shabuas*. That is seventy seven-year periods, or 490 years, after the Babylonian captivity. As Figure 4 shows, the first 483 of those years were fulfilled precisely as God said they would be beginning with the command to restore and rebuild Jerusalem in 444 BC (Daniel 9:25a; cf. Nehemiah 2:1-8) and concluding with the arrival of Messiah corresponding to the historical date of Christ's triumphal entry (Daniel 9:25b; March 30, AD 33).

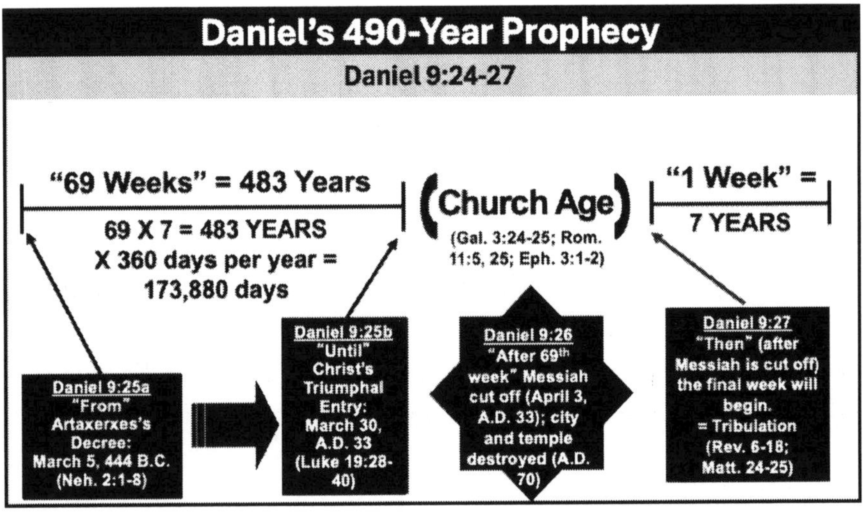

Figure 4

Without getting too far into the weeds here, the late New Testament scholar Dr. Harold Hoehner has shown that using the Hebrew calendar of 360 days per year, Christ's triumphal entry occurred exactly 483 years (173,880 days) to the day after the clock began ticking on Daniel's prophecy. (See Figure 4.)

Moreover, the prophecy further predicted after the conclusion of the 483-year segment, the Messiah would be cut off and the city and temple would be destroyed. Unsurprisingly, God's Word came true again! Just days after His triumphal entry, Christ was crucified (i.e., "cut off") and almost forty years later, Jerusalem was ransacked by the Romans and the temple was destroyed. Both events occurred, as God told Daniel they would, after the 483rd year of the prophecy but prior to the start of the 484th year. The final seven years of this prophecy (years 484-490) await future fulfillment in the end times. The clock will start ticking on this final *shabua,* the 70th of Daniel's 70 "weeks," when the Antichrist confirms the covenant that allows Israel to resume their sacrificial customs.

Returning to Figure 4, you will notice the prophecy demands a gap of time between the 69th and 70th weeks. In the New Testament, God revealed additional revelation about things that would take place in this gap of time. Specifically, God revealed the church age—a new group center stage on the earth. Yet, this does not mean that God is finished with Israel. As discussed, there is a future for national Israel. After the Rapture, which brings the church age to an end, Israel returns to center stage and will remain there until the closing act of God's plan of the ages, when the long-awaited Messianic Kingdom is inaugurated.

The notion that the church has somehow replaced Israel in God's program, and that Israel no longer plays a role in God's plan of the ages is utterly foreign to Scripture. We will address this in more detail in Chapter Four. For now, it is enough to point out that both Israel and the church have significant roles to play in God's plan.

How God Is Using Israel

There are at least five ways God is using or has used Israel to advance His plan. First, He used Israel to testify to the unity of Yahweh amid universal idolatry and paganism.

> *"You are My witnesses," says the Lord, "And My servant whom I have chosen, That you may know and believe Me, And understand that I am He. Before Me there was no God formed, Nor shall there be after Me. I, even I, am the Lord, And besides Me there is no savior. I have declared and saved, I have proclaimed, And there was no foreign god among you; Therefore you are My witnesses," Says the Lord, "that I am*

> *God." (Isaiah 43:10–12)*

The *Shema,* which served (and still serves for Orthodox Jews) as a centerpiece of the morning and evening Jewish prayers, is central to this witness. "Hear, O Israel: The Lord our God, the Lord is one" (Deuteronomy 6:4)!

A second way God used Israel during their time on stage is to be an example to the nations of the benefits of serving Yahweh.

> *"There is no one like the God of Jeshurun, Who rides the heavens to help you, And in His excellency on the clouds. The eternal God is your refuge, And underneath are the everlasting arms; He will thrust out the enemy from before you, And will say, 'Destroy!' Then Israel shall dwell in safety, The fountain of Jacob alone, In a land of grain and new wine; His heavens shall also drop dew. Happy are you, O Israel! Who is like you, a people saved by the Lord, The shield of your help And the sword of your majesty! Your enemies shall submit to you, And you shall tread down their high places." (Deuteronomy 33:26–29)*

As pagan nations saw how God blessed Israel, they would seek to learn more about Him. This was God's plan from the beginning when He called Israel out of Egypt. Unfortunately, Israel failed to obey God and instead capitulated to the false gods of surrounding cultures. This brought God's discipline on the nation. One day, however, when Christ takes the throne and Israel returns to the land in obedience and belief, they will fulfill this purpose to the utmost. "Many nations shall come and say, 'Come, and let us go up to the mountain of the Lord, To the house of the God of Jacob; He will teach us His ways, And we shall walk in His paths.' For out of Zion the law shall go forth, And the word of the Lord from Jerusalem" (Micah 4:2).

Third, God used Israel to receive and record His special revelation; that is, the Scriptures. Every human author of the books of the Bible was Jewish except possibly Luke. The Bible says, "What advantage then has the Jew, or what is the profit of circumcision? Much in every way! Chiefly because to them were committed the oracles of God" (Romans 3:1–2). Fourth, not only did God use Israel to produce His living written Word, but He also used Israel to produce the living Incarnate Word, Jesus! Jesus said, "...salvation is of the Jews" (John 4:22). God's entire redemptive plan runs through Israel. Jesus, being the ultimate Seed of Abraham (Galatians 4:16), came into the world to save sinners (1 Timothy 1:15).

A fifth way God will use Israel in His plan is to be center stage in the coming global Kingdom of peace.

> *For unto us a Child is born, Unto us a Son is given; And the government will be upon His shoulder. And His name will be called Wonderful, Counselor, Mighty God, Everlasting Father, Prince of Peace. Of the increase of His government and peace There will be no end, Upon the throne of David and over His kingdom, To order it and establish it with judgment and justice From that time forward, even forever. The zeal of the Lord of hosts will perform this. (Isaiah 9:6–7)*

There can be no doubt Israel has played a central role in God's plan of the ages, and He is not through with them yet. Figure 5 below summarizes how God is using Israel in His plan of the ages.

How God is Using Israel in His Plan

1. **To testify to the unity of Yahweh amid universal idolatry and paganism (Deut. 6:4; Is. 43:10-12)**
2. **To be an example to the nations of the benefits of serving Yahweh (Deut. 33:26-29)**
3. **To receive and record God's revelation (i.e. the Scriptures; Deut. 4:5-8; Rom. 3:1-2)**
4. **To produce the Savior (Gen. 3:15; 12:3; 22:18; Is. 7:14; 9:6; Rom. 1:1-6)**
5. **To be center stage in a global Kingdom of peace (Isa. 9:7; Jer. 23:5; Zech. 14:9; Rev. 11:15; 21:1-2)**

Figure 5

How God Is Using the Church

Similarly, God is using the church to advance His plan in the present age in at least five ways. First, through the church God is calling out a people for His name. The Bible says God visited the Gentiles "to take out of them a people for His name" (Acts 15:14). This is why we are called "Christians." The very label God gave to believers in the church age points others to Christ. "...The disciples were first called Christians at Antioch" (Acts 11:26).

Second, God is using the church to showcase the exceeding riches of His grace and mercy. Although God's grace and mercy have always been manifested on earth, after the cross, with the onset of the church age, God's grace is on display more vividly than ever (Ephesians 2:7; Romans 11:11-15, 31). Third, God is using the church to get Israel's attention. "I say then, have they [Israel] stumbled that they should fall? Certainly not! But through their fall, to provoke them to jealousy, salvation has come to the Gentiles" (Romans 11:11).

Israel rejected Messiah the first time He came. But after seeing the blessings given to Christians, and the intimacy we have with God the Son and God the Father through the indwelling Holy Spirit, the Jews will be clamoring to receive Him upon His return. This is another reason the great last days apostasy is so devasting. It not only negatively impacts those Christians who are falling away, but it also impacts unbelieving Jews who see the church acting so much like the world and wonder, "Why would we want that?!"

God is using the church in a fourth way, and this one is very significant considering the degree to which spiritual warfare is intensifying the closer we get to the Rapture. God is using the church to showcase His wisdom to Satan and his demons. "To the intent that now the manifold wisdom of God might be made known by the church to the principalities and powers in the heavenly places, according to the eternal purpose which He accomplished in Christ Jesus our Lord" (Ephesians 3:10–11). When Christians fall away, Satan scoffs. When Christians stand firm, Satan shrieks!

The fifth way God is using the church converges with the fifth way He is using Israel. God is using the church to prepare a body that will help rule and reign in the future Messianic Kingdom when Israel takes center stage once more. Jesus promised the disciples, "...when the Son of Man sits on the throne of His glory, you who have followed Me will also sit on twelve thrones, judging the twelve tribes of Israel" (Matthew 19:28). One of the rewards distributed to Christians at the Bema judgment will be positions of service in the Kingdom (Luke 19:11-27). If we endure persecution and fulfill our role as believers in the church age, God will give us the right to reign over geographic portions of Christ's Kingdom. If we fall away, and do not fulfill our duty, He will deny us this right to reign, even though we will still enter the Kingdom (2 Timothy 2:12-13).

Figure 6 below summarizes how God is using the church in his plan of the ages.

How God is Using the Church in His Plan

1. **To call out a people for His name (Acts 15:14; cf. 11:26)**
2. **To showcase the exceeding riches of God's grace and mercy (Eph. 2:7; Rom. 11:11-15, 31)**
3. **To get Israel's attention (Rom. 11:11)**
4. **To showcase God's wisdom to Satan (Eph. 3:10)**
5. **To prepare a body that will help rule the Messianic Kingdom (Matt. 19:28; Lk. 19:11-27; 22:28-30; 2 Tim. 2:12; Rev. 20:4-6)**

Figure 6

The Remnant Principle

Before we turn our attention to seven manifestations of apostasy in the American church, I want to address a biblical principle that is often overlooked. Many Christians assume the Lord works in the majority. In other words, movements of God are identified by their size and scope, making them stand out. And sometimes this is true. There are many examples of moves of God that impacted the masses, both in the world at large and in America in particular. In America, one might point to the First Great Awakening and the ministries of men like George Whitefield and Jonathan Edwards in the 18th century.

Yet, a survey of human history will show more often than not God moves in the minority—the remnant. I call this the Remnant Principle. This principle has two implications. First, it reminds us that if everyone is jumping on the latest Christian bandwagon, it probably is wise to pause and evaluate it more closely. Sometimes the majority simply means all the fools are on the same side. When Jesus was crucified, only a faithful remnant cried, "Hosanna! Hosanna!" The larger crowds cried, "Crucify Him! Crucify Him!" When Noah shut the doors to the ark there were vastly more people outside than inside. Lot and his family escaped the fire and brimstone that rained down on Sodom and Gomorrah, while the rest of the inhabitants of those cities perished. Jesus changed the world with only eleven faithful followers. You get the idea.

Second, the Remnant Principle reminds us at any given time, no matter how bad things are, there is always a remnant of God-fearing believers on planet Earth. During this present evil age (Galatians 1:4), a vast minority of people are believers in Jesus Christ, and even fewer are Spirit-filled, mature believers who are awake to what is really going on in the world. There is a great falling away taking place in the church the closer we get to the Lord's return. Yet, no matter how small the number, the faithful remnant is there.

Will God's people ever constitute a majority on planet Earth? Yes, but not until Christ takes the throne. At the Rapture, the church is caught up to meet the Lord in the air (1 Thessalonians 4:13-18). There are roughly eight billion people in the world today. Let us suppose, for the sake of illustration, that a billion people are Christians and are rescued from the earth at the Rapture. One billion constitutes a *remnant* of roughly twelve percent out of a world population of eight billion.

There will be another remnant of believers that will come out of the seven-year Tribulation, having heard and believed the Gospel during that awful time on earth. Revelation 7 talks about people from every nation, tribe, tongue, and language getting saved during that time. Those believers constitute a *remnant,* a minority. Most of the world will be deceived into taking the mark of the Beast and will pledge their allegiance to the Antichrist. God works in the remnant. His people are often outnumbered but never outmatched. Just ask Gideon (cf. Judges 7:1-25).

When Christ inaugurates the long-awaited Kingdom, for the first time since the days of Noah and his family after the flood, everyone on planet Earth will be a believer. Believers will be in the majority, and Christ will reign in perfect peace and justice. A better day is coming. But until then, we must not ignore the great last days apostasy. Recognizing the dangers of falling away could mean the difference between awaiting the Rapture with a remnant in the ark versus getting swept away in a tidal wave of deception.

In the next chapter, we will focus on one of the most obvious manifestations of apostasy in the church today: biblical apostasy.

3

FALLING AWAY BIBLICALLY

For the time will come when they will not endure sound doctrine, but according to their own desires, because they have itching ears, they will heap up for themselves teachers; and they will turn their ears away from the truth, and be turned aside to fables. (2 Timothy 4:3–4)

* * *

Eight-year-old Jimmy had been raised in a solid, biblically minded family. He learned in Sunday school the Bible was true, and with all the beauty of a child's faith, he believed it. He had never conceived of questioning the truth of God's Word. That is why he was astounded when Mrs. Harris, his second-grade teacher at Roosevelt Elementary School, mocked the Bible. The class had been discussing their favorite animal stories and Jimmy mentioned the biblical account of Jonah's encounter with the great fish. Mrs. Harris scoffed, "You know, Jimmy, there is no way a man could have survived three days inside the belly of a fish!" Surprised but self-assured, Jimmy said, "Yes, he could! The Bible says so!"

This provoked Mrs. Harris even further. "Jimmy," she said, with an air of condescension, "there is no way to prove the story of Jonah being swallowed by a great fish is true." Undeterred, Jimmy retorted, "Why yes there is! When I get to heaven, I will just ask Jonah directly." Mrs. Harris snapped, "What if Jonah is not in heaven?" Jimmy paused for a moment and then replied, "Well, then I guess you'll have to ask him!"

Skeptics outside the church are nothing new. The secular world has long ridiculed the Bible as the standard of absolute truth. What is new in these last days of the church age, however, is the degree to which attacks on the Bible have made their way inside the church. One of the biggest indications the American church is falling away is the presence of denigrating remarks about the Bible reverberating from America's pulpits.

The Secularization of the Christian Worldview

Everyone has a worldview, even if we do not always realize where it comes from, how to define it, or when we are accessing it. Our worldview is essentially the lens through which we see life and validate or invalidate truth claims we encounter every day. Not only does everyone have this lens, this belief system, but also it is often on autopilot. We seldom stop to think about why we believe what we believe, we just believe it.

The Bible speaks often of the importance of the mind. Paul exhorts the believer to "be renewed in the spirit of your mind" (Ephesians 4:23). Elsewhere he writes, "And do not be conformed to this world, but be transformed by the renewing of your mind, that you may prove what is that good and acceptable and perfect will of God" (Romans 12:2). It all comes down to a battle for the mind. The minds of unbelievers are debased, futile, and blinded (Romans 1:28; 2 Corinthians 4:4; Ephesians 4:17; Colossians 1:21). Once we are born again by faith (John 3:3), our minds are no longer alienated from God (Romans 5:8-11; Ephesians 4:18), yet the enemy still targets our minds (2 Corinthians 11:3).

The Bible warns, "Beware lest anyone cheat you through philosophy and empty deceit, according to the tradition of men, according to the basic principles of the world, and not according to Christ" (Colossians 2:8). The word "cheat" in this verse is the Greek word *sulagōgeō*. This is the only time the word is used in the New Testament. It means "to take captive," "to plunder," or "to carry off as booty." That is exactly what Satan is trying to do.

He wants to plunder the minds of Christians, so we do not see life through the lens of Scripture.

Sadly, many Christians today have been taken captive. Their minds have been conformed to the world (Romans 12:2). The worldview of these Christians is the result of layer upon layer of worldly influences that build up over time. These influences are inconsistent, contradictory, and even incoherent at times, yet most Christians remain unaware of the flawed nature of their worldview. There is only one unfailing standard on which to base one's beliefs: the Bible.

It is a sign of the times that so few people are raising an alarm about the secularization of the church's worldview. Before taking a closer look at some of the invalid influences on our worldview, let us first examine the cultural milieu in which we find ourselves. Everything happens in a context, and this certainly is true of the development of one's worldview. To understand how we arrived at a place where the average Christian's worldview is so inherently convoluted, we must understand postmodernity.

Postmodernism in Historical Perspective

Broadly speaking, scholars have divided history into three time periods classified as: *premodern, modern,* and *postmodern.* The premodern world encompasses all ages prior to the scientific revolution and the Age of Enlightenment. Most historians mark the end of the premodern era around 1789 with the French Revolution. The modern era ran from 1789 until roughly 1989. We currently are living in the postmodern era (though some would say we have progressed to a "post-truth" or "post-Christian" era). The rate of change in the postmodern era has increased exponentially over previous periods due primarily to technological advancements such as the Internet.

How has the postmodern mindset influenced our worldview? Figure 7 illustrates the shift in thinking as we moved from a premodern to a modern and finally to a postmodern world.

Postmodernism in Historical Perspective		
PREMODERN	**MODERN**	**POSTMODERN**
Up to 1789	1789-1989	1989-present
FAITH	REASON	BIAS
Supernatural Explanations	Natural Explanations	No Explanations
5 senses incomplete	5 senses complete	5 senses incomplete
Efficiency	Solutions	Convenience
Revelation	Scientific Method	No Absolute Truth
High view of Bible	Low view of Bible	Self-serving view of Bible
Duty: You are your function.	Desire: You are your feelings.	Definition: You are your Facebook profile.
Fulfill your duty.	Find your dream.	Frame your disguise.

Figure 7

In this postmodern age, all truths (little "t") are equally valid. Truth is in the eye of the beholder. There is no grand metanarrative that is always true for all people. There is no capital "T" Truth. Luciferian Klaus Schwab admitted as much in his 2022 book, *The Great Narrative.* He wrote, "…nothing is more effective than the power of narratives, that is to say, developing stories that are both pertinent and convincing to others. This is the best way to motivate those with whom we interact socially, politically, and economically, and to move the agenda forward." In other words, it is better to create false narratives that further your agenda rather than accept a universal metanarrative such as the narrative of Scripture. Adolf Hitler once boasted, "The victor will never be asked if he told the truth."

When conflicting views arise, contradictions are explained away as a matter of personal bias. For this reason, most people are unconcerned when told their worldview contains inconsistencies. They respond with an indifferent yawn, since, after all, the postmodern mindset allows for two contradictory propositions to be true at the same time. In Figure 8 below, we zoom in on a few significant differences between the mindset of the modern world versus today's postmodern mindset.

Then versus Now

	MODERN	POSTMODERN
Goal of Communication	Knowledge	Participation & Acceptance
Art	Skill	Outrage
Emphasis	Truth	Image
Media	Fact & Fiction Distinct	"Reality" TV & Spin
Entertainment	Wisdom	Escapism
Ultimate Authority	Gov't or Religion	Self
Worldview	Anthropocentric	Egocentric
Education	Individual Book Learning	Group Work
Key Word	What?	Whatever!

Figure 8

Image is valued much more highly in today's world than truth. The makeup artist is more important than the speechwriter. Style supersedes substance. It is not *what you say,* but *how you say it,* that matters most. As Louis Kronenberger put it, "The trouble with our age is that it is all signpost and no destination."

This is why most pastors today are evaluated on their style and oratory skills rather than the accuracy of their sermons. When a pastor delivers a riveting sermon, and there is no doubt America's pulpits are filled with exceptional speakers, few people have the ability or inclination to validate the truthfulness of what was said. What starts out as a mist in the pulpit thus becomes a fog in the pew, to paraphrase the late Howard Hendricks.

Why Do You Believe What You Believe?

Someone has correctly noted, "Most people cling to what doesn't matter and don't believe what does!" These days, few Christians stop to think about why they believe what they believe. The technical term for this subject is *epistemology*. Academicians ask, what is your epistemology? A more common term for this is *worldview*. By examining various influences on our worldview, we can begin to recognize how the American church has drifted away from the centrality of the Scriptures as the only standard for our beliefs, attitudes, and practices. Only then will we be able to strip away false beliefs and replace them with a coherent biblical worldview.

Sociological Influences

Many of the beliefs we hold dear arise from our social interactions. We believe what we believe because someone told us to believe that way. For example, in many cases, parents have a profound impact on the mindset of their children. Of course, this is not always the case because many children grow up in dysfunctional homes where there is no steady parental presence. In such cases, other sociological influences hold sway. But in traditional family settings, one's parents yield considerable influence.

Allow me to illustrate. I grew up in a conservative Christian home where I was taught the fundamentals of the Christian faith. My family attended mostly Dispensational churches. My father also was a devoted Dallas Cowboys fan and a diehard Republican. It should come as no surprise then to learn that as I graduated from college and entered adulthood, I too was a Dispensationalist, a Republican, and most importantly, a passionate fan of the Dallas Cowboys!

Had I grown up in Philadelphia, perhaps I would have been (perish the thought!) a fan of the Philadelphia Eagles. Or had I been raised in Commiefornia, er, uh, I mean, *California*, I might be a Democrat. Perhaps most horrifying? If my parents had been Presbyterian, I might be.... [gulp].... a Calvinist! My point is our social setting affects our worldview. This is true not only of one's family, but also of his friends, classmates, and even geography.

My high school and college years were spent in Texas, where I have fond memories of hunting deer, turkey, and dove with my dad. With his influence, I became, and remain to this day, a gun-loving outdoorsman. My wife and I have some friends from a large city in Canada who visited us in the States a few years ago. As we sat around our family room discussing our upbringings, they were enthralled by the fact that I had not only *seen* a real gun but had actually *touched* one. They had grown up in a social environment where gun possession was relegated almost entirely to law enforcement.

Sociological influences, like the others we will discuss below, can change over time. As our friends, coworkers, neighbors, acquaintances, etc., change, so too does our worldview. When exposed to new traditions, thoughts, and ideas, we often assimilate them into our thinking. It is easy to see how sociological factors should not serve as the ultimate standard for our worldview. While such influences can be positive, such as parents leading their children to faith in Christ, or a friend encouraging you to read the Bible, other social influences can lead to harmful or sinful activities. This is why the Bible reminds us, "The righteous should choose his friends carefully, for the way of the wicked leads them astray" (Proverbs 12:26).

As we evaluate our worldview, we must take note of the ways in which sociological components have impacted our thinking. Those beliefs that are validated by the truth of Scripture should be retained. Those that are contrary to God's Word must be removed, no matter how sentimental we may feel about the source of those false views.

Psychological Influences

Another factor in formulating our worldview is what we might categorize broadly as psychological influences. We often hold certain beliefs because they bring us comfort or peace of mind. Perhaps we find meaning in life by holding on to certain emotional memories or experiences from the past. The heart is a seedbed of many false hopes and beliefs. For this reason, you must "keep your heart with all diligence, for out of it spring the issues of life" (Proverbs 4:23).

Emotions like fear, joy, and anger can lead to serious thinking errors. Take fear, for example. Even secular, humanistic psychologists recognize the power of fear. In a September 23, 2009, article for *Psychology Today*, Robert Evans Wilson, Jr. writes, "There are many things that motivate us. But the most powerful motivator of all is fear." Satan knows this, which is why fear is one of his favorite weapons. My friend and colleague, L.A. Marzulli, put it this way, "Fear is always the calling card of darkness!" Believers are "sons of light and sons of the day. We are not of the night nor of darkness," and fear has no place in the heart of a Christian (1 Thessalonians 5:5). When we are afraid, we are not thinking properly. "For God has not given us a spirit of fear, but of power and of love and of a sound mind" (2 Timothy 1:7).

Similarly, joy can lead us astray. There are many things that can bring pleasure for a season, but they are not all healthy and good. Feelings can be misleading. According to *Medical News Today*, endorphins are a type of "feel-good brain chemical" the body releases during pleasurable activity. These endorphins can trick us into thinking what we are doing is appropriate when it may not be. Opioids, for example, function similarly to endorphins, and we all know how horrific and deadly the opioid crisis in America has become. Moses is an example of right thinking in this area. The Bible says he chose "rather to suffer affliction with the people of God than to enjoy the passing pleasures of sin" (Hebrews 11:25).

Think of our feelings like a child's security blanket. It brings the child comfort, but it is powerless to protect the child. It is a false sense of security. The only true source of peace is the Lord. "Be anxious for nothing, but in everything by prayer and supplication, with thanksgiving, let your requests be made known to God; and the peace of God, which surpasses all understanding, will guard your hearts and minds through Christ Jesus" (Philippians 4:6–7). Artificial sources of peace, joy, comfort, etc., are not from the Lord.

Yet, like sociological influences on our worldview, psychological factors can be positive if they are validated by the Word of God. Human beings are made in the image of God (Genesis 1:26-27), which means we have a mind, will, and emotions. Thus, emotions, in and of themselves, are not evil. They only become a problem when we look to our emotions as the ultimate standard for our beliefs.

We must believe what we believe based on the empirical standard of Scripture, not whimsical feelings that are subject to change. Godly sorrow (2 Corinthians 7:10), inner peace (Philippians 4:7), true joy (Nehemiah 8:10;

Galatians 5:22), etc., are all emotions the Holy Spirit uses to draw us closer to the Lord. However, Satan can use those same emotions to lead us astray. "Beloved, do not believe every spirit, but test the spirits, whether they are of God; because many false prophets have gone out into the world" (1 John 4:1).

Theological Influences

In arriving at this third category of influences on our worldview, some might think I have moved from preaching to meddling. But rest assured, I am still preaching; I am just preaching to myself. I am a theologian by trade, and I recognize the value of pastors, teachers, and academicians in helping people formulate a biblical worldview. But in these great last days of apostasy, we must remember not all theologians are Biblicists. As Charles Ryrie reminds us, anyone can be a theologian. A theologian is simply someone who thinks about God and expresses those thoughts in some way. If not tethered to the truth of the Bible, theology is like a wheel spinning off its axis. Like the previous two influences, theological factors, when standing alone, are insufficient as a basis for our worldview. Let me explain.

As I mentioned previously, I had the distinct privilege of growing up in a Christian home. By the time I started attending Dallas Theological Seminary (DTS) at age twenty-two, I already had a solid dispensational framework built into my worldview. However, I learned very quickly that when a DTS professor asked me why I believe in the pre-tribulation Rapture or in the distinction between God's program for the church and His program for Israel, "because I am a Dispensationalist" or "because my Dad said so" were insufficient answers! The professor was looking for more than that. He was looking for biblical justification for my beliefs.

Like the previous two factors that shape our worldview, theological influences are only helpful to the extent they can be validated by the Bible. In other words, although I am an unapologetic Dispensationalist, I must always be a Biblicist first. Why? Because—and this may come as a shock—pastors, theologians, and other religious leaders can be *wrong*. We are not infallible.

One of the occupational hazards of being a professor is that students tend to adopt their teacher's viewpoint without taking the time to validate it. They often accept what their instructor is saying, hook, line, and sinker. After all, the professor is an authority figure and he or she *must* be right, right?

I experienced this phenomenon firsthand while spending twelve years as a professor in full-time academics at the baccalaureate and graduate levels. One of the comments from students that always made me feel a bit uncomfortable was, "You've convinced me, Dr. Hixson." Sure, there was a part of me that loved hearing that (the prideful part!). But deep down I knew if a student's belief was based solely upon my arguments, then sooner or later another theologian or teacher was going to come along who was a better communicator, funnier, or otherwise more compelling, and the student was going to waffle on his or her views like a straw in the wind.

What I would much rather hear from students is, "We have searched the Scriptures and come to the same conclusion as you, Dr. Hixson." In that way, the Bible is the ultimate basis for our conclusions. Now, of course, we may both be wrong if we have mishandled Scripture, but at least the starting point is correct. With faithful hermeneutics and diligence over time, we will get it right more than we get it wrong (2 Timothy 2:15).

Theological influences have woven their way into the worldview of most people these days. During the Middle Ages, the Catholic Church held sway over millions worldwide as Councils, Creeds, and *ex cathedra* papal declarations ruled the day. Thus, to this day, people tend to believe what they believe because their pastor said so, or their priest said so, or their favorite Christian author, or their rabbi, or their guru, or their channeler, or their imam, etc. Such influences on our thinking can be even more dangerous than the sociological factors mentioned previously because they come with inherent authority. But titles, credentials, and positions of authority, even within conservative evangelicalism, are no guarantee of sound teaching.

The Bible warns, "My brethren, let not many of you become teachers, knowing that we shall receive a stricter judgment" (James 3:1). The most effective theologians are those who point people to the authoritative Word of God, not their own systems and speculations. "All Scripture is given by inspiration of God, and is profitable for doctrine, for reproof, for correction, for instruction in righteousness, that the man of God may be complete, thoroughly equipped for every good work" (2 Timothy 3:16–17).

Philosophical Influences

Many people base their worldview on philosophical factors like rational argumentation, reasoning, and logic. To be sure, evidential and rational arguments have their place. Indeed, God uses language and logical rules of grammar to reveal Himself to us in the written Scriptures. But even rationality and reasoning cannot trump God's Word as the ultimate standard for our beliefs, attitudes, and behaviors. Let me explain.

There are many biblical truths that defy logic. For example, it is not logical, nor is it rational, for a virgin to give birth to a child. But the Bible says this is exactly what happened at the incarnation (Isaiah 7:14; Matthew 1:18-24). Similarly, everyone knows that a person cannot be 100% God and 100% man at the same time. 50/50 maybe, but not simultaneously fully God and fully man. The philosophical law of non-contradiction disallows such a scenario. But again, the Bible tells us this is precisely the case with Jesus Christ and the doctrine of the hypostatic union.

Speaking of the law of non-contradiction, if we were to allow it to rise to the level of the supreme arbiter of truth, the doctrine of the Trinity also would go out the window. After all, God cannot be three yet one at the same time—at least not according to sound reasoning and logic. Yet, once again, the Bible plainly teaches this foundational doctrine and standard of orthodoxy. If we base our worldview on philosophical argumentation, the same problems arise with historical miracles revealed in Scripture such as a literal, six-day creation; a global flood; the parting of the Red Sea; Jonah and the great fish; and the resurrection of our Lord. Logic disproves all these things, does it not?

The Bible is, and must always be, the only standard for our belief system. Regarding biblical truths that seem to confound logic, the Bible addresses this very issue. "Oh, the depth of the riches both of the wisdom and knowledge of God! How unsearchable are His judgments and His ways past finding out" (Romans 11:33)! In other words, just because something does not make sense to us does not mean it is not true. God, and God alone, determines truth from error. "Let God be true and every man a liar" (Romans 3:4).

Political Influences

I am certain I stepped on the toes of a few of my apologetics-minded colleagues in the previous section. So, while I am toe-stomping anyway, I may as well address the arena of politics. In the United States, it is inevitable that one's worldview will be influenced by the sphere of politics. As I have discussed in my three-book series, *Spirit of the Antichrist Volumes One* and *Two* and *Spirit of the False Prophet,* the Luciferian elite are working behind the scenes to usher in a one-world system (cf. Psalm 2; Revelation 13). Often called the "deep state" or "global elite" or "shadow government," these nefarious co-conspirators developed the two-party political system to keep Americans arguing even though nothing ever changes much. It is a technique known as the Hegelian Dialectic, or *controlled opposition.* Here is how it works.

They polarize Americans into two camps: left/right; liberal/conservative; Democrat/Republican, etc. In so doing, they give the impression we have a voice. We believe there is someone in Washington, D.C. who represents our values. Sadly, this is far from the case. As I have documented extensively in my books, the global powers that be control both sides of the aisle. The 2020 presidential election confirmed for many what I had been pointing out for years. We do not have *elections* in this country; we have *selections.* It has always puzzled me how so many conservatives think elections are rigged when the Democrat wins, but when the Republican wins, inexplicably, the digital vote tabulation machines were all untampered-with and worked fine!

Even though more and more people are waking up to the controlled two-party system in the United States, the sphere of politics remains a driving force behind the worldview of the average American. We believe what we believe because "I'm a Republican!" or "I'm a Democrat!" It is true the underlying values behind the two major parties in the U.S. political system are real and represent opposing perspectives on a variety of important issues. However, when debating moral values with others, most people simply parrot what they heard from their favorite media talking head without getting to the crux of the matter.

We must learn to think critically and analytically using the lens of Scripture. Blindly trusting in our political leaders is a dead-end street. The Bible says, "For our leaders are stupid. They have not sought the Lord's advice. So they do not act wisely, and the people they are responsible for have all been scattered" (Jeremiah 10:21, NET Bible). "Confidence in an unfaithful man in time of trouble is like a bad tooth and a foot out of joint" (Proverbs 25:19). "Do not put your trust in princes or other people, who cannot save you" (Psalm 146:3, NCV).

What matters most is what the Bible says. Most news shows today have become little more than raucous name-calling and *ad hominem* attacks. Criticizing those "liberal democrats" or those "hateful fascists," etc., is symptomatic of a worldview influenced more by political discourse than moral principles. Like the previous influences on our worldview, political influences are inevitable, but invalid when it comes to serving as an ultimate standard for our beliefs.

Biblical Influences

Although our worldview is undeniably influenced by sociological, psychological, theological, philosophical, and political factors, none of these are reliable. They may have some merit when validated by the truth of Scripture, but they can never stand alone. The only valid basis to believe what we believe is: What does the Bible say? Figure 9 summarizes the invalid influences on our worldview discussed above.

Why do you believe what you believe?

INVALID!	INVALID!	INVALID!	INVALID!	INVALID!	VALID!
SOCIO-LOGICAL INFLUENCES	PSYCHO-LOGICAL INFLUENCES	THEO-LOGICAL INFLUENCES	PHILO-SOPHICAL INFLUENCES	POLITICAL INFLUENCES	BIBLICAL INFLUENCES
Parents Friends Society Culture Tradition	Comfort Peace of mind Meaning Purpose Hope Feelings Experience Counselors	Pastor Church Theological System Guru Rabbi Channeler Imam	Consistency Coherence Rationality Reason Logic	Republican Democrat Libertarian Green Party Constitution Independent	WHAT DOES THE BIBLE SAY?

Figure 9

As we go through life, various inputs from a variety of sources add layer upon layer to our convoluted belief system. In these great last days of apostasy, it is more important than ever that we overhaul our worldview and make sure, as much as possible, that it aligns with the infallible Word of God. "Your word is a lamp to my feet and a light to my path" (Psalm 119:105). "The law of the Lord is perfect, converting the soul; the testimony of the Lord is sure, making wise the simple; the statutes of the Lord are right, rejoicing the heart; the commandment of the Lord is pure, enlightening the eyes" (Psalm 19:7–8).

Where Has the Bible Gone?

Listening to some popular evangelical preachers these days, one might get the impression, "The Bible has left the building!" The word of God has been under attack since the beginning of time. Satan maligned God's Word in the Garden ("Has God indeed said…?"), and it has been in his crosshairs ever since. These attacks reached new heights during the Enlightenment Period and made their way into academia. We will have more to say about how Christian colleges and seminaries are falling away in Chapter Eight.

Today most "Christian" colleges and universities reject the authority of Scripture. Apparently, so too do highly regarded evangelical leaders who, frankly, should know better.

In 2018, Andy Stanley, pastor of one of the largest evangelical churches in America, preached a sermon entitled, "The Bible Told Me So." In it, he explained how Christians should *not* base their beliefs on the Bible. According to Stanley, "...perhaps you were taught, as I was taught, 'Jesus loves me, this I know, for the Bible tells me so.' That is where our trouble began." He added, "Christianity does not hang by the thread of 'The Bible told me so.' ...It is next to impossible to defend the entire Bible." Sharing a bit about his journey, he elaborated, "We went off to college and discovered that even though it [the Bible] was sacred, it wasn't scientific. ...it wasn't necessarily something that was factual. ...[The Bible's stories] ...weren't necessarily true." Later he tweeted, "The Christian faith does not rise and fall on the accuracy of 66 ancient documents."

If that does not illustrate how the American church is falling away, I do not know what does. When you abandon the authority of God's Word, the slope quickly becomes slippery. In 2023, North Point Community Church, where Stanley serves as the lead pastor, hosted and led a controversial two-day conference geared toward "support[ing] parents and LGBTQ+ children in their churches." The *Unconditional Conference*, as it was called, was billed as a place "for ministry leaders looking to discover ways to support parents and LGBTQ+ children in their churches." Featured speakers included two men who are married to other men, and additional keynoters who are openly supportive of same-sex relationships and marriage.

Stanley is not alone. More and more pastors and evangelical leaders are equivocating on the authority of God's Word. Randy Alcorn rightly asks, "Does the word 'evangelical' mean anything anymore?" Historically, evangelicalism developed as a reaction to the modernist movement of the early 20th century and referred to Christians and churches who believe in the inerrancy of Scripture. Evangelicals were known for defending the authority of the Bible as the only standard for our beliefs, attitudes, and practices. This is no longer the case. As Alcorn laments, "the decline of biblical knowledge and the erosion of sound doctrine in churches have only become more obvious" in recent years.

A Straw in the Wind

Lauren Daigle is another popular evangelical Christian personality who has compromised on the truth of God's Word. A contemporary Christian singer, Daigle has led worship at North Point Community Church and was part of a band signed to the church's music label. Given her connection to Andy Stanley and Northpoint, it should come as no surprise that she could not give a straightforward answer when asked if homosexuality is a sin. During an appearance in November of 2018 on *The Domenick Nati Show,* just days after her appearance on *The Ellen DeGeneres Show,* Daigle told Nati, "I can't honestly answer on that, in the sense of I have too many people that I love, and they are homosexuals." She continued, "I can't say one way or the other, I'm not God." I guess when your pastor denies the authority of God's Word, this is all you can say when someone asks you if homosexuality is a sin.

Daigle is correct that she is not God. However, God has revealed His Word to us in the Scriptures and His view on homosexuality is not ambiguous in the least. "You shall not lie with a male as with a woman. It is an abomination" (Leviticus 18:22). "Likewise also the men, leaving the natural use of the woman, burned in their lust for one another, men with men committing what is shameful, and receiving in themselves the penalty of their error which was due" (Romans 1:27). That someone like Daigle, who is surrounded by Christian influences, active in a Christian church, and sitting under the teaching of an accomplished Christian pastor, cannot understand something as basic as the doctrine of human sexuality, is a glaring sign of the great last days apostasy.

When you remove the Bible as the authoritative standard of truth, you become like a straw in the wind. Every whim of worldly wisdom becomes a new launching pad for moral speculations. Questions like, "Is homosexuality a sin?" leave you speechless with a bewildered look in your eyes. Absent an objective source to answer these and other moral questions, we are left to our own opinions, biases, and assumptions. Daigle's answer to Domenick Nati's question illustrates this point. Her answer was not built upon objective truth; it was born out of her desire not to offend. In other words, she was looking to the world to validate her answer. Truth is never defined as the absence of offense. To rephrase Ben Shapiro, the truth does not care about your feelings. God's truth has a long history of being "a stone of offense" (1 Peter 2:8). When we stand on the Word of God, we are always in good company! "Let God be true but every man a liar" (Romans 3:4).

Not surprisingly, apostasy in the pulpit and among evangelical leaders has had a profound effect on Christians in the pew. According to a recent study by the American Bible Society, more and more Christians are leaving their Bibles on the shelf.

> *When researchers for the American Bible Society's annual State of the Bible report saw this year's survey statistics, they found it hard to believe the results. The data said roughly 26 million people had mostly or completely stopped reading the Bible in the last year.*
>
> *"We reviewed our calculations. We double-checked our math and ran the numbers again ... and again," John Plake, lead researcher for the American Bible Society, wrote in the 2022 report. "What we discovered was startling, disheartening, and disruptive."*
>
> *In 2021, about 50 percent of Americans said they read the Bible on their own at least three or four times per year. That percentage had stayed more or less steady since 2011.*
>
> *Top of Form*
>
> *Bottom of Form*
>
> *But in 2022, it dropped 11 points. Now only 39 percent say they read the Bible multiple times per year or more. It is the steepest, sharpest decline on record.*
>
> *According to the 12th annual State of the Bible report, it wasn't just the occasional Scripture readers who didn't pick up their Bibles as much in 2022 either. More than 13 million of the most engaged Bible readers—measured by frequency, feelings of connection to God, and impact on*

day-to-day decisions—said they read God's Word less.

Currently, only 10 percent of Americans report daily Bible reading.

If only ten percent of Americans read the Bible daily, can we really be considered a Christian nation any longer?

According to a 2023 study by the Cultural Research Center at Arizona Christian University, only four percent of Americans have a biblical worldview. Meaning, when making moral decisions, the question of, "What does the Bible say?" only weighs into their decision four percent of the time! The report, led by the center's Director of Research, Dr. George Barna, shows precipitous "declines in biblical understanding throughout American society since [2020]." According to Barna, a startling 82% of Americans say they "embrace a few biblical principles but generally believe and behave in ways that are distinct from biblical teaching." This group has grown substantially from the 69% in 2020. The American church is falling away from God's Word faster and faster the closer we get to the Rapture.

Hell? Yes!

Another manifestation of the last days apostasy is the growing trend in American churches to eliminate hell. Benjamin L. Corey is an author, speaker, and scholar, who holds graduate degrees from two highly regarded evangelical institutions: Gordon-Conwell Theological Seminary and Fuller Seminary. In an article for *Time* entitled, "5 Reasons Christians Are Rejecting the Notion of Hell," Corey put it bluntly, "More and more Christians are beginning to reject the traditional view of hell which states the unjust will experience 'eternal, conscious torment.'"

Like all false doctrines, the rejection of hell derives from either the rejection of the Bible altogether, or in some cases, the mishandling of the Bible by evangelicals who have not quite reached the bottom of the slippery slope, wanting to retain at least the appearance of a respect for God's Word. Benjamin Corey is in the latter category. He blatantly mishandles the Word of God and asserts, "The concept of eternal, conscious torment runs contrary to the whole testimony in scripture." Bart Ehrman, a New Testament scholar, stunningly comes to the same conclusion. "Neither Jesus, nor the Hebrew Bible He interpreted, endorsed the view that departed souls go to paradise or everlasting pain," Ehrman insists, contrary to the plain, straightforward teaching of Scripture.

Corey and Ehrman are by no means alone. There is a growing chorus of Christian leaders who deny the reality of eternal punishment. For example, popular evangelical pastor, Rob Bell, infamously espoused a "no hell" view in his 2012 best seller, *Love Wins*. The book took the American church by storm, spawning a *Love Wins Companion Study Guide* and a *Love Wins for Teens* edition aimed at promoting this false doctrine to Christian teenagers. The subtitled of the teenage version of the book is particularly troubling. "If God Threw a Party, Would Everyone Be Invited?" The notion that God is nothing more than a cosmic party planner, and there is no eternal penalty for sin, is disturbing. If there is no hell, why did God's Son, our Savior Jesus Christ, have to die on the cross? Jesus did not die for your sins so that you could be happy, healthy, and wealthy *in this life*. He died to rescue you from the *everlasting lake of fire*!

Jesus said, "Then He will also say to those on the left hand, 'Depart from Me, you cursed, into the everlasting fire prepared for the devil and his angels'" (Matthew 25:41). The Bible says, "Then Death and Hades were cast into the lake of fire. This is the second death. And anyone not found written in the Book of Life was cast into the lake of fire" (Revelation 20:14–15). During His earthly ministry, Jesus told the true story of an unbelieving rich man who died and was in torment in hell (Luke 16:19-31). The concept of eternal life and eternal punishment is in fact a central part of the "whole testimony of Scripture," notwithstanding Mr. Corey's assertions to the contrary. The same word used to describe our *eternal* home in heaven, (Gk. *aiōnios*, "eternal") is used to describe the *eternal* punishment of those who refuse to accept the free gift of salvation by faith alone in Christ alone. In Jude 7 and Matthew 25:41, *aiōnios* is used to describe the "eternal" or "everlasting" fire of hell.

The idea that people can reject the free gift of eternal life, paid for by the atoning blood of Jesus, and yet avoid hell when they die is a lie that began in the Garden when Satan told Eve, "You will not surely die" (Genesis 3:4). In other words, Satan wants us to think sin has no eternal consequence. The Bible says otherwise, "Therefore, just as through one man sin entered the world, and death through sin, and thus death spread to all men, because all sinned" (Romans 5:12). "For the wages of sin is death, but the gift of God is eternal life in Christ Jesus our Lord" (Romans 6:23). Jesus warned, "Therefore I said to you that you will die in your sins; for if you do not believe that I am He, you will die in your sins" (John 8:24). Such a warning is meaningless unless the penalty for sin has eternal consequences.

The good news is no one has to go to hell. The free gift of eternal salvation is available to anyone and everyone who, in simple, child-like faith, receives Jesus Christ as their one-and-only Savior. No one else has the power to forgive sin and give eternal life. Only Jesus. He said, "Most assuredly, I say to you, he who believes in Me has everlasting life" (John 6:47). Elsewhere He promised, "Most assuredly, I say to you, he who hears My word and believes in Him who sent Me has everlasting life, and shall not come into judgment, but has passed from death into life" (John 5:24). If you are trusting in anything or anyone else to get you to heaven—your works, your religion, your church, your baptism, your wealth, etc.—you will have hell to pay one day. Faith alone in Christ alone is our only hope. Have you trusted in Jesus Christ as your Savior?

The degree to which the church has marginalized, mishandled, and even mocked the Bible is a sign of the great last days apostasy. In the next chapter, we will take a closer look at one specific area of Bible doctrine: eschatology. The burgeoning fascination with end times Bible prophecy has spawned no shortage of bizarre and unbiblical views that obscure God's plan of the ages as revealed in Scripture. This proliferation of false eschatological views is further evidence the American church is falling away.

4

FALLING AWAY ESCHATOLOGICALLY

Knowing this first: that scoffers will come in the last days, walking according to their own lusts, and saying, "Where is the promise of His coming? For since the fathers fell asleep, all things continue as they were from the beginning of creation."
(2 Peter 3:3–4)

* * *

"We should go see him," my friends said when we learned Edgar C. Whisenant was going to be speaking at a church in Houston, TX. It was the summer of 1988, and I had just finished my sophomore year in college. Whisenant had been making quite a splash around the country with his book, "88 Reasons Why the Rapture Will Be in 1988." According to his calculations, the Rapture was sure to happen sometime between September 11-13, 1988, corresponding with the Jewish Feast of Trumpets (Rosh Hashanah). The venue was not far from us, so we all hopped in my Honda Accord and drove across town to attend the Wednesday night service where Whisenant was the featured speaker. I have had an interest in Bible prophecy since I was a young boy. The idea the Rapture could happen very soon excited me, and I was eager to hear

Whisenant's arguments.

The church was smaller than I expected, and it was packed. The four of us squeezed into a wooden pew near the back of the sanctuary. The crowd size overwhelmed the building's air conditioning system, especially on that hot, humid summer evening in Houston. It was stifling in the room, but few seemed to mind. The Rapture is a subject that draws a crowd no matter the environment, especially with all the hype surrounding Whisenant's book. When he began speaking all eyes were fixed on the pulpit. After only twenty minutes of listening, I was ready to leave, and so were my friends. In the first place, he was not a good speaker. More than that, his arguments were convoluted and strained. He did not connect the dots very well, and it seemed to us like he was only trying to sell books. We lasted another ten minutes or so before awkwardly slipping out of our row and exiting through the back door.

Whisenant is a classic example of the sensationalist brand of Bible prophecy teachers: lots of hype, very little substance. When September 1988 came and went with no sign of the Rapture, Whisenant revised his calculations and claimed 1989 was the year of the Lord's return. Newsflash: The Rapture did not happen in 1989 either. Each year thereafter, for several years as I recall, the author released new versions of his speculative teaching. "90 Reasons Why the Rapture Will Be in 1990," "91 Reasons...," and so on. With his failed predictions, Edgar C. Whisenant joins a long list of prophecy "experts" who created a stir only to ride off into the sunset with nothing to show for their efforts but a worn-out calculator and an eraser.

As my friend Dr. Tommy Ice says, "They often have complicated schemes and reasons why they believe they are right, even though everyone has been wrong in the past." No one will ever be able to predict the date of the Rapture because according to the Bible, the Rapture is imminent; that is, it could happen at any moment. The Rapture is the next event on God's prophetic calendar. There are no prophecies that must be fulfilled prior to the Rapture. Figure 10 provides an overview of the End Times.

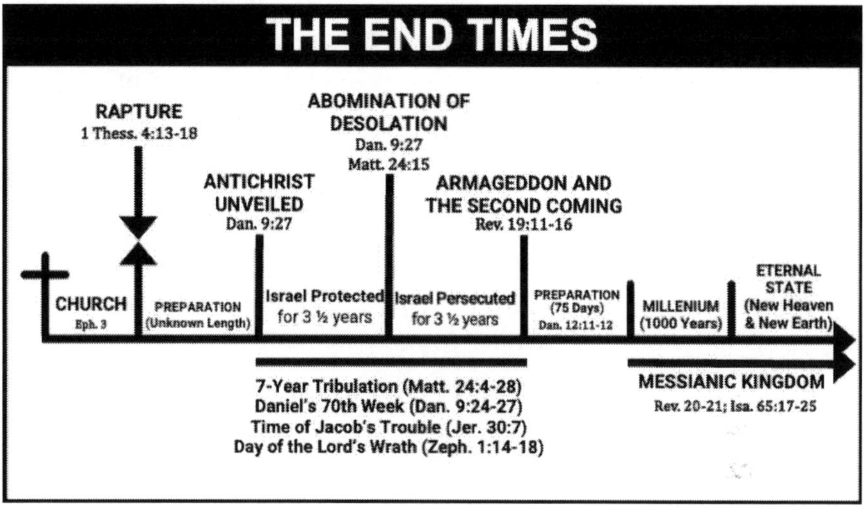

Figure 10

Appendix B at the end of this book provides a sequential order of ends times events. You will notice the Rapture is the first item on that list. I explain the doctrine of imminency in more detail in my book *What Lies Ahead: A Biblical Overview of the End Times.*

The desire to set a date for the Rapture is understandable. Marc Laclear correctly points out, "It's human nature to want certainty, especially about momentous future events. The idea that we could know exactly when Jesus will return is incredibly appealing. It gives a sense of control and allows us to prepare." Throughout church history, many believers have been influenced by often well-intentioned date-setting prophecy teachers. They bet the farm on some sensationalist scheme, sell their possessions, move to a mountaintop, and count the days waiting to be caught up to meet the Lord in the air.

One famous example is William Miller, a Baptist preacher, who predicted the Rapture would occur on March 21, 1844. After Christ did not return on that date, the Millerites, as they came to be called, then revised William Miller's prediction to October 22 of the same year, claiming he had made a few miscalculations. Charles Taze Russell is another notable example. His teachings laid the foundation for what became the Watchtower Society

(Jehovah's Witnesses). Russell predicted the Rapture would occur in 1874. When that year had come and gone, he reinterpreted his prediction to say Jesus had indeed returned in 1874, but in invisible form. Before his death in 1916, Russell concluded, "...the battle of the great day of God Almighty... The date of the close of that 'battle' is definitely marked in Scripture as October 1914. It is already in progress, its beginning dating from October 1874."

Date-setting is not the only form of eschatological error. Eschatology is a branch of systematic theology that refers to the study of the end times. The closer we get to the return of the Lord, the more the church seems to deviate from sound, biblical truth in the area of end times prophecy. Although eschatological inaccuracies are nothing new, the increase and intensity of these mistakes are a clear sign of the great last days apostasy.

Mishandling Prophetic Passages

Almost all doctrinal error begins with a mishandling of Scripture. A faulty hermeneutic is the seedbed of shaky theology. Such is certainly the case with end times fallacies. One way some Christians mishandle the biblical text is to suggest all prophecies have been fulfilled in the past, including the return of Christ. According to this view, known as *preterism*, the Second Coming of Christ occurred in AD 70. By allegorizing Scripture, rather than interpreting it in its plain, normal, literal sense, preterists conclude Jesus returned metaphorically in the sky in AD 70, as symbolized by the smoke and fire billowing up from Jerusalem after the Roman general, Titus, ransacked the city. That historical event, they say, fulfilled Jesus' words in the Olivet Discourse, "For as the lightning comes from the east and flashes to the west, so also will the coming of the Son of Man be" (Matthew 24:27).

Such an interpretation is embarrassingly false. In no sense did the fall of Jerusalem in AD 70 fulfill the Second Coming passages in the Bible. A comparison of Scripture with Scripture shows there will be literal cosmic signs in the heavenlies when Christ returns at the end of the seven-year tribulation to inaugurate the Kingdom. Jesus said, "Immediately after the tribulation of those days the sun will be darkened, and the moon will not give its light; the stars will fall from heaven, and the powers of the heavens will be shaken" (Matthew 24:29). The prophet Isaiah put it this way:

> *Behold, the day of the Lord comes, Cruel, with both wrath and fierce anger, To lay the land desolate; And He will destroy its sinners from it. For the stars of heaven and their constellations Will not give their light; The sun will be darkened in its going forth, And the moon will not cause its light to shine. "I will punish the world for its evil, And the wicked for their iniquity; I will halt the arrogance of the proud, And will lay low the haughtiness of the terrible. I will make a mortal more rare than fine gold, A man more than the golden wedge of Ophir. Therefore I will shake the heavens, And the earth will move out of her place, In the wrath of the Lord of hosts And in the day of His fierce anger. (Isaiah 13:9–13)*

Joel used similar language when describing the Second Coming. "The sun shall be turned into darkness, and the moon into blood, before the coming of the great and awesome day of the Lord" (Joel 2:31). Throughout human history, God has frequently used supernatural, cosmic signs to announce major events in His plan of the ages. Such will be the case when Christ comes back to usher in the long-awaited Kingdom of peace, righteousness, and justice (cf. Isaiah 24:23; Ezekiel 32:7-8; Joel 2:10; 3:15; Amos 5:20; 8:9; Zephaniah 1:15; Revelation 6:12-17; 8:12; etc.).

Preterists point to Jesus' words in Matthew 24:34 to suggest that all end times prophecy must have been fulfilled in the first century AD. In that passage, Jesus said, "Assuredly, I say to you, this generation will by no means pass away till all these things take place" (Matthew 24:34). However, contrary to the assertion of preterists, "this generation" does not refer to the generation *to whom* Jesus was speaking. Rather, it refers to the generation *about whom* Jesus was speaking. This is the normal way in which prophecies are revealed. The prophet, in this case, Jesus, gives a prophecy to a historical audience that represents the future generation who will see the fulfillment of that prophecy. For example, Isaiah's audience did not see the virgin give birth to Messiah (Isaiah 7:14), even though they were the ones who received that prophecy. Micah's audience did not see the Messiah born in Bethlehem, even though Micah addressed that prophecy to them (Micah 5:2). And so on.

In Matthew 24, Jesus is answering the question from His disciples, "What will be the sign of your coming and of the end of the age" (Matthew 24:3)? He answers their question by giving detailed signs that will precede His Second Coming during the seven years just prior to His return. He then explains the generation that sees all these signs will be the generation that sees His return (Matthew 24:34). The entire preterist interpretation hangs on their misinterpretation of Matthew 24:34. "This generation" does not refer to Jesus' first century audience. It refers to the eschatological audience that will be alive at the time of His return. For an overlay of Jesus' teaching in the Olivet Discourse in an eschatological context, see Figure 11.

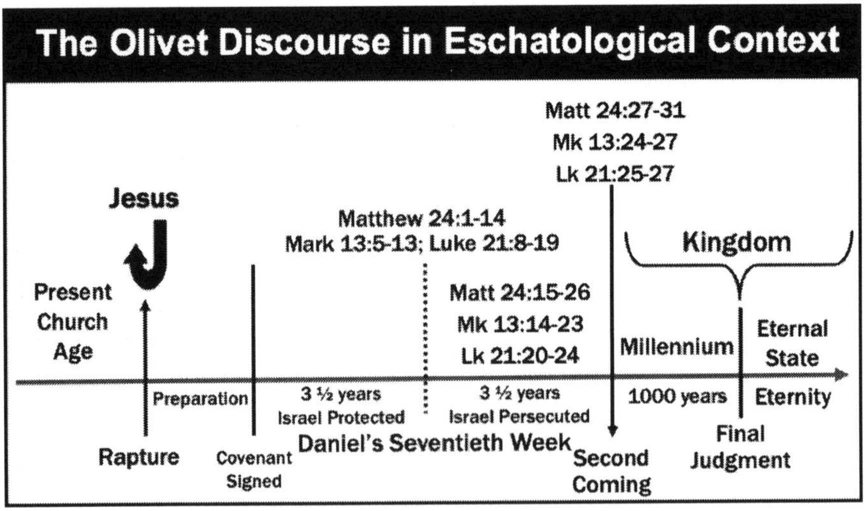

Figure 11

The entire Olivet Discourse is eschatological in nature. It does not refer to the present church age. Indeed, the church age was still future at this point in history, as discussed in Chapter Two.

Allegorizing Prophetic Passages

A key principle of Bible interpretation, indeed of literary interpretation in general, is a consistent literal, grammatical, and historical approach. In other words, when interpreting the written text, we must understand the words on the page the way they were intended in their normal, natural setting, taking into account the grammar and syntax of the original language, and maintaining a keen sensitivity to the historical setting of the author. Meaning always originates with the author, not the reader. We cannot come up with some fanciful, creative interpretation and then force it on the text.

When Bible interpreters arrive at highly symbolic interpretations of the text that do not emanate clearly from the words on the page, they are practicing what theologians call an allegorical hermeneutic. The number of Christians who routinely allegorize the Scriptures has reached epidemic proportions—a striking manifestation of the great last days apostasy. With allegorical interpretation, meaning originates in the mind of the reader rather than with the written text. The interpreter is asked to get inside the mind of the author and seek his *true* meaning, rather than letting the writer's words speak for themselves. Allegorizing essentially says, "This is what the author wrote, but let me imagine what he *really* means." This is dangerous hermeneutical ground. If meaning originates in the mind of the reader, there can be an endless number of interpretations, with no stake in the ground to which to tether the one true meaning. Those Bible teachers who falsely spiritualize the eschatological portions of Scripture do so against all sound Bible study methodology.

The opposite of allegorical interpretation is the literal-grammatical-historical (LGH) method of Bible study. The LGH method is the only proper way to handle Scripture. Paul wrote, "Be diligent to present yourself approved to God, a worker who does not need to be ashamed, rightly dividing the word of truth" (2 Timothy 2:15). The phrase "rightly dividing" is one verb in Greek, *orthotoméō*. This is the only time this word is used in the New Testament. It means, "to cut or make straight." The idea is that we are to cut a straight path from the words on the page to the original meaning, without straying off course into spiritualized and imaginative speculation. We get the English word *orthodontia* from this Greek word. Orthodontists are paid a lot of money to make our teeth *straight*, not point them in several directions! Allegorical interpretation sends the reader off on multiple tangents with no way to land on the correct meaning of the text.

A growing number of Christians today are falling away eschatologically because they fail to practice a consistent LGH method of Bible interpretation. Notice I said, "consistent." This is because almost all Bible teachers use the LGH method when studying the historic portions of Scripture. For example, Isaiah 7:14 is interpreted as meaning a literal virgin will give birth to the Christ child, because historically this is precisely what happened. The same is true for all prophecies that relate to Christ's first advent. However, when dealing with prophecies pertaining to Christ's return, Christians in these last days are increasingly deviating from sound hermeneutics and allegorizing the text. In other words, they are *inconsistent* in the way they handle Scripture. Sometimes they are literal, sometimes they are allegorical.

We could look at several examples of this error, but one should suffice to make the point. Consider Gabriel's announcement to Mary in Luke.

> *Now in the sixth month the angel Gabriel was sent by God to a city of Galilee named Nazareth, to a virgin betrothed to a man whose name was Joseph, of the house of David. The virgin's name was Mary. And having come in, the angel said to her, "Rejoice, highly favored one, the Lord is with you; blessed are you among women!" But when she saw him, she was troubled at his saying, and considered what manner of greeting this was. Then the angel said to her, "Do not be afraid, Mary, for you have found favor with God. And behold, you will conceive in your womb and bring forth a Son, and shall call His name JESUS. He will be great, and will be called the Son of the Highest; and the Lord God will give Him the throne of His father David. And He will reign over the house of Jacob forever, and of His kingdom there will be no end." (Luke 1:26–33)*

There is no doubt that Mary literally "found favor with God." There is equally no doubt that she literally "conceived in her womb and brought forth a Son." No one denies that Joseph and Mary literally "called His name Jesus," and He is the "Son of the Highest." Yet, when it comes to the last part of Gabriel's pronouncement, according to which Jesus will take "the throne of His father David," "reign over the house of Jacob forever," and preside over an everlasting Kingdom, many interpreters in these last days turn aside from the plain meaning of the text and allegorize Christ's reign. He is reigning "in our hearts," they say. Nothing in Gabriel's words, however, suggests the last part of His proclamation was intended to be symbolic while the first part was clearly literal.

When we consistently employ the LGH method of Bible interpretation, we will inevitably arrive at a dispensational understanding of God's Word. The late Charles Ryrie, who was a friend and colleague of mine, pointed out that consistent literal interpretation is part and parcel of dispensationalism. According to Ryrie, "What marks off a person as a dispensationalist? What is the *sine qua non* (the absolutely indispensable part) of the system? ... Consistently literal, or plain, interpretation...." He calls this consistency in literal interpretation "the strength of dispensational interpretation." Without a consistent literal interpretation of the Bible, we would not recognize a distinction between God's program for Israel and His program for the church, as discussed in Chapter Two. Conversely, those Christians who allegorize the Bible arrive at the erroneous conclusion the church has replaced Israel in God's plan of the ages.

Confusing Prophetic Passages

In these great last days of apostasy, there is great confusion over the relationship between the church and Israel. The false teaching that the church is "spiritual Israel" and there is no prophetic future for national Israel is called covenant theology, or sometimes supercessionism. More commonly it is referred to as "replacement theology." According to this view, the nation of Israel played an important role historically in the past but will not play a significant role in God's plan in the future. Adherents to replacement theology believe the church has replaced Israel in God's plan. See Figure 12 for more contrasts between dispensationalism and replacement theology.

	DISPENSATIONALISM	REPLACEMENT THEOLOGY
Bible Study Method	Literal-Grammatical-Historical	Allegorical
Israel & The Church	Distinct Programs	Church has replaced Israel
Purpose of God in Human History	Bring God Glory	Redeem mankind
End Times	Literal earthly kingdom	No earthly kingdom
Salvation	Free Grace	Calvinism

Figure 12

The resurgence of replacement theology means many Christians now conclude when Israel exited the world stage, as we discussed in Chapter Two, it left the stage for good. Israel will never play a role in God's program again, or so they say. Dispensationalists correctly understand, according to the Bible, that one day the church is going to exit the world stage (at the Rapture), and Israel once again will take center stage. God is not through with the people of Israel; they are just in the dressing room waiting for the right time to come back on stage. God has a future for national Israel on earth.

The word eschatology causes many Christians to think of the Book of Revelation. However, eschatology starts with the Old Testament not the New Testament. It begins with the unconditional promises of God to Israel. When understood in their plain, normal sense (LGH), these promises demand a literal future for national Israel. They demand a literal earthly Kingdom, a rebuilt temple in Jerusalem, and a physical throne from which Jesus will reign over a global Kingdom someday. "Of the increase of His government and peace there will be no end, upon the throne of David and over His kingdom, to order it and establish it with judgment and justice from that time forward, even forever. The zeal of the Lord of hosts will perform this" (Isaiah 9:7).

The Lord Jesus Christ made the teaching of His Kingdom a part of His public ministry. The Sermon on the Mount, in Matthew 5–7, is the first major recorded discourse Jesus preached in His public ministry. The Gospel of Matthew was written to a Jewish audience with the intention of proving Jesus is the Messiah. The central message during this discourse was the Kingdom of Heaven. In Matthew, the term *kingdom* always refers to the promised Kingdom of Israel. It should be noted there is no distinction between the *Kingdom of Heaven* and the *Kingdom of God*. These two terms are used interchangeably in the Gospel of Matthew. The Kingdom of Heaven simply means the Kingdom that comes from heaven. The Kingdom of God refers to the Kingdom that belongs to God (cf. Matthew 19:23-24). The point of both expressions is to convey the idea of God's earthly Kingdom which will be inaugurated at Christ's triumphant return.

The historical setting of the Sermon on the Mount is riveting. The Jewish people were deeply concerned about getting into the Kingdom of God. Rumors were beginning to swirl that perhaps this man, Jesus, was the long-awaited Prophet of Israel. "Could He be the One who would usher in the Kingdom of Israel?" many thought. Jesus had been proclaiming the Kingdom of Heaven was at hand (Matthew 4:17). So too had Christ's forerunner, John the Baptist (Matthew 2:2). This led to a very natural question, "Who would make it into the Kingdom?" The only group who appeared to have a standard of righteousness necessary for entrance into the Kingdom was the religious leaders of Israel. Who would dare to question their ability to get into the Kingdom? Even a quick reading of the Gospels reveals Jesus had many run-ins with the Pharisees. The miracles Jesus performed had already stirred up a lot of trouble. Against this backdrop, Jesus began discussing the Kingdom in Matthew 5.

Matthew 5:20 is a key verse within the Sermon on the Mount. Jesus said, "For I say to you, that unless your righteousness exceeds the righteousness of the scribes and Pharisees, you will by no means enter the kingdom of heaven" (Matthew 5:20). These were powerful words. What a rebuke to the religious leaders of Israel! In effect, Jesus was teaching, "If you really want to get into the Kingdom, let me tell you how. You must be righteous, but not just any kind of righteousness. You must be more righteous than even the Pharisees and the scribes." What a shocking statement this was. It was common knowledge to the people of Israel that their leaders were arrogant, but there was still respect for their service to God. No one could argue their leaders did not have a deep reverence for the laws of God. The Jewish people in Jesus' day assumed the Pharisees and the scribes were on the correct path to getting into the Kingdom.

In His customary masterful way, Jesus pointed out how woefully inadequate the self-righteousness of the Jewish leaders was. The people certainly knew the teaching of the Old Testament forbidding murder (Exodus 20:13), but Jesus told them, "But I say to you that whoever is angry with his brother without a cause shall be in danger of the judgment" (Matthew 5:22). The people also knew Exodus 20:14 instructed them not to commit adultery, but again Jesus told them, "But I say to you that whoever looks at a woman to lust for her has already committed adultery with her in his heart" (Matthew 5:28). Jesus was breaking down their misconceptions in the Sermon on the Mount. He was trying to get the people to understand the focus should be on the status of their hearts rather than their outward behavior. Jesus wanted them to see what was taking place within their hearts was more significant than the external actions that men could see.

The highpoint of the teaching, in this section of Scripture, is when Jesus proclaimed, "Not everyone who says to Me, 'Lord, Lord,' shall enter the kingdom of heaven, but he who does the will of My Father in heaven" (Matthew 7:21). This raises an important question, what is the will of His Father? The answer is found in John 6:40, "And this is the will of Him who sent Me, that everyone who sees the Son and believes in Him may have everlasting life; and I will raise him up at the last day." By believing in Jesus Christ, we become righteous. Paul expounded on this later, in the church age, by saying, "Christ is the end of the law for righteousness to everyone who believes" (Romans 10:4).

Set aside our look at the Sermon on the Mount for a moment. In Romans 9, the Apostle Paul gave us the doctrinal foundation for what Jesus alluded to in the Gospels. Paul put together the pieces theologically for us, and it synthesizes perfectly with everything Jesus said in the Sermon on the Mount (as well as the teaching of our Lord throughout the Gospels). The Gentiles were considered by the Jews to be dirty, rotten, filthy people who had no respect for the sacred Law. Yet, Paul teaches, "What shall we say then? That Gentiles, who did not pursue righteousness, have attained to righteousness, even the righteousness of faith; but Israel, pursuing the law of righteousness, has not attained to the law of righteousness. Why? Because they did not seek it by faith, but as it were, by the works of the law. For they stumbled at that stumbling stone" (Rom. 9:30–32).

Building off this point, Paul continued to teach about Israel. He said, "I bear them witness that they have a zeal for God, but not according to knowledge. For they being ignorant of God's righteousness, and seeking to establish their own righteousness, have not submitted to the righteousness of God. For Christ is the end of the law for righteousness to everyone who believes" (Romans 10:2–4).

When Jesus presented Himself to the nation of Israel, He offered the Jews the Kingdom. The bottom line is that Israel had drifted. It had been roughly 400 years since Malachi, the last writing prophet. Over the generations, the people of Israel had wandered and gotten off track with their understanding of the Kingdom promises. Traditions had been added, the Scriptures reinterpreted, and the Law had been recast into man's image. This all had a devastating effect. The Jews had turned the Law into a legalistic standard for entrance into the Kingdom. The Jewish leaders then turned around and proclaimed their own righteousness because they lived by the same rules they had created. How convenient this was for them!

This is what Jesus was up against. Jesus stepped onto the scene and completely opposed this line of thinking. Jesus taught if a person wanted to be righteous, *it must be faith righteousness, not self-righteousness*. If the people of Israel would have turned from the misconceptions they had created about the Kingdom, they would have received their King and His Kingdom.

What is so truly remarkable about this passage is the nature of the Kingdom. There is no hint anyone in Jesus' audience on the hillside, nor the original Jewish recipients of Matthew's Gospel, thought the Kingdom was anything other than literal. If you had been listening to Jesus as He first spoke these words, what would you have understood the Kingdom to be? Or, if you were reading about these events after the Gospel of Matthew started circulating in the churches in the late 40s AD, what would you have recognized the Kingdom to be? There was only one answer for the Jewish people living at that time. It was the Kingdom that was promised to David, the Kingdom that was reiterated through the prophets, the Kingdom that was proclaimed when Gabriel announced the birth of Christ, and the Kingdom that Jesus had referred to in the Sermon on the Mount. No one would have had any reason to think this Kingdom was spiritual.

Overlooking Prophetic Passages

Immediately after the Sermon on the Mount in Matthew, we see the Lord's interaction with a centurion. The eschatological details of this encounter are often overlooked. Matthew records, "Now when Jesus had entered Capernaum, a centurion came to Him, pleading with Him, saying, 'Lord, my servant is lying at home paralyzed, dreadfully tormented.' And Jesus said to him, 'I will come and heal him.' The centurion answered and said, 'Lord, I am not worthy that You should come under my roof. But only speak a word, and my servant will be healed'" (Matthew 8:5–8).

This was an incredible response by the centurion in verse eight. He understood he was not even worthy to have Jesus come under his roof. At the very heart of this was the recognition that when Jesus spoke, it was God speaking. The centurion acknowledged who Jesus was, and how unworthy he was before God. What a contrast this was with the Pharisees, who were counting on their own righteousness to justify themselves before God. The definitive teaching of the Word of God, regarding our eternal salvation, is that we are completely unworthy before a Holy God. There is absolutely nothing that we can muster up, in our own self-righteousness, to make us worthy before God.

Jesus' dialogue with the centurion continues, "For I also am a man under authority, having soldiers under me. And I say to this one, 'Go,' and he goes; and to another, 'Come,' and he comes; and to my servant, 'Do this,' and he does it. When Jesus heard it, He marveled, and said to those who followed, 'Assuredly, I say to you, I have not found such great faith, not even in Israel!'" (Matthew 8:9–10). This is the key—faith righteousness. Verse eleven is a significant verse, "And I say to you that many will come from east and west, and sit down with Abraham, Isaac, and Jacob in the kingdom of heaven" (Matthew 8:11). All who have faith in Jesus Christ, and Him alone for eternal life, Jew and Gentile alike, will sit at the banquet table in the Kingdom of Heaven.

This same verse also contains another key teaching on the Kingdom. This will be a global Kingdom, not merely a Jewish Kingdom. Jesus was teaching that when He comes back a second time, many people will come from around the world including many Gentiles like the centurion. They will sit down in the Kingdom with Abraham, Isaac, and Jacob. Matthew 8:11 forces us to recognize the global nature of the Kingdom; this is the point Jesus was making. It was for the benefit of everyone who could hear Him. He wanted them to know the Gentile centurion understood this critical truth: it is faith righteousness that is essential for getting into the Kingdom. Jesus was trying to tell the people there will be many Gentiles in the Kingdom of God.

In the very next, verse Jesus mentions the "sons of the kingdom," which is a reference to Jews, and in this context, it obviously refers to unbelieving Jews. They will be, "cast out into outer darkness" (Matthew 8:12). This was sure to rattle the people of Israel! Jewish people without faith righteousness would not make it into the Kingdom. Jesus was testifying that if the Jewish people had faith, like the centurion, they would be there with Abraham, Isaac, and Jacob. Without this faith, they would become like the Pharisees and Sadducees who will be cast into outer darkness.

Misunderstanding Prophetic Passages

When God promised David, in 2 Samuel 7:16, that his descendant will reign forever upon the throne, what did David envision? David himself was a king who sat upon a literal throne. David did not picture some mystical, spiritual, hypothetical throne. He understood the throne the only way it was ever understood at that time, as a literal throne. Likewise, when the Messianic King had come, He was also talking about a literal Kingdom. This is exactly what the people were expecting. By the time we reach chapter 13 of Matthew's Gospel, it is evident the nation of Israel was not going to receive Jesus as their King. The only crown the people would give Jesus was a crown of thorns before they crucified Him. It is precisely for this reason there is a dramatic shift in Matthew 13. At this point, Jesus began to speak the parables of the Kingdom.

Great misunderstanding has crept into the church surrounding this chapter. It is often thought the parables of the Kingdom are about the church age. The idea proposed is that Jesus introduced a *mystery form* of the Kingdom, according to which the church would replace Israel in God's plan. Such an idea is utterly foreign to the text. Indeed, an examination of the text reveals Matthew 13 does not contain the word *form*. In context, this chapter does not say anything about the church at all. The purpose of this section of Scripture is to show since Israel had clearly rejected Christ, the earthly Messianic Kingdom would be postponed.

In Matthew 13 Jesus also was explaining, through parables, that when the Kingdom did arrive, it would be slightly different from what many of the Jews were expecting. There will be unbelievers living in the Kingdom (because eventually there will be some unbelievers in the Millennium). The Kingdom will start small like a mustard seed and then explode. This points us to the understanding (just as we see elsewhere in Scripture) that at the end of the Tribulation, the earth will be sparsely populated because most people on earth will have died. It will be a small remnant of people that enter the Kingdom. We discussed the remnant principle in Chapter Two.

The future, literal Kingdom is not just the subject of the Sermon on the Mount and the Parables of the Kingdom, it is a major theme throughout Jesus' earthly ministry. The subject comes up again and again. It is almost as if the disciples were obsessed with the Kingdom. In Matthew 18:1 the disciples asked Jesus, "Who then is greatest in the kingdom of heaven?" In chapter 19 Peter asked a bold question, "See, we have left all and followed You. Therefore what shall we have?" (Matthew 19:27). The Lord's response was astounding, "Assuredly I say to you, that in the regeneration [i.e., the Kingdom], when the Son of Man sits on the throne of His glory, you who have followed Me will also sit on twelve thrones, judging the twelve tribes of Israel" (Matthew 19:28). Then there is the request from the mother of two of Jesus' disciples. "Then the mother of Zebedee's sons came to Him with her sons, kneeling down and asking something from Him. And He said to her, 'What do you wish?' She said to Him, 'Grant that these two sons of mine may sit, one on Your right hand and the other on the left, in Your kingdom'" (Matthew 20:20–21). None of these passages sounds like a spiritual Kingdom. The reason is remarkably simple—all these people were expecting a literal Kingdom.

As we approach the Olivet Discourse, the crucifixion was drawing near. It was only a matter of hours before Jesus would be betrayed, arrested, and crucified. Within Matthew 23, Jesus had given some scathing rebukes to the religious leaders (this is seen with the eight *woes* listed in verses 13–36). In verse 37, we have a powerful and passionate lament by Jesus. This is a key display of emotion by our Savior for His people of the nation of Israel when He cried out, "O Jerusalem, Jerusalem, the one who kills the prophets and stones those who are sent to her! How often I wanted to gather your children together, as a hen gathers her chicks under her wings, but you were not willing" (Matthew 23:37)! The repetition of a noun (Jerusalem mentioned twice) is a demonstration of great emotion in Hebrew culture. Our Lord was agonizing over the reality that His people had rejected Him and His Kingdom.

Jesus continues, "See! Your house is left to you desolate; for I say to you,

you shall see Me no more till you say, *'Blessed* is *He who comes in the name of the Lord!'*" (Matthew 23:38–39). The *house* of Israel was the Temple (1 Kings 9:7–8). The words of Jesus came true within forty years when Jerusalem was ravaged and the Temple destroyed by the Roman general, Titus. Jesus specifically told the first-century Jewish leaders they would not see Him until they said, *"Blessed* is *He who comes in the name of the Lord*!" (Matthew 23:39). This quote is from Psalm 118, which is a Messianic Psalm. Most Christians recognize the words of part of this Psalm, "This is the day the Lord has made; we will rejoice and be glad in it" (Psalm 118:24). The *day* referred to is the Second Coming of Christ. This is the day when the Messiah will come and usher in the Kingdom.

Just two days before Jesus taught the Olivet Discourse, at the Triumphal Entry, the people had cried out as Jesus entered Jerusalem, "Hosanna to the Son of David! Blessed is He who comes in the name of the Lord! Hosanna in the highest" (Matthew 21:9). Before long those calls of, "Hosanna! Hosanna!" turned into, "Crucify Him! Crucify Him!" Jesus had predicted a delay in the coming of His Kingdom in the parables of the Kingdom, as mentioned earlier. He also alluded to a delay in the parable of the minas (Luke 19:11-27), which He gave the day before the Triumphal Entry. In Matthew 23:39, Jesus was now making this delay in His Kingdom explicitly clear. He revealed Israel would not see Him again until the people as a nation come together and receive Him by faith as their King crying out, "Hosanna! Hosanna!"

The disciples were quite troubled by this. They still did not comprehend everything the Lord was teaching them. Despite the Old Testament prophecies of the suffering Messiah, and the Lord's teaching about His death, the disciples were still confused. In Matthew 24:1 it appears the disciples were alarmed over the Lord's statement about the Temple being left desolate. Their response was curious. They approached Jesus and pointed out how beautiful the Temple was. Jesus responded with an even more troubling statement regarding the Temple, "Do you not see all these things? Assuredly, I say to you, not one stone shall be left here upon another, that shall not be thrown down" (Matthew 24:2).

This definitely got the disciples' attention and raised another question.

Mark 13:2 informs us that it was Peter, James, John, and Andrew questioning the Lord. There was one basic question, "When will this happen?" They wanted to know when the Kingdom would be ushered in, but they asked it three different ways, "Tell us, when will these things be? And what will be the sign of Your coming, and of the end of the age?" (Matthew 24:3). If the Kingdom was not going to come immediately, when would it come? The disciples were asking for some signs so they could be ready. The entire Olivet Discourse is in response to verse 3. It answers the disciples' questions and reveals signs which will precede His coming so they would know what to look for. The Olivet Discourse relates to the Tribulation—that seven-year period immediately preceding Christ's return to inaugurate the Kingdom. It is a mistake to try to fit the church and the Rapture into the Olivet Discourse. Jesus was talking about the signs of His Second Coming, not the Rapture.

Jesus said, "When the Son of Man comes in His glory, and all the holy angels with Him, then He will sit on the throne of His glory" (Matthew 25:31). What kind of throne is this? This is a reference to a literal throne. Is there any reason to believe, from anything Jesus said in three and a half years of ministry, that He was talking about a spiritual, nonliteral Kingdom? There is nothing to suggest this at all. The only way you can arrive at this conclusion is by allegorizing the text.

Fast forward in time. Jesus was betrayed, arrested, crucified, and had risen again. Forty days later, in Acts 1, Jesus was talking with His disciples on the day of His ascension. Unsurprisingly, the disciples were still obsessed with the Kingdom. Notice what they said in Acts 1:6, "Lord, will You at this time restore the kingdom to Israel?" If, as many supposed today, the Kingdom is not literal, this would have been the perfect opportunity for Christ to set the record straight. Christ could then have broken the news to them that the Kingdom would be different from what they expected. He could have explained He was going to reign figuratively in their hearts from the clouds of heaven. But Jesus did not do this! Instead, He affirmed the literalness of the Kingdom when He responded, "It is not for you to know times or seasons which the Father has put in His own authority" (Acts 1:7). The Father has determined the timing, but Jesus confirmed the Kingdom is still going to come.

The wording in Luke's account of the ascension is fascinating. "Now when He had spoken these things, while they watched, He was taken up, and a cloud received Him out of their sight. And while they looked steadfastly toward heaven as He went up, behold, two men stood by them in white apparel" (Acts 1:9–10). The disciples were standing there gazing up into heaven. It leaves us wondering if they understood at this point there would be a long delay (the church age) before Christ ushers in His Kingdom. Did they think Jesus would ascend to heaven, grab the keys to the Kingdom, and head right back down to earth to usher in His Kingdom? This is when the men in white apparel said to the disciples, "Men of Galilee, why do you stand gazing up into heaven? This same Jesus, who was taken up from you into heaven, will so come in like manner as you saw Him go into heaven" (Acts 1:11). Jesus left in bodily form and will return in bodily form (not spiritually or figuratively, but literally).

The disciples made their way back to Jerusalem and met in the upper room. One of the first acts of business was to choose a new disciple. Judas had proven himself to be an unbeliever (and had killed himself) so they needed a replacement. This was an urgent matter of business for them. Remember, Jesus had promised them that in the Kingdom the disciples would reign with Him upon twelve thrones (Matthew 19:28). Could it be the disciples' urgency in replacing Judas was because they did not want the twelfth throne to be left empty? Regardless, there is no hint they expected anything other than a literal Kingdom.

Early in the church age, Peter was preaching in Solomon's Porch. We read in Acts:

> *But those things which God foretold by the mouth of all His prophets, that the Christ would suffer, He has thus fulfilled. Repent therefore and be converted, that your sins may be blotted out, so that times of refreshing may come from the presence of the Lord, and that He may send Jesus Christ, who was preached to you before, whom heaven must receive until the times of restoration of all things, which God has spoken*

by the mouth of all His holy prophets since the world began. (Acts 3:18–21)

The disciples were still looking for Christ to come back. We see this continued focus on the promised return of Christ in the New Testament epistles.

There is never a single hint, in all of Scripture, that the Kingdom of Christ is a spiritualized Kingdom. For this reason, replacement theology needs to be replaced with a proper understanding of biblical eschatology. The Kingdom in the Bible has one meaning, an eternal Kingdom that was first promised in the Old Testament. The Word of God always refers to a literal earthly Kingdom over which Jesus Christ, the eternal Son of God, will rule and reign with a rod of iron in perfect peace and justice. This Kingdom, according to Bible prophecy, will be inaugurated when Christ returns at the Second Advent. This eternal Kingdom will be on the old earth for one thousand years (the Millennium). After the old heaven and old earth are destroyed, this Kingdom will continue for all eternity in the new heaven and new earth.

Misapplying Prophetic Passages

Another sign the church is falling away is the way so many Christians misapply prophecy to current events. Many Christians think we are living within a momentous bubble of prophetic fulfillment. This idea stems from what is sometimes called "newspaper exegesis." It describes those Christians who hold a Bible in one hand and a newspaper in the other, claiming every news item is the fulfillment of prophecy. This tendency is particularly prevalent in the American church, where the penchant for wearing red-white-and-blue sunglasses when reading the Bible is so common. I have addressed the hazards of American exceptionalism in some of my other books, so I will not belabor the point here. It is worth noting, however, that "newspaper exegesis" is almost entirely an American phenomenon.

Date-setters fall into this category, but they are not alone. Even Christians who rightly shy away from setting a date for the Rapture can be guilty of connecting current events to Bible passages and suggesting prophecy is being fulfilled before our very eyes. As mentioned, the Rapture is the next event on God's prophetic calendar. While there are many events occurring today that are *setting the stage* for the fulfillment of prophecy, we must be cautious not to assign chapter and verse to every headline in the news. We should interpret the newspaper through the lens of Scripture, not the other way around.

For many years, prophecy teachers have gone out on a limb by claiming some new geo-political development or scientific advancement fulfills a particular end times prophecy. For example, when UPCs first hit the market, we were told they constituted the mark of the beast. So too with RFID chips. Today, many are pointing to brain-computer interfaces or messenger RNA vaccine technology as the mark of the beast. While such advancements in technology could be setting the stage for the future beast system, we cannot know this with certainty.

Another example of misapplying prophetic Scriptures relates to the establishment of the European Union many years ago. Some of you may be old enough to remember the chorus of prophecy pundits proclaiming the ten-nation confederacy of Daniel and Revelation had arrived. We see similar declarations today. "Obama is the Antichrist!" "No, Trump is the Antichrist!" "The United States is Mystery Babylon!" Yet, at the end of the day, all we can really do is look to the signs of the times and recognize the end times stage is rapidly taking shape (cf. Matthew 16:3).

Neglecting Prophetic Passages

Some Christians in these last days ignore end times Bible prophecy altogether. This is another form of eschatological apostasy. Peter warned this would happen in the last days. "Knowing this first: that scoffers will come in the last days, walking according to their own lusts, and saying, "Where is the promise of His coming? For since the fathers fell asleep, all things continue as they were from the beginning of creation" (2 Peter

3:3–4). This increasing ridicule of Bible prophecy teachers has been aided and abetted by the date-setting miscalculations mentioned above. When Bible teachers, well-intentioned though they may be, suggest Jesus is going to return on a particular date, they discredit the entire Bible prophecy community. So too with those who suggest all (or most) of Bible prophecy has been fulfilled in the first century. Such erroneous conclusions lead Christians to ask, "Why bother studying the end times? What difference does it make to me now?"

By failing to "cut straight" (2 Timothy 2:15) when it comes to eschatological portions of Scripture, Christians in these last days find an excuse to ignore the reality of future end times prophecy. Since, in their view, it is all spiritual or metaphorical, why waste time studying it? There is nothing tangible to look forward to, or so they think. Like the scoffers Peter warned would come in these last days (2 Peter 3:3-4), these Christians think everything will stay the same and the promise of Christ's coming is not literal.

If more Christians understood the literal nature of the future Kingdom, they would not neglect biblical teaching about the end times. Unfortunately, this has become the predominant view in the church. To believe in a *literal* return of Christ to establish a *literal* Kingdom on earth with a *literal* throne from a *literal* rebuilt temple in Jerusalem places you in the vast minority of Christians today. As I have pointed out elsewhere, to neglect end times Bible prophecy is to abandon roughly 16% of the Bible. This estimate is derived from the fact that about one-third of the Bible is prophetic, with half of that being unfulfilled end times prophecy. Thus, about 16% of Scripture is unfulfilled prophecy. Those who ignore the subject of eschatology are part of the "84% Club," content to study only 84% of the Bible. That this club has so many members is surely a sign of the great last days apostasy.

Abusing Prophetic Passages

The stranglehold replacement theology has on the church in these last days has given rise to another serious sign of the times: the rise of antisemitism in the church. The further the church drifts away from the Lord, the more it will abandon His chosen nation, Israel. A profound increase in anti-Israel sentiments swept across America following the Hamas terrorist attacks of October 7, 2023. According to the Anti-Defamation League (ADL), "In the three months since the Oct. 7 massacre in Israel, U.S. antisemitic incidents have skyrocketed, reaching a total of 3,291 incidents between Oct. 7 and Jan. 7... This represents a 361% increase compared to the same period one year prior, which saw 712 incidents."

This was particularly prevalent on college and university campuses. My wife, Wendy, and I had the opportunity to visit three Ivy League campuses in 2024. While on the campus of Brown University in Providence, RI, we witnessed a gathering of students in the quad making large pro-Palestinian signs and preparing for an anti-Israel protest later that night. It is one thing to see antisemitism in the culture at large. It is quite another when it finds its way into the church. Most American pulpits were deathly silent after the attacks in Israel, and they refused to call out the antisemitic protests across the land that followed. It was a sad reflection on the state of the American church.

Jonathan Greenblatt, in a March 21, 2024, article for *TIME* entitled, "The Growing Antisemitism Among Young Americans," wrote, "Negative attitudes about Jews, and negative experiences for Jews, by every metric, are growing, not fading. And most troubling, antisemitism—for the first time—is growing among younger generations of Americans, portending a very different and dark future for the American Jewish community." Citing an ADL study, Greenblatt points out, "Millennials now [lead] the way, harboring the most antisemitic views" including "conspiracies about Jewish control of the media and Wall Street, or beliefs that Jews are insular or irritating." According to the study, "This upsurge in antisemitism among the younger generations is driving an overall jump in antisemitic attitudes." Chad Roberts, writing for *Christianity.com*, comments, "Hamas set the world on fire in the fall of 2023, and things have not looked the same since. There is an unprecedented rise in antisemitism. ... From major cities to college campuses, the spirit of antisemitism is raging."

The rise of antisemitism in the last days should not surprise us. The enemies of God's chosen people have long sought to destroy Israel. Psalm 83 is a lament song with a note of imprecation written by Asaph. He wrote, "For behold, Your enemies make a tumult; and those who hate You have lifted up their head. They have taken crafty counsel against Your people, and consulted together against Your sheltered ones. They have said, "Come, and let us cut them off from being a nation, that the name of Israel may be remembered no more" (Psalm 83:2–4). Jesus warned that during the seven years prior to His return to establish the long-awaited Kingdom the Jewish people would experience unprecedented persecution. "Then they will deliver you up to tribulation and kill you, and you will be hated by all nations for My name's sake. And then many will be offended, will betray one another, and will hate one another" (Matthew 24:9–10). With the rise of antisemitism in these last days, the stage is being set for this end times persecution of Israel by the Antichrist and False Prophet.

While the rise in antisemitism in general may not be surprising, what *is* surprising is the prevalence of antisemitic rhetoric coming from evangelical pulpits and conservative Christian pundits. Some Christians who have an interest in end times prophecy have been led astray into a false conspiratorial world where the Jewish people are the enemy. Again, this is because they have been taught for so long that the church has replaced Israel and there is no prophetic future for national Israel. Popular conservative talk show hosts like Alex Jones, Mike Adams, and Rick Wiles espouse and disseminate widely debunked antisemitic conspiracy theories about how the Zionists control the world. What they fail to realize, however, is that Zionists will not control the world until the Chief Zionist and Prince of Peace, Jesus Christ, returns to take the throne.

"Antisemitism is not disliking a person who happens to be Jewish. It is disliking a person *because* they are Jewish," writes Ty Perry in an article for *The Friends of Israel Gospel Ministry*. There is no doubt some (many?) of today's secular Jewish leaders in Israel are aiding and abetting the globalist agenda in the same way many American political leaders are part of the broader globalist conspiracy, and many Chinese, Russian, and British leaders are as well. But this does not mean, in any way, that the grand conspiracy to usher in a one-world system at the behest of Satan is a "Jewish" conspiracy, nor is it an "American," "Russian," "Chinese," or "British" conspiracy. The Jews began returning to the land in unbelief in 1948. They will not return in belief until they first accept Jesus Christ as their Savior and King and cry out, "Hosanna! Hosanna" (Cr. Matthew 23:37-39; Romans 10:1-14)!

Antisemitic ideology in the American church is by no means new. As one secular writer put it, "Christian theology has ...gone hand-in-hand with anti-Semitism for centuries, dating back long before Martin Luther." What is new, however, is the pervasiveness of such views in these last days. Many of the same New Testament passages used to defend Israel's prophetic future and centrality in the coming Kingdom are abused by replacement theologians in support of their antisemitic conclusions. The American church is undoubtedly falling away from sound, biblical eschatology.

In the next chapter, we will examine another manifestation of the great last days apostasy: moral compromise.

5

FALLING AWAY MORALLY

But know this, that in the last days perilous times will come: For men will be lovers of themselves, lovers of money, boasters, proud, blasphemers, disobedient to parents, unthankful, unholy, unloving, unforgiving, slanderers, without self-control, brutal, despisers of good, traitors, headstrong, haughty, lovers of pleasure rather than lovers of God, having a form of godliness but denying its power. And from such people turn away! (2 Timothy 3:1–5)

* * *

A young preacher was eager to preach his first sermon at the little country church where he had accepted a call as pastor. He decided to use his inaugural message to address the growing moral decline in society. On and on he went, bemoaning various examples of moral turpitude running rampant in the culture. He ended his sermon by stepping on the toes of the casual drinkers in the congregation with a crescendo of condemnations about alcohol.

"Why, if I had all the beer in the world, I would take it and throw it into the river!" he exclaimed. With even greater emphasis, he said, "And if I had all the wine in the world, I would take it and throw it into the river too!!" And finally, with much exuberance, he concluded, "And if I had all the whiskey in the world, I would take it and throw it into the river as well!!!" With that, he sat down, satisfied he had made his point. A worried look came over the song leader's face as he mounted the pulpit to lead the closing hymn. Hesitantly, he said, "For our closing song, let us stand and sing hymn #365, *Shall We Gather At the River*!"

In these last days of the church age, more and more Christians are gathering at the river to engage in and celebrate all sorts of immoral behaviors. What was once done in secret is now openly embraced. Christians who used to steal away secretly to the river of debauchery can now march there unashamedly with affirming pastors at their sides. The attitude of the American church is growing increasingly permissive towards homosexual and heterosexual sin, transgenderism, the breakdown of marriage and traditional family values, pornography, and other forms of immorality.

This shift away from biblical morality is yet another indication of the great last days apostasy. The church's moral decay stems from the biblical departure we addressed in Chapter Three. Britt Mooney explains, "The growing influence of secularism and relativism has led to a rejection of absolute truth and moral absolutes, resulting in moral relativism and the acceptance of diverse lifestyles and beliefs." In this chapter, we will expose several ways the American church is falling away morally.

Moral Failures in the Pulpit

Pastors are human and struggle with the same sins of the flesh every believer does. In fact, it could be said ministers are even more susceptible to moral failure than the average Christian because Satan knows he can get more bang for his buck if he gets a pastor to fall away. The damage done to the body of Christ when a preacher falls can be catastrophic. Any believer who caters to the old nature instead of walking in the Spirit is capable of the worst forms of immorality, and members of the clergy are no exception. This is why Paul warned all Christians, "I say then: Walk in the Spirit, and you shall not fulfill the lust of the flesh. For the flesh lusts against the Spirit, and the Spirit against the flesh; and these are contrary to one another, so that you do not do the things that you wish" (Galatians 5:16–17). When high-profile ministry leaders engage in immoral behavior it brings shame to the cause of Christ and discredits the church. While such moral failures in America's pulpit sadly are nothing new—they are as old as our country itself—the frequency and blatancy of such hypocritical actions are a sign of growing apostasy.

The 1980s saw a tidal wave of renowned American pastors who ventured into the moral abyss. 1988 in particular was a bad year for preachers. Televangelists Jimmy Swaggart and Jim Bakker both made headlines for their extra-marital affairs that year. The Catholic Church's sex abuse scandals that began emerging in the mid-eighties only added to the disrepute brought upon American Christianity. By 2004, more than four thousand Catholic priests had been accused of child sexual abuse dating back as far as 1950, according to a report compiled by the John Jay College of Criminal Justice. Protestant or Catholic, it seems immorality is an equal opportunity temptation. The Southern Baptist Convention has experienced its own ignominy when it comes to moral failures in their pulpits and churches. Widespread sexual abuse cases in Southern Baptist churches were reported by the *Houston Chronicle* and *San Antonio Express-News* in 2019.

Moral failure is no respecter of denominations. Pastors and ministry leaders in a multitude of Christian organizations have fallen from grace. Genevieve Carlton, in a July 3, 2024, article entitled, "Legendary Pastors Who Fell From Grace," adds another name to this infamous list. Michael Hintz was a youth counselor at the First Assembly of God Church in Des Moines, Iowa. According to Carlton, in 2004, "Hintz, who was 35, married, and had four kids, became sexually involved with a 17-year-old girl whom he had been counseling." Ted Haggard, former president of the National Association of Evangelicals and once considered one of America's most charismatic and powerful evangelical leaders with an audience of more than thirty million people, was caught in a gay sex scandal in 2006. In 2014, more than thirty women accused conservative evangelist Bill Gothard of molestation and assault, including underage girls. Gothard eventually resigned from the Institute in Basic Life Principles (IBLP). The IBLP board of directors claimed Gothard had acted inappropriately but not criminally and accused the media of propagating false and misleading statements. Regardless, the damage was done.

Also in 2014, Mark Driscoll, pastor of the enormous Mars Hill Church in Seattle, WA, resigned amid a cavalcade of allegations involving plagiarism, emotional abuse, misogyny, and more. Craig Welch, in a September 13, 2024, article for the Seattle Times entitled, "The rise and fall of Mars Hill Church," writes, "For years the edgy, blue-jeaned, hipster preacher used charisma and combativeness to barrel through turmoil, once bragging that he'd mow down all who questioned his vision: 'There is a pile of dead bodies behind the Mars Hill bus, and by God's grace, it'll be a mountain by the time we're done,' he once said in a meeting. 'You either get on the bus or you get run over by the bus.'" I guess Solomon was correct. "Pride goes before destruction, and a haughty spirit before a fall" (Proverbs 16:18). In 2020, evangelical leader Jerry Falwell Jr. resigned as president of Liberty University amid an unfolding sex scandal. The details about the ménage à trois involving Falwell's wife, Becki, and a younger man they met at a hotel in Miami Beach are beyond sordid.

Pornography and Promiscuity

Moral apostasy in the church is further indicated by the pornography and promiscuity epidemics. According to a study commissioned by Josh McDowell and conducted by the Barna Research Group, 57% of pastors in the United States struggle with pornography personally, and 68% of youth pastors. McDowell calls the pornography crisis a "spiritual cancer in the church." Ross McCall, in an article for *Cru.org*, sounds the alarm. "The Barna Group study put hard numbers on a problem many have known was afflicting the church for decades," McCall writes. He summarizes the research:

> *Barna's research demonstrates that:*
>
> *62% of teenagers (ages 13-17) have received a sexual image via their*

cell phones.

72% of Christian young adults (ages 18-24) actively seek out pornography on the internet.

3 out of 5 divorces cite the use of porn as a major factor.

The study also shows that the most worrying numbers are all increasing at an alarming rate.

It is this alarming rate of increase that marks pornography as a major sign of moral apostasy in these last days. The Internet and social media have exasperated the problem. No longer is it necessary for teenage boys to shoplift a copy of *Playboy* from the local 7-Eleven; pornography is just a click away in the palm of their hands.

Austin Fruits points out, in a September 9, 2022, article for *Josh McDowell Ministry*, "Our culture is so sexually saturated that porn is now included in top-selling books, advertising, and social media. We don't even realize how many pornographic images we are exposed to daily, without our even trying to see them." Josh McDowell laments, "[Pornography is] available, accessible, affordable, anonymous, appealing, aggressive, and addictive." It also objectifies the human body and leads to animalistic behaviors in an attempt to gratify the flesh. The Apostle Paul warned, "But put on the Lord Jesus Christ, and make no provision for the flesh, to fulfill its lusts" (Romans 13:14). He describes the depraved mind as conducting itself "in the lusts of our flesh, fulfilling the desires of the flesh and of the mind" (Ephesians 2:3). When Christians cater to the flesh we are acting like unbelievers, who "dishonor their bodies among themselves" (Romans 1:24).

Josh McDowell Ministries points out that pornography causes a person to: (1) think it is okay to use, abuse, or mistreat others for self-gratification; (2) think it's okay to view and participate in the use, mistreatment, or abuse of a person; (3) think it's okay to treat others with indifference; and (4) believe the lie that pleasure guides principle, meaning sexual passion trumps moral objectives. Pornography creates a lack of empathy toward others. It leads to sexual aggression, incest, and age-inappropriate relationships. And it causes concentration problems, low motivation, depression, social anxiety, negative self-perceptions, and a litany of other spiritual and psychological problems.

The massive influence of the pornography industry is hard to wrap our minds around. Fruits reports, "One study found that pornography sites receive more regular traffic than Netflix, Amazon, and Twitter [now known as X] combined each month. Porn now accounts for a third of all Internet traffic! More than 91 percent of men and 60 percent of women have reported consuming pornography in the past month." It is unsurprising then that pornography has given rise to another manifestation of moral apostasy in the church: promiscuity. Once relegated to the arena of whispers and gossip, sexual promiscuity has become normalized in the apostate church.

I can still remember when revelations of fornication (sex before marriage) or adultery (sex outside of marriage) engendered gasps and shocked looks. Not anymore. Today such revelations are met with a collective yawn by the American church, which is undoubtedly a sign of moral apostasy in the last days. We are witnessing the death of shame. The Bible predicted this day would come. "But you, beloved, remember the words which were spoken before by the apostles of our Lord Jesus Christ: how they told you that there would be mockers in the last time who would walk according to their own ungodly lusts" (Jude 17–18).

Homosexuality and Gay Marriage

As I mentioned in Chapter Three, many mainstream evangelical churches and pastors are embracing the homosexual lifestyle over and against the clear teaching of the Bible on this subject. Carlyle Murphy from the Pew Research Center writes, "Acceptance of homosexuality is rising across the broad spectrum of American Christianity, including among members of churches that strongly oppose homosexual relationships as sinful, according to an extensive Pew Research Center survey of U.S. religious beliefs and practices." According to Murphy, "A majority of U.S. Christians (54%) now say that homosexuality should be accepted, rather than discouraged, by society." This trend has given rise to websites like *GayChurch.org* where apostate Christians can find churches in their geographic region that affirm homosexuality and gay marriage.

In 2024, the United Methodist Church (UMC) officially abandoned the plain truth of God's Word about homosexuality. Chelsea Bailey, in a May 5, 2024, article for *CNN.com,* explains, "The church's governing body marked a new era of LGBTQ inclusion by voting to lift the bans on LGBTQ clergy and on pastors performing same-sex unions. They also removed the language that said homosexuality was 'incompatible with Christian teaching.'" Apostate methodists hailed this moment as creating a "better church." Not true. The UMC is much, much worse for this decision. The United Methodist Church is one of the largest mainline Protestant Christian denominations in the United States, according to the Pew Research Center. As of 2022, the UMC says it has more than 5.4 million members in the US, across nearly 30,000 active churches. Hopefully, any remnant members of the church will run, not walk, away from this apostate denomination.

Another example of this kind of moral apostasy comes from the Mennonites. The governing body of the largest Mennonite denomination in the United States passed a resolution in 2022 committing to LGBTQ inclusion. The Mennonite Church USA also repealed instructions to pastors not to officiate at marriages between people of the same sex. Kathryn Post reports, "Nearly 83% of the delegates meeting at a special assembly in Kansas City, Missouri, voted in favor of repealing the guidelines barring marriage for same-sex couples, while the resolution for LGBTQ inclusion passed by a narrower margin, with 55.7% in favor." *WesternChurch.net* lists another denomination that has fallen away morally: the Presbyterian Church USA (PCUSA). The PCUSA officially voted in 2015 to allow ministers to perform same-sex marriages and amended its constitution to define marriage as being between "two people," rather than "a man and a woman." Additionally, the PCUSA also allows LGBTQ+ individuals to be ordained as ministers, elders, and deacons.

The Evangelical Lutheran Church in America (ELCA) was an early adopter when it came to welcoming and affirming the sin of homosexuality. LGBTQ+ ministers have been ordained by the ELCA since 2010. Today, church programs include summer camps and homeless shelters for LGBTQ+ youth, and pastor participation in the "It Gets Better" campaign. Both Sexual Orientation & Gender Identity have been included in their "Human Sexuality: Gift and Trust" Social Statement. The list of apostate churches and denominations that condone homosexuality and gay marriage would take dozens of pages to cite.

One only needs to look at a few Scriptures from God's infallible Word to see how wrong this is. "You shall not lie with a male as with a woman. It is an abomination" (Leviticus 18:22). "Likewise also the men, leaving the natural use of the woman, burned in their lust for one another, men with men committing what is shameful, and receiving in themselves the penalty of their error which was due" (Romans 1:27). "Nevertheless, because of sexual immorality, let each man have his own wife, and let each woman have her own husband" (1 Corinthians 7:2).

The Transgender Movement

As I have written about in my *Spirit of the Antichrist* book series, the Luciferians are pushing transgenderism because they want to destroy the uniqueness of mankind. I call this the "gender surrender movement." Transhumanists want to obliterate the *Imago Dei*. The Bible says, "So God created man in His own image; in the image of God He created him; male and female He created them" (Genesis 1:27). Eliminating gender paves the way for what they call the singularity, the final merging of man and machine into one "created" being. It is the creation of artificial life, that is, artificial intelligence or *AI*. AI has no gender because AI needs no gender. Mankind is the crown jewel, the highest pinnacle, of creation. When God created mankind, He saved the best for last. Biological gender is an indispensable component of God's divine design for humanity (Genesis 1:26-27).

By convincing people today to give up their gender, or that they have no gender to begin with, the Luciferians are mocking God. The gender surrender movement is their attempt to eradicate biological sex and show God that His prized creation is flawed. One's gender, to the Luciferians, is a blight that must be eliminated. Their transhumanist agenda seeks to purge mankind of the affliction of biological sex. Sadly, this demonic worldview has infiltrated the church. The way American churches are embracing the LGBTQ+ agenda must surely grieve our Heavenly Father. As Wendy and I drive across the country for speaking engagements, it saddens us to see so many churches with rainbow flags hanging from their porticos and marquees extolling the virtues of the transgender ideology.

The disgusting trend of men dressing up as women and participating in church services is sweeping across the American church. In December 2021, St. Luke's Lutheran Church of Logan Square in Chicago, invited a drag queen into the pulpit to read a book to children. According to a Facebook post from the church, attendees were encouraged to "wear garments/accessories that make you feel 100% like the best version of yourself!" In January 2022, Austin Congregational UCC and Spirituality Center in Austin, Minnesota held a Sunday morning service that doubled as a drag show. The church dubbed the event "Drag Me to Church." In June 2023, people came to Calvary Presbyterian Church in San Francisco one Sunday for a "Drag Queen Bible Story Hour."

In his inaugural address on January 20, 2025, President Trump promised to put an end to the lunacy of the transgender movement. This surprised me since his support of the transgender community is widely known. Meredith McGraw, in a December 16, 2022, article for *Politico.com*, writes, "On December 16, 2022, hundreds of guests sipped on Trump-branded champagne and martinis at Mar-a-Lago. Between courses of steak and bite-sized Key lime pie, they danced to 'YMCA' and 'Macho Man.'" The gala in the main ballroom of Donald Trump's Mar-a-Lago beachfront club was a joyous celebration of gay rights and the historic same-sex marriage law signed by President Joe Biden days earlier. The event in honor of the LGBTQ movement brought in Republican notables like Kari Lake from Arizona and a host of other pro-LGBTQ Republicans.

The main attraction, obviously, was Trump. He received a standing ovation after delivering an enthusiastic and passionate speech affirming LGBTQ+ rights. Trump told the crowd, "We are fighting for the gay community, and we are fighting and fighting hard. With the help of many of the people here tonight in recent years, our movement has taken incredible strides, the strides you've made here is [sic] incredible." That statement is in stark contrast to Trump's remarks three years later at the 2025 Presidential Inauguration. Time will tell if his words constitute empty rhetoric or a genuine promise.

The Sanctity of Life

When gender is marginalized and sexual purity is mocked, the value of life in general becomes maligned. We are no longer precious human beings made in the image of God. Rather, we are mere biological algorithms that can be manipulated and discarded at will. In order to explain how the church has compromised on the crucial moral issue of the sanctity of human life, we must first understand the history of the diabolical eugenics movement. I covered this in my book *Spirit of the Antichrist Volume One*. I wrote,

> *The Luciferians love death. God's Word says, "All those who hate Me love death" (Proverbs 8:36). Although Satan's murderous agenda goes all the way back to the Garden, the Luciferian plan to depopulate the earth gained steam with the eugenics programs of the nineteenth century.*
>
> *Sir Francis Galton, a cousin of Charles Darwin, is known as the founder of eugenics, coining the term himself in 1883. Galton wrote, "Eugenics is the study of all of the agencies under social control." He was heavily influenced by his cousin Darwin's works, The Origin of the Species: The Preservation of Favored Races in the Struggle for Life, and The Descent of Man. In The Descent of Man, published in 1871, Darwin explained how most people are evolutionary dead ends and only a small elite is actually evolving. Everyone else just gets in the way.*
>
> *Galton and Darwin both felt that, by any means, we must rid the world of the "feeble-minded." The process of depopulation must involve "all agencies under social control," as Galton said. There were eugenics offices in every town of any size across the U. S. in the early part of the*

twentieth century. Eugenics is an outgrowth of Darwin's ethic that says we must get rid of all the people we do not like, those who do not look like us, or have illnesses, ailments, or disabilities. We must wipe them off the face of the earth. That has been the Luciferians' goal from the beginning. They want this earth for themselves.

Margaret Sanger was one of the early well-known and highly influential eugenicists in our country. She founded the American Birth Control League in 1921, now known as Planned Parenthood. At a March 1925 International Birth Control gathering in New York City, one of the speakers warned of the menace posed by the "black and yellow peril." The man was not a Nazi or a Klansman. He was Dr. S. Adolf Knopp, a member of Margaret Sanger's American Birth Control League. Sanger herself spoke of "sterilizing those that she designated as unfit," a plan she said would be the "salvation of American civilization." She also spoke of those who were "irresponsible and reckless." Among whom she included those "whose religious scruples prevent their exercising control over their numbers." Sanger further contended, "There is no doubt in the minds of all thinking people that the procreation of this group should be stopped."

She considered Americans of African origin particularly unfit. She wrote in a letter to Dr. Clarence Gamble, December 10, 1939, "We do not want word to get out that we want to exterminate the Negro population." Modern defenders of Sanger's worldview, according to which unwanted unborn children should be murdered, have suggested that what she meant by that statement was, "We do not want people to think that we want to exterminate the Negro population." Such an assertion is absurd. Sanger's entire corpus of writings and speeches makes the meaning of her comments to Dr. Gamble unambiguous.

Sanger said, "Birth control is often denounced as a violation of natural law, but it is nothing more than the facilitation of the process aiding human evolution, the facilitation of the process of weeding out the unfit and preventing the birth of defectives or of those who will become defective." Notice that she said not just those who have a deformed leg.

> *It is those that we think might become unfit, mentally, or otherwise. She said, "The most merciful thing that a large family does to one of its members is to kill it." Sanger wrote, "Remember our motto, if we must have welfare, give it to the rich not the poor. We are paying for and even submitting to the dictates of an ever-increasing, unceasingly spawning class of human beings who never should have been born at all."*

While most Christians today have a negative visceral response when they hear, "Planned Parenthood," if you dig a little deeper into their worldview, you will see compromise at every turn when it comes to abortion. This is largely due to over one hundred years of indoctrination through the government-controlled public school system. I will have more to say about the relationship between Christians and public schooling in the next chapter.

George Barna points out in a 2021 article, "Only six out of ten theologically determined born-again Christians (60 percent) say that human life is sacred." The fact that four out of ten self-proclaimed born-again Christians think human life is *not* sacred is bad enough. What is worse is that 34% said "abortion is morally acceptable if it spares the mother from financial or emotional discomfort or hardship." The notion that a Christian, or anyone else for that matter, can espouse the sanctity of human life and yet affirm the right to murder innocent children in the womb for financial reasons is inherently illogical. Paraphrasing Brian Rohrbough, in an interview with NBW Ministries on December 17, 2024, any argument that ends with the phrase, "…and then it's okay to kill the baby" is wrong. It is morally unacceptable.

Because most American Christians do not hold a consistent biblical view on the sanctity of *all* human life, the church at large celebrated the June 24, 2022, Supreme Court ruling on abortion, *Dobbs v. Jackson Women's Health Organization*, as a positive development. As I explained in *Spirit of the Antichrist Volume Two*, this is by no means the case. I wrote,

> *In Dobbs, SCOTUS ruled definitively that the unborn have no Constitutional right to life.*

The United States Constitution grants equal protection to all human beings. By granting individual states the right to decide whether they will allow the murder of unborn children, SCOTUS denied the unborn their Constitutionally protected right to life. The Court essentially enshrined the contention of Luciferians that unborn children are not human beings. The Dobbs decision was a geographical one, not a Constitutional one. It effectively told Americans where we can murder our unborn children, not whether we can.

According to the 14th Amendment, all citizens are guaranteed "equal protection of the laws." According to the 10th Amendment of the U.S. Constitution ("States' Rights"), only those powers not delegated to the federal government by the Constitution are reserved to the States. SCOTUS had an opportunity, based on these explicit Amendments, to settle the issue once and for all by affirming the rights of the unborn. Yet, because Supreme Court justices are controlled, like most Senators, Congressmen, and the President, so-called "conservative" justices lacked the courage to do the right thing.

Dobbs has created abortion tourism. The ruling created sanctuary states for the killing of the unborn. A growing number of companies have begun not only encouraging the murder of the unborn, but also incentivizing, aiding, and abetting it. Companies like Dick's Sporting Goods, Levi's, Disney, JPMorgan Chase, Tesla, Starbucks, and many more are offering their employees up to four thousand dollars and paid leave to travel across state lines and murder their unborn children. They are calling it "abortion travel benefits."

If *Dobbs* was such a victory for the pro-life movement; if it "overturned Roe v. Wade," as so many proclaim, we should have seen a reduction in the number of abortions in the U.S. as a result. Yet, predictably, the United States recorded its *highest number of abortions in over a decade during 2023, the first full calendar year after the Dobbs decision*. I think Satan has a good laugh when he watches Christians celebrate a decision that leads to the murder of *more* innocent children, not less! Moral apostasy is everywhere in the church; unfortunately, when it comes to abortion, most Christians cannot see it.

Nibbling Leads to Swallowing

My family and I live in the Colorado mountains where free-range cattle ranching is common. It is not unusual for a forest road to be closed off to traffic for several minutes during roundup season while cowboys and wranglers herd cattle. For someone like me who has not spent much time on a ranch, it is quite a sight to behold. I love cowboys, but the ones I am accustomed to watching have blue stars and shoulder pads. The ones herding cattle are *real* cowboys, with Stetsons and spurs. After all the cows have been collected and loaded into pens or on trucks, sometimes the ranchers will discover one or two cows missing. This is because occasionally, a cow will get separated from the herd and it takes a lot of extra time and effort for the ranchers to find it.

You can learn a lot about life by watching cows. For instance, ask a cowboy how a cow gets separated from the herd and he will tell you the cow starts nibbling on a tuft of green grass, and when it finishes, it looks ahead to the next tuft of green grass and starts nibbling on that one. Then it moves on to the next patch of grass to nibble some more. Before long, the cow has nibbled itself away from the herd and is lost. Such is the condition of the American church today. Christians have nibbled and nibbled on enticing moral compromise until finally, the church has swallowed it completely, utterly departing from its biblical foundations. It is not some outside enemy that is the greatest threat to the church. It is moral compromise from within. As J. Vernon McGee put it, "Today we are witnessing the destruction of the church from the inside—it's an inside job."

In the next chapter we will look at some ways the church is falling away socially. Rather than changing the world with the Gospel, the church has allowed the world to change it.

6

FALLING AWAY SOCIALLY

And do not be conformed to this world, but be transformed by the renewing of your mind, that you may prove what is that good and acceptable and perfect will of God. (Romans 12:2)

* * *

Having grown up in New England, I have many fond memories of visiting New York City. The Big Apple. The city that never sleeps. What an amazing place! Notwithstanding the usual criticisms—traffic, crowds, crime, etc.—the City holds a special place in my heart. Maybe it is nostalgia. Whatever it is, the sights, sounds, and smells of NYC beckon me whenever our ministry travels take us to the northeast. My father worked in Manhattan for almost six years when I was a boy. He rode the train every day from our suburban neighborhood in western Connecticut to Grand Central Terminal, where he would emerge from the subway and walk the few remaining blocks to his office. Sometimes my mom, sisters, and I would go with him to spend the day sightseeing or shopping. Other times it was a class field trip that took me to the City. Whatever the purpose, NYC never disappointed.

My memories include the Staten Island Ferry, the Statue of Liberty, the observation deck at the top of the World Trade Center (This was the '70s, well before the events of September 11, 2001.), Times Square, the ice rink at Rockefeller Center, the New York Public Library, FAO Schwarz, Macy's, hotdog vendors, pretzels, Italian ice, the chess tables in Central Park, the three-card monte street hustlers (My parents would never let me try to find the lady, though I was certain I could!), and so much more. Wendy and I have visited the city several times over the years, and every time it takes me back to those boyhood memories. One of my favorite activities was watching the live mannequins in the store windows at Saks Fifth Avenue. My sisters and I would make faces, knock on the glass, anything we could think of to get them to smile. It never worked. You had to watch very closely to catch even the slightest blink. They were amazing!

It was hilarious watching tourists pause to look at the window displays, completely unaware the mannequins were live fashion models. When one of them would blink or take a breath, the tourists would lurch back from the window, startled to realize they had been looking at live human beings! Once the secret was out, a crowd would quickly gather in front of the model, and everyone would try their hand at getting the "mannequins" to move, usually with no success. There was no way the models were going to let the spectators on the other side of the glass keep them from doing their job.

As I think about that childhood memory, it occurs to me the church is a lot like those mannequins. If the church is going to remain untouched by worldliness, we will have to ignore the people on the other side of the glass. We must live our lives unaffected by the pagan world around us and remain focused on the task at hand. The church is called to change the world, not conform to the world. Paul said, "And do not be conformed to this world, but be transformed by the renewing of your mind, that you may prove what is that good and acceptable and perfect will of God" (Romans 12:2). Sadly, the church in these last days is taking its cue from the world and failing in its mission. In this chapter, we will examine several ways the church is falling away socially.

Agents of Light in a Dark World

On the night Jesus was betrayed, He shared a private moment with His disciples. This intimate interchange between Jesus and His disciples is recorded in John 13-17 and is called the Upper Room Discourse. At the conclusion of the conversation, Jesus prays for Himself (John 17:1–5), then for His apostles (vv. 6–19), and finally for future believers. Here is part of that prayer.

> *I have given them Your word; and the world has hated them because they are not of the world, just as I am not of the world. I do not pray that You should take them out of the world, but that You should keep them from the evil one. They are not of the world, just as I am not of the world. Sanctify them by Your truth. Your word is truth. As You sent Me into the world, I also have sent them into the world. And for their sakes I sanctify Myself, that they also may be sanctified by the truth. (John 17:14-19)*

Jesus spoke these encouraging words just hours before He was betrayed, arrested, tried, crucified, and rose again. He knew the church age was about to be established. He had predicted it a few weeks earlier (cf. Matthew 16). He knew dark days were on the horizon.

Jesus also knew Satan was to be the prince of this world and that his deception and evil scheming would reach levels never experienced in human history. He knew in the church age, the last age before the Kingdom, "evil men and imposters would grow worse and worse, deceiving and being deceived" (2 Timothy 3:13). He knew Satan's aim in this present age would be "to steal, kill, and destroy" (John 10:10); that he would prowl around throughout the church age "like a roaring lion seeking whom he may devour" (1 Peter 5:8). Jesus knew God's people were about to enter an age of unprecedented spiritual warfare in which the schemes of the Devil would require us to "wrestle not against flesh and blood, but against principalities, against powers, against the rulers of the darkness of this age, against spiritual hosts of wickedness in the heavenly places" (Ephesians 6:11–12). He knew we would need the Spirit's help, guidance, and advice if we were to "withstand in the evil day" (Ephesians 6:13). This advice comes through His written Word, the Bible.

Jesus also knew He was going to be leaving this "present evil age," as it would later be called by the Apostle Paul (Galatians 1:4), but that believers in the church age could not leave. They had a job to do. They were to be God's agents of light in a dark world. In every age, God always has His chosen people who are to be His witnesses to pagan nations. In this age, it is the church. So, knowing all this, Jesus prayed that God would protect us from the evil one. How amazing! Jesus prayed for you and me two thousand years before we were even born. And what did He pray? He prayed that God the Father would protect us from the evil one. He knew the present evil age would be far more sinister, wicked, and unrestrained than any other age in human history.

The Separation Principle

One of the ways God has always safeguarded His people, in every age, from the influences of the world is by the principle of separation. There is a divine tension, throughout Scripture, between God's command for His people to evangelize the rest of the world, and God's command for His people to remain separate from the rest of the world. The idea of separation is perhaps best illustrated by the command God gave the Israelites just prior to their entering the Promised Land.

> *"When the Lord your God brings you into the land which you go to possess, and has cast out many nations before you, the Hittites and the Girgashites and the Amorites and the Canaanites and the Perizzites and the Hivites and the Jebusites, seven nations greater and mightier than you, and when the Lord your God delivers them over to you, you shall conquer them and utterly destroy them. You shall make no covenant with them nor show mercy to them. Nor shall you make marriages*

> *with them. You shall not give your daughter to their son, nor take their daughter for your son. For they will turn your sons away from following Me, to serve other gods; so the anger of the Lord will be aroused against you and destroy you suddenly. But thus you shall deal with them: you shall destroy their altars, and break down their sacred pillars, and cut down their wooden images, and burn their carved images with fire. "For you are a holy people to the Lord your God; the Lord your God has chosen you to be a people for Himself, a special treasure above all the peoples on the face of the earth."* (Deuteronomy 7:1-6)

Elsewhere God told the Israelites, "Consecrate yourselves therefore, and be holy, for I am the LORD your God. ...And you shall be holy to Me, for I the LORD am holy, and have separated you from the peoples, that you should be Mine" (Leviticus 20:7, 26).

Although Israel was called to be separate, they were also called to be a witness to the pagan nations of the world. They were to witness to the unity of Yahweh amid universal idolatry and paganism (Deuteronomy 6:4; Isaiah 43:10-12) and to be an example to the nations of the benefits of serving Yahweh (Deuteronomy 33:26-29). Isaiah records these Words of the Lord, "Look to Me, and be saved, all you ends of the earth! For I am God, and there is no other" (Isaiah 45:22). This divine tension between separation and evangelism is repeated extensively in the New Testament. And it is given even greater importance in light of the age in which we live, the present evil age (Galatians 1:4).

Paul warned, "But know this, that in the last days perilous times will come: For men will be lovers of themselves, lovers of money, boasters, proud, blasphemers, disobedient to parents, unthankful, unholy, unloving, unforgiving, slanderers, without self-control, brutal, despisers of good, traitors, headstrong, haughty, lovers of pleasure rather than lovers of God, having a form of godliness but denying its power. And from such people stay away" (2 Timothy 3:1-5)! And yet, we are told to preach the Gospel to all the world. How can we fulfill the Great Commission and simultaneously "stay away" from them? Is God playing games with us? Not at all.

In the World but Not of It

A careful reading of the Bible in its plain, normal, grammatical sense, makes it clear how God intends for us to obey both commands. First, we must recognize God has not changed His plan for His people to be a holy, set apart, distinct, and special people in the present age. Sometimes I hear people say something like, "Well, that separation stuff, that was just for Israel in the Old Testament. But today, why, we're supposed to immerse ourselves in the world's culture. After all, how else can we relate to them and win them to Christ?" Yet, the New Testament is clear the church, like Israel, is to remain separate from the world. Consider the following passages:

> *But you are a chosen generation, a royal priesthood, a holy nation, His own special people, that you may proclaim the praises of Him who called you out of darkness into His marvelous light; (1 Peter 2:9)*

> *Pure and undefiled religion before God and the Father is this: to visit orphans and widows in their trouble, and to keep oneself unspotted from the world. (James 1:27)*

> *Do not be unequally yoked together with unbelievers. For what fellowship has righteousness with lawlessness? And what communion has light with darkness? And what accord has Christ with Belial? Or what part has a believer with an unbeliever? And what agreement has the temple of God with idols? For you are the temple of the living God. As God has said: "I will dwell in them And walk among them. I will be their God, And they shall be My people." Therefore "Come out from among them And be separate, says the Lord. Do not touch what is unclean, And I will receive you." "I will be a Father to you, And you shall be My sons and daughters, Says the Lord Almighty." (2 Corinthians 6:14-18)*

> *Adulterers and adulteresses! Do you not know that friendship with the*

> *world is enmity with God? Whoever therefore wants to be a friend of the world makes himself an enemy of God. (James 4:4)*

> *For you were once darkness, but now you are light in the Lord. Walk as children of light (for the fruit of the Spirit is in all goodness, righteousness, and truth), finding out what is acceptable to the Lord. And have no fellowship with the unfruitful works of darkness, but rather expose them. (Ephesians 5:8-11)*

These church age commands are in keeping with the timeless wisdom principles of Psalms and Proverbs that apply to all people of all ages. "My son, do not walk in the way with [sinners], keep your foot from their path" (Proverbs 1:15). "The righteous should choose his friends carefully, for the way of the wicked leads them astray" (Proverbs 12:26). "He who walks with wise men will be wise, but the companion of fools will be destroyed" (Proverbs 13:20). "Blessed is the man who walks not in the counsel of the ungodly, nor stands in the path of sinners, nor sits in the seat of the scornful" (Psalm 1:1).

The Apostle Paul said it about as succinctly and plainly as it can be said: "Do not be deceived: Evil company corrupts good morals" (1 Corinthians 15:33). Notice Paul's reference to deception. That brings us right back to the motive for God's call to separation in the Bible. He knows, just as Jesus said in His prayer in John 17, that the world is evil; that Satan is the great deceiver, and that it is going to get worse and worse until the Kingdom finally comes. Therefore, we must choose our friends wisely.

As we think about how we are to be a light to a dark world, perhaps it will be helpful to think about the distinction between being "friendly" and being a "friend." The Bible clearly prohibits friendship with the world. Yet, we use the term "friend" in a much broader sense than the Bible does. Just like we use the word "love" in a much broader sense than the Bible does. We can love our wife, love football, love ice cream, and love roller coasters—but we recognize in each instance the word "love" has a different nuance. Similarly, we call everyone from mere acquaintances to life-long, intimate relationships "friends." But the Bible speaks of a friendship that goes beyond mere superficial acquaintance, and it reserves the term "friend" only for those who share a bibliocentric worldview; those whose affections, attitudes, and shared experiences all flow out of a relationship with God through His Son Jesus Christ.

As we interact with the world, we are to be loving and friendly and kind and compassionate. That is what will make us stand out, and that is what will make our message attractive. But there is an important difference between being "friendly" and establishing "close friendships." When we allow unbelievers to occupy a place in our inner circle of closest friends, we have compromised God's principle of separation. We have opened the door to worldly influences of this present evil age, and inevitably, our good morals will become corrupt. Our pathway will be led astray, our wisdom will become tainted, and our worldview will be influenced negatively. When you get too close to the world, it cannot help but rub off on you. That is why God wants us to remain separate. He knows *we will never become like the people we don't hang around.*

The separation principle not only regulates our interaction with the world, but it applies to our interaction with fellow believers as well. There are times when we are to shun believers who are engaging in sinful behavior. Why? Precisely because they are behaving like the world! "Now I urge you, brethren, note those who cause divisions and offenses, contrary to the doctrine which you learned, and avoid them. For those who are such do not serve our Lord Jesus Christ, but their own belly, and by smooth words and flattering speech deceive the hearts of the simple" (Romans 16:17-18). "But we command you, brethren, in the name of our Lord Jesus Christ, that you withdraw from every brother who walks disorderly and not according to the tradition which he received from us" (2 Thessalonians 3:6). "And if anyone does not obey our word in this epistle, note that person and do not keep company with him, that he may be ashamed" (2 Thessalonians 3:14).

It always has been God's design that His people, in every age, serve as witnesses to His glory. The present age is no different. We are to "make disciples of all nations" (Matthew 28:18-20). This does not contradict

God's command to remain separate. Rather, the evangelistic enterprise is enhanced by God's principle of separation. That is right; separation enhances evangelism. How could this possibly be the case? It is simple, really. When we look like the world, act like the world, and intermingle with the world to the extent that we are indistinguishable from the world, it makes it more difficult to evangelize the world. When we lose our distinction, there is nothing compelling about our message. Jesus said,

> *"You are the salt of the earth; but if the salt loses its flavor, how shall it be seasoned? It is then good for nothing but to be thrown out and trampled underfoot by men. "You are the light of the world. A city that is set on a hill cannot be hidden. Nor do they light a lamp and put it under a basket, but on a lampstand, and it gives light to all who are in the house. Let your light so shine before men, that they may see your good works and glorify your Father in heaven." (Matthew 5:13-16)*

Paul echoes the same thought. "I beseech you therefore, brethren, by the mercies of God, that you present your bodies a living sacrifice, holy, acceptable to God, which is your reasonable service. And do not be conformed to this world, but be transformed by the renewing of your mind, that you may prove what is that good and acceptable and perfect will of God" (Romans 12:1-2).

As we seek to win the world to Christ, we do so by being friendly, loving, kind, and compassionate in our interaction with the lost. And we do it by making sure that our affections, attitudes, values, experiences, and worldview remain distinct, lest we lose our testimony, and our witness becomes marginalized. In the New Testament, when Jesus or the early church age apostles interacted with unbelievers, it was always for the purpose of evangelizing them. Jesus interacted with the woman at the well—to get her to believe in Him. Jesus interacted in Zacchaeus' home—to get him to believe in Him. Jesus sat with tax collectors and harlots and sinners—to win them to Him. Similarly, the early Apostles were singularly focused on evangelism as they interacted with the lost. They did not befriend them for months in hopes that when they finally shared the Gospel with them it would be more favorably received. The Gospel was front and center.

The Gospel does not need our help. It is the power of God to salvation (Romans 1:16). To the extent we develop relationships with the lost, our singular focus, at the forefront of our minds and the center of our radar screens, ought to be to proclaim the Gospel to them. That is, after all, what the word "evangelize" means. When the interaction between believers and unbelievers yields no evangelistic fruit, the believer needs to be careful not to allow the relationship to develop into something more intimate or close than God intends. It is unbiblical to maintain prolonged interpersonal relationships with unbelievers, under the guise of evangelism, when no real evangelism is taking place. Consider Paul's example.

> *And he went into the synagogue and spoke boldly for three months, reasoning and persuading concerning the things of the kingdom of God. But when some were hardened and did not believe, but spoke evil of the Way before the multitude, he departed from them and withdrew the disciples, reasoning daily in the school of Tyrannus. And this continued for two years, so that all who dwelt in Asia heard the word of the Lord Jesus, both Jews and Greeks. (Acts 19:8-10)*

God wants the church to be distinct, separate, set-apart, and unique in this fallen world. Christians should be careful not to engage in close, intimate relationships with unbelievers in the world.

Remember, "Whoever therefore wants to be a friend of the world makes himself an enemy of God" (James 4:4). This teaching is sorely neglected in these great last days when the church is falling away socially. Considering the deception of this present evil age, our goal should be to join the Psalmist in saying, "I am a companion of all who fear You, and of those who keep Your precepts" (Psalm 119:63). As we look at the state of the church in the world today, and our failure to practice the biblical doctrine of separation, is it really any wonder why the church has become so indistinguishable from the world? Remember the principle: Bad company corrupts good morals.

You'll never become like the people you don't hang around.

Social Clubs in Church Clothing

Instead of being in the world and not of it, the church today has become indistinguishable from the world. So much so that most churches resemble little more than social clubs, and like social clubs, these churches will do whatever it takes to get people through their doors. As sound doctrine gave way to social acceptance, churches began developing growth strategies that had little, if anything, to do with the biblical purpose of the church in the present age. The modern church growth movement in America grew out of this social club mentality.

Donald McGavran is widely considered the father of the church growth movement. He was the founding Dean of the School of World Mission at Fuller Theological Seminary in Pasadena, California. McGavran's 1970s book, *Understanding Church Growth*, became a go-to text for those wishing to build "successful" churches. The book was later revised and expanded by his successor in the church growth movement, C. Peter Wagner. McGavran suggested three questions when evaluating the health of a church. (1) When a church is growing, why is it growing? (2) What barriers, obstructions, or sicknesses prevent the natural life, vitality, and growth of churches? And (3) What reproducible principles operative in growing churches can be used elsewhere? Church ministry thus became more driven by the scientific method than the word of God. If you want to grow your church, you gather data, construct a hypothesis (i.e., a potential solution), test the hypothesis, and establish a proven principle.

Conspicuously absent from this approach is any reference to biblical principles. McGavran's emphasis was on numbers. He had a pragmatic approach wherein the end justifies the means. His philosophy created a new field called the "church growth strategist." Two evangelical leaders who trace their philosophical lineage to McGavran, and later Wagner, include Bill Hybels and Rick Warren. This social club mentality ignores the power and presence of the Gospel as the central component of the local church. Any church that is more interested in growth analytics than Gospel attainments is nothing more than a social club in church clothing.

The great American preacher, Donald Grey Barnhouse, pastored the Tenth Presbyterian Church in Philadelphia, Pennsylvania from 1927 until his death in 1960. Barnhouse saw the writing on the wall with the church growth movement. He wrote,

> *To preach a social gospel without the redemptive background of the individual salvation from sin of the individual sinner is like launching a glider instead of a high-powered plane. A glider may soar for a while on the fickle currents of the wind, and climb high on some sudden up-draft, but it is the four whirl-wind motors that will carry a bomber to the stratosphere and jet-propulsion and rockets that will take a plane beyond the speed of sound.*

A church that does not make the Gospel central to its ministry is like an automobile that emphasizes its shiny door handles and neglects its engine.

Do You Seek Here Often?

The church growth movement eventually birthed what came to be called the "seeker-sensitive movement." In keeping with the social club model, seeker-sensitive churches make it a priority to avoid anything in their services, facilities, and ministry programs that might offend a "seeker." The church, according to this model, must change the way it does things if it is going to attract new people. The world is not attending church because the church is boring, outdated, and offensive. Rather than change the world, the seeker model seeks to change the church to conform to the world. Such an approach is more evidence the church is falling away from its biblical mandate in these last days.

According to the Bible, Jesus is a "rock of offense" (Romans 9:33; 1 Peter 2:8), and the cross itself is considered an "offense." The Greek word translated "offense" is *scandalon,* meaning "stumbling block." This is precisely the way the NKJV translates the word in 1 Corinthians 1:23 where Paul says the crucifixion of Christ is a *scandalon*, a "stumbling block." To avoid offending the world, the church would have to stop preaching the Gospel. Predictably, this is precisely what has happened. The seeker-sensitive model suggests the way in which the Gospel message is packaged can have a dramatic effect on whether or not the lost respond to it. I will have more to say about this in the next chapter

Several years ago, I had the opportunity to visit a large church in the suburbs of Houston, Texas. The church was a seeker-sensitive church. In the atrium, there were two large bowls resting on a table. One was labeled "seeker" and the other was labeled "follower." Attendees who considered themselves to be seekers (i.e., non-Christians) were encouraged to write their name on an index card and place it in the seeker bowl. The pitch was, "No pressure.... no urgency. No one will contact you. Just put your name in the bowl and give our church a try." The theory was that after attending the church for a while, the seeker would experience a period of soul-searching and personal introspection wherein he would become convinced the church is the way to find meaning and purpose to his life. When that happened, he was encouraged to move his index card from the seeker bowl to the follower bowl. Meanwhile, the pastor and staff point to the increasing number of cards in the follower bowl as a validation of the church's methodology.

In true postmodern form, the entire equation is hazy, individually defined, and subjectively experienced. There is no definitive line in the sand drawn whereby the lost person is warned of the eternal consequences of sin and its singular solution through faith alone in Christ alone. There is no urgency—no sense that "today might be the day" or "what if you died today?" Carl F. H. Henry was right when he said, "The gospel is only good news if it gets there in time." Reflecting on this lack of urgency, Ajith Fernando comments,

> *Traditionally, Christians have been motivated to evangelism through their belief that the gospel is absolutely true and is the only hope for salvation. However, the aptness of thinking in such categories as "absolutely true" and "only hope for salvation" is being questioned by*

> *today's pluralistic thinking. The postmodern mood is thus hostile to the idea of urgency as it is portrayed in the Bible.*

In other words, seekers in these last days of the church age dismiss out of hand any notion of a universally applicable salvation message. "Who are you to tell me that your way is the only way to eternal life?!" they exclaim.

In response, the seeker-sensitive model has devised a way to counteract this rejection of an all-encompassing metanarrative for salvation by repackaging the Gospel in a misguided and unnecessary effort to make it appear softer, friendlier, and more appealing. Fernando continues,

> *I would go so far as to say that entertainment has replaced urgency as a primary means of attracting people to the gospel. Therefore, we do not strive to let the truth shine forth in all its glory, an enterprise that calls for dedication and hard work. Instead, the hard work goes to producing an entertaining program. We often find that Christian worship is characterized by an entertaining and technically excellent program of music, drama, worship, and sharing, followed by a ministry of the Word that is comparatively inferior and unimaginative....*
>
> *As a result of this focus on entertainment, people come to worship looking to have an entertaining time. Songs and stories and humor are chosen so that the people might be entertained. In the process, truth is subordinated to an inferior position. So today when many Christians inquire about the value of a worship service they ask, "Did you enjoy the worship there?" But what they really mean is, "Did you get an emotional lift from the spiritual entertainment provided there?"*

Thus, in endeavoring to convince a lost person that what the church has to offer is more fulfilling and meaningful than the emptiness of a life without it, entertainment becomes the primary tool. Whatever you do, do *not* offend! If this describes your church, it is time to find another church. For a list of non-negotiables when choosing a local church, see Appendix C.

The Secularization of Worship Music

This brings up another example of worldliness infiltrating the church: music. Music is quite a lightning rod in churches these days. The issue of music style has undoubtedly led to more church splits than just about any other issue. My approach to music in church is sure to bother some of you. I am neither in the "only hymns/piano/organ" camp nor the "rock band/lights/smoke" camp. In my mind, there is a clear distinction between style and substance when it comes to music. Regarding substance, if the lyrics to a song are unbiblical or theologically in error, it should not be sung in church. Period. Many times over the years I have asked the worship leader at our church to tweak the words to an otherwise good song in order to correct a phrase that is doctrinally inaccurate or misleading.

On the other hand, style is largely a preference issue, not a moral one. There is nothing unbiblical about drums, electric guitars, soloists, and various other aspects of so-called contemporary worship teams, provided the style is not so divergent from established and culturally acceptable rules of musical etiquette that it distracts from worship instead of aiding it. Too many Christians today have elevated their personal preference in worship music to a level of moral absolutism. There is a word for this. It is called *legalism*. Whenever I impose my personal, non-moral, preference upon others I am being legalistic. If a particular style of music does not appeal to you, you may need to find another church. Better yet, stay put and allow the Lord to stretch you in your preferences. You might find that a style of music you have not previously favored touches your heart in new and meaningful ways.

By its very nature, music is culturally driven. The style of worship in Russian churches differs from the style in Latin American churches. The underground church in China has a different style of music in their gatherings than a Calvary Chapel meeting on the beach in Los Angeles. A church with an older congregation in a midwestern farming community likely will have a musical style that differs dramatically from one in downtown Chicago. This is not only true geographically, but also historically. It is a mistake to assume that "new" means "unbiblical." Hymns in the Middle Ages undoubtedly sounded different than hymns in the 1960s American church, yet both eras have a beauty all their own.

Jesus had a thing or two to say to those in His day who rejected His message because it was new. When the Pharisees questioned Jesus' views on fasting, which differed from their traditions, Jesus said, "And no one puts new wine into old wineskins; or else the new wine will burst the wineskins and be spilled, and the wineskins will be ruined. But new wine must be put into new wineskins, and both are preserved" (Luke 5:37–38).

In the first century, wineskins would have been made of goatskin or sheepskin taken from the neck area of the animal. To put new wine into a used wineskin would be a disaster, a needless and costly waste of wine. The new wine would ferment and cause the old wineskins, already stretched to their limit, to burst. The new wine would be lost, and the wineskin would be ruined. Christ's point was that the Pharisees' forms and traditions were obsolete. If they were to accept Christ's offer of the Kingdom, it would necessitate abandoning their current forms altogether. Christianity, like new wine, has such inherent vigor and life that it cannot function in the restrictive atmosphere of legalism.

Some Christians today are like the Pharisees when it comes to their preference in music style. If it does not suit their traditions, they reject it. If it is "new" it must be "wrong." Yet, as I pointed out, this is by no means the case. People often have a natural tendency to resist new things. It is alleged that Martin Van Buren, Governor of New York, wrote a letter to then-President Andrew Jackson in 1829 expressing his concern over a new form of transportation called the "railroad." In the letter, Van Buren supposedly said, "As you may well know, Mr. President, 'railroad' carriages are pulled at the enormous speed of fifteen miles per hour by 'engines' which, in addition to endangering life and limb of passengers, roar and snort their way through the countryside, setting fire to crops, scaring the livestock, and frightening women and children." Historians dispute the authenticity of the letter, but it still makes the point.

While worship music can and should be rejected if the lyrics violate sound biblical doctrine, music is neither moral or immoral, right or wrong, based merely upon its style. There is one notable exception to this, as I referenced above. If a particular style or genre of music causes a distraction or is otherwise inappropriate for the setting, it should be avoided. In other words, you cannot simply take a sound biblical lyric and attach it to *any* style. Some styles pose a hindrance to worship for a variety of reasons, especially when the church borrows styles from the secular world. Perhaps the rhythmic beat or tempo has a counterproductive impact on the audience. It has been medically proven certain styles of music can adversely affect the brain's impulses or heartbeat or otherwise impact human physiology. There is a reason NBA basketball players take the court with Metallica blaring over the arena loudspeaker, not Barry Manilow.

We might also reject a particular worship song, even though the lyrics in and of themselves are biblically sound, because the song's composers or original singers have become associated with something immoral, and singing the song will cause a distraction. Such is the case with the groups like Hillsong, Bethel, and Elevation. An examination of these groups reveals shocking issues related to false doctrine, immorality, and other scandals. Although some of the songs produced by these groups are enormously popular in churches today, and may contain doctrinally sound lyrics, their usefulness is tainted by the reputation of these artists. That so many churches show no discernment when choosing worship songs is another sign of apostasy.

Bob Smietena, in a July 12, 2023, article for *ChristianityToday.com*, explains,

> *For the past decade, a handful of megachurches have dominated worship music, churning out hits such as "Goodness of God," "What a Beautiful Name," "King of Kings" and "Graves Into Gardens."*
>
> *And though churches like Australia-based Hillsong and Bethel Church in California have met with scandal and controversy, worship leaders still keep singing their songs.*
>
> *A new study released Tuesday found that few worship leaders*

avoid songs from Hillsong and Bethel, two of the so-called Big Four megachurches that dominate modern worship music.

The study found that most worship leaders connect with songs because they've experienced them firsthand at a conference or by listening to them online, or because a friend or church member recommended them—rather than seeing the song at the top of the charts or on a list of new songs.

Selecting worship songs based on experience or feeling is unwise, to say the least, and it is another example of worldly philosophy superseding biblical principles.

Bursting the Bubble of Pop Psychology

Not only has worldliness infiltrated the Christian music arena, but it also has a firm grip on the Christian counseling business. I say "business" because indeed Christian counseling has become a huge financial enterprise in the church today. Many churches have their own counseling departments and there is no shortage of licensed Christian counselors who hang out a shingle and meet with clients to provide advice. To be sure, there is a place for sound biblical counseling in churches. The Bible speaks often of the benefit of wise counsel. "Where there is no counsel, the people fall; but in the multitude of counselors there is safety" (Proverbs 11:14). "Without counsel, plans go awry, but in the multitude of counselors they are established" (Proverbs 15:22). "Listen to counsel and receive instruction, that you may be wise in your latter days" (Proverbs 19:20). "The way of a fool is right in his own eyes, but he who heeds counsel is wise" (Proverbs 12:15).

Unfortunately, most "Christian" counseling today is not biblically based. It is simply pop psychology warmed over. The integrationist model that combines biblical principles with humanistic behavioral science is prevalent in the apostate church today. Like oil and water, the timeless truths of Scripture can never be mixed with the godless ideas of Freud or Jung. The Bible contains everything we need for life and godliness (2 Peter 1:3). It is sufficient for all our counseling needs. Secular psychology has no place in the biblical counseling model.

A recent example of the merging of secular psychology with Christian church ministries is the widespread popularity of the Enneagram personality test in American churches. Joe Carter, in an August 18, 2018, article entitled, "What Christians Should Know About the Enneagram," explains the demonic origins of the enneagram.

> *The earliest mention of the Enneagram is found in the writings of the Russian occultist P. D. Ouspensky, who attributes it to his teacher, the Greek American occultist Georges I. Gurdjieff. Gurdjieff considered the Enneagram a symbol of the cosmos, but made no connection with it to personality types.*
>
> *It was left to another occultist, Óscar Ichazo, to connect the Enneagram to personality. Ichazo claimed to have discovered the personality type meaning of the Enneagram when it was taught to him by the Archangel Metraton while he was high on mescaline.*
>
> *One of Ichazo's students, a Chilean-born psychiatrist named Claudio Naranjo (another occultist) was the first to connect the nine points of the Enneagram to nine basic personality types. (Naranjo also appears to be the one to connect the mention of the Enneagram by Gurdjieff and Ouspensky to ancient sources.)*
>
> *In the 1970s, students of Naranjo spread the Enneagram to various Catholic communities, especially in mystical and contemplative circles. Some of the promoters of the Enneagram include the former Jesuit Don Riso, the Franciscan friar Richard Rohr, and late Benedictine nun Suzanne Zuercher.*
>
> *In 1997, Riso co-founded the Enneagram Institute, an organization that helped bring the Enneagram to a broader audience.*

This certainly does not sound like a tool biblical Christianity should be embracing or using.

Godless Government Schooling

Another example of the merging of sacred and secular worldviews in the church is the way most Christians have embraced pagan government-controlled schooling for their children. They have abandoned their biblical duty to raise up their children in the Lord and subcontracted out this task to a godless institution. Even worse, this godless institution is hellbent on indoctrinating America's youth with Satanically inspired ideologies like transgenderism, Darwinism, and humanism. See *Episode 1146* of the *NBW Ministries Podcast,* entitled, "Doctrines of Demons in Public Schools," released February 18, 2025. In that podcast I interviewed Alex Newman who gives sickening examples of what goes on behind closed classroom doors in America's schools.

At a young age, children in the Luciferian-controlled compulsory government schooling system are taught that gender is a choice, and they are steered toward deviant and unnatural behavior. Even preschoolers are targeted. Planned Parenthood has distributed guidelines for parents on how to talk to their preschoolers about gender. If your four-year-old asks you why boys and girls are different, the guidelines say you should tell them, "Your genitals don't make you a boy or a girl." With the help of Luciferian foundations, agencies, and corporations, the concept of synthetic sex identities (SSI) is being forced upon our children in a massive mind-control program under the guise of "sex education." As I discussed in my book, *Spirit of the Antichrist Volume Two,* one of the most influential backers of SSI is the Pritzker family empire.

James Nicholas Pritzker is a retired lieutenant colonel from the Illinois Army National Guard who now goes by the name, Jennifer Natalya Pritzker. She is the world's first transgender billionaire. Her cousins are J.B. Pritzker, the current governor of Illinois, and Penny Pritzker, former U.S. Secretary of Commerce under President Barack Obama. They hail from one of the richest and most powerful Luciferian families in the United States today, yet few know about them. They amassed their billions through the Hyatt hotel chain and are using it to destroy America's youth.

In August 2021, Governor Pritzker signed into law a new sex education bill for all public schools in Illinois with the goal of eliminating what he calls the "myth" of biology and replacing it with the lie that a child's biological sex is "fluid." It was required to be implemented on or before August 1, 2022. The law is already having a widespread impact. For example, in Naperville, IL, Nick Cosme, a third-grade teacher, paints his nails and teaches boys how to act like girls. The *North Cook News* reports that Pritzker's State Schools Superintendent, Carmen Ayala, has been replacing classic literature with books that promote LGBTQ+ themes. New Illinois K-12 library books include *Gender Queer*, a cartoon pornography book that depicts high school boys engaging in oral sex; *Flamer*, another book that promotes gay sex between high school boys; and *My Shadow Is Pink*, a book aimed at second and third graders that encourages child cross-dressing.

Sadly, this perverse curriculum is not unique to Illinois. The National Sex Education Standards (NSES) is seeking to make this a nationwide policy. Bilek writes, "the NSES manual was crafted by The Future of Sex Education Initiative," with the financial backing of major foundations like Packard and Ford, to institute WISE (Working to Institutionalize Sex Education), "a national initiative that supports school districts in implementing sex education—throughout the country." If you think a Republican president or a Republican congress will change this, do not get your hopes up. Remember, it was Republican-appointed Supreme Court justices that gave us gay marriage and the right to murder unborn children so long as your state says it is okay.

The attempt on the part of the Luciferians to capture the minds of our young people and fill them with this filth is utterly despicable. Even twenty years ago such blatant lewdness would never have been tolerated. The words of the prophet Isaiah come to mind. "Woe to those who call evil good, and good evil; who put darkness for light, and light for darkness; who put bitter for sweet, and sweet for bitter" (Isaiah 5:20). Woe indeed. And woe to those Christian parents who think their public school is different. No matter how good you think your school is, or your school's principal, or your child's teacher, there is an overarching, top-down control grid that makes any attempt to redeem the government-controlled school system impossible. As my friend Col. E. Ray Moore has pointed out, it is time for Christian parents to tell the taxpayer-funded, government-run, mind-control enterprise, "Let my children go!"

In the next chapter, we will examine an area of apostasy in the American church that surely grieves our Lord as much or more than any we have addressed thus far. The church is failing in its most vital mission: evangelism.

7

FALLING AWAY EVANGELISTICALLY

I marvel that you are turning away so soon from Him who called you in the grace of Christ, to a different gospel, which is not another; but there are some who trouble you and want to pervert the gospel of Christ. But even if we, or an angel from heaven, preach any other gospel to you than what we have preached to you, let him be accursed. (Galatians 1:6–8)

* * *

At a young age, I learned the importance of the clarity, accuracy, and urgency of the Gospel. I was scarcely twenty-two years old when I packed up my things, headed north on I-45, and moved into Lincoln Hall on the campus of Dallas Theological Seminary. I was the youngest student on campus, having just graduated from college three months earlier. By God's providence, within my first few weeks on campus, I crossed paths with a man whose passion for getting the Gospel right started me on a lifelong pursuit of Gospel precision that serves as the central motif of our ministry to this day. The name of our ministry, *Not By Works* (i.e., NBW Ministries), comes from Titus 3:5, "not by works of righteousness which we have done, but according to His mercy He saved us." *Not By Works* reflects our unwavering allegiance to the freeness of God's grace in salvation and our rejection of any message or methodology that includes works or performance as a means of obtaining eternal life.

Because of this preoccupation with the fidelity of the biblical Gospel, I have gathered quite a large collection of anecdotes and experiences over the years that illustrate just how far the American church has drifted from the pure and simple Gospel. It is not that I intentionally search for false gospels or expend much effort in finding them. Attacks on the Gospel, some subtle, others much more blatant, are ubiquitous. Stand on any street in the American Bible Belt, with a church on every corner, cover your eyes, spin around and open them again. Your gaze will almost certainly land upon a church that preaches a false gospel. Go to any seminary library, stand in the theology section, and throw a fistful of confetti up into the air. Upon coming to rest, virtually every shard will settle upon a book that espouses an unbiblical view of salvation.

I recall sitting in the greenroom at a conference where I was scheduled to speak. There were several keynoters in the lineup, and I was waiting my turn to go on stage. As I listened to the two preachers who spoke just before me, I noticed something troubling. The first speaker gave a salvation invitation at the conclusion of his message that was more muddled and confusing than a Joe Biden press conference. The speaker who followed him, and immediately preceded me, also ended his presentation with a Gospel plea. It was equally off base, and what is worse, it directly contradicted the salvation message articulated by the previous speaker. Now, what bothered me was not so much that each of those men had fumbled the ball so egregiously when giving the Gospel, it was that the crowd in the auditorium, in both cases, clapped enthusiastically and approvingly after both messages.

How could this be? I thought to myself. Did they not hear what I heard? Were they just being polite? How could they express equal admiration for both messages when the sermons directly and obviously contradicted each another? Moreover, neither message hit the target when it came to the simple message of grace as revealed in God's Word. Over the years, this same experience has repeated itself literally hundreds of times at conferences where I have spoken. It is like the movie *Groundhog Day*, only with more serious, indeed *eternal*, implications.

Right on cue, speaker after speaker comes to the podium, obliterates the Gospel in disturbingly innovative and bewildering ways, and then walks off the stage to hearty applause—sometimes even to a standing ovation! It is stunning to watch auditoriums packed with Christians respond to false gospel presentations like a room full of *Stepford Wives.* Their eyes glaze over, their brains turn off, and any old gospel will do, it seems. A famous dictator once said, "What luck for rulers that men do not think." Looking at the apostate church, we could rephrase that, "What luck for Satan that Christians do not think." In this chapter, we will examine one of the most serious aspects of the great last days apostasy: how the American church is falling away evangelistically.

The Gospel: Lost in the Shuffle

The word *evangelism* comes from the Greek word, *euangélion.* It means, "good news." The verb form is *euangelízō,* "to announce good news" or "preach the Gospel." This is the church's mission in the present age (cf. Mark 16:15; 1 Corinthians 1:17-25; 2 Corinthians 5:18-21). Yet, somehow, the Gospel has gotten lost in the shuffle, obscured by various church policies, programs, and potlucks. This most definitely should not be the case. If there is one thing more than any other that indicates the church is falling away it is the church's ambivalence toward the Gospel.

My friend Gregg Jackson pointed out something recently that likely was lost on the majority of American Christians. Not one Christian-oriented commercial or program he heard or watched over the month of December 2024 ever mentioned anything about who Jesus is and what He accomplished on the cross. Who could imagine such a thing? Christian messages, at Christmastime, ignoring the most important aspect of Christianity! As I thought about Jackson's observation, I realized he was right. These so-called Christian ads and television shows had a lot to say about love, family, or joy, but absolutely nothing about the Savior's atoning work at Calvary. The Christmas message has been all but stripped of its salvific content.

The Gospel is first and foremost the good news about how a person can be rescued from the penalty of sin. In his book, *Salvation*, Lewis Sperry Chafer wrote,

> *Preaching the Gospel is telling men something about Christ and His finished work for them, which they are to believe. This is the simplest test to be applied to all soul-saving appeals. The Gospel has not been preached until a personal message concerning a crucified and living Savior has been presented, and in a form which calls for the response of a personal faith.*

The Bible says, "So then faith comes by hearing, and hearing by the word of God" (Romans 10:17). A person must hear and understand the Gospel before they can believe it and receive eternal life.

According to God's Word everyone is a sinner. "Indeed, there is not a righteous man on earth who continually does good and who never sins" (Ecclesiastes 7:20, NASB). "For all have sinned and fall short of the glory of God" (Romans 3:23). The consequence of our sinful condition is eternal separation from God in a literal place of torment called hell. "For the wages of sin is death..." (Romans 6:23). If a person never accepts God's free gift of salvation, that person will die in his sins. Jesus said, "Therefore I said to you that you will die in your sins; for if you do not believe that I am He, you will die in your sins" (John 8:24). Those who reject God's free offer of forgiveness will hear Jesus say the awful words, "Depart from Me, you cursed, into the everlasting fire prepared for the devil and his angels" (Matthew 25:41).

What makes the Gospel "good news" is it provides information on precisely how individuals can be rescued from the penalty of sin and receive eternal life. "The gift of God is eternal life in Christ Jesus our Lord" (Romans 6:23). "But God demonstrates His own love toward us, in that while we were still sinners, Christ died for us" (Romans 5:8). Those who believe the Gospel can be "justified freely by His grace through the redemption that is in Christ Jesus" (Romans 3:24). Jesus said, "Most assuredly, I say to you, he who believes in Me has everlasting life" (John 6:47). Once a person trusts in Jesus Christ, and Him alone, for forgiveness and eternal life, he is "justified by faith," and has "peace with God through our Lord Jesus Christ" (Romans 5:1).

The Gospel message is simple. "For God so loved the world that He gave His only begotten Son, that whoever believes in Him should not perish but have everlasting life" (John 3:16). Jesus Christ, the Son of God, took your place on the cross. He died for you personally, taking your sin debt upon Himself. The moment you place your faith in Him, and Him alone, for forgiveness and eternal life, you are saved eternally. There is nothing difficult whatsoever to understand about the Gospel. In fact, it is so simple, a child can understand it. That is why Jesus often said, "Let the little children come to Me, and do not forbid them; for of such is the kingdom of God" (Mark 10:14).

Unfortunately, Satan is hard at work blinding people's minds to the Gospel (2 Corinthians 4:4). As the American church has drifted further and further away from sound biblical truth, it has begun adding new and false information to the pure Gospel message. We might call this new information "footnotes." Although these manmade footnotes are intended to clarify the Gospel message, they have the opposite effect. The first footnote that contaminated the pure Gospel is personal happiness and success. Downplaying the eternal aspect of the Gospel, salvation has become about how to live your best life now or how to find purpose in this earthly life. The need for salvation is couched in terms of the search for meaning in *this life*. The result of salvation, according to this modified view of the gospel, is not so much the gaining of ultimate *eternal* life in heaven, but rather a newfound sense of fulfillment and direction in the *present life*. God is viewed as a new "best friend" rather than the One who can rescue us from hellfire.

Over time, this false gospel further devolved by adding another footnote, suggesting it is about character development and personal improvement. "You can be a better person if you'll just come to Jesus!" Next came the influence of new age and mystical ideas suggesting the gospel is about some vague spiritual experience, rather than about a literal heaven and hell. David Wells summarizes this evangelistic apostasy in the American church.

> *This rearrangement of meaning around the self, around its moods, needs, intuitions, aches, and ambiguities, has entered the church. Its presence is signaled wherever there are those who think, or act, as if the purpose of life is to find ways of actualizing the self, realizing it, and crafting it through technique or purchase... Where Christian faith is offered as a means of finding personal wholeness rather than holiness, the church has become worldly.*
>
> *There are many other forms of worldliness that are comfortably at home in the evangelical church today. Where it substitutes intuition and feelings for biblical truth, it is being worldly....*
>
> *What I have been describing is, of course, the loss of the church's needed otherworldliness and its consuming preoccupation with its this-worldly life. ...Soon there is very little that cannot be incorporated into the faith or even become the center around which that faith gets reorganized. As it becomes worldly in these ways, it also becomes anthropocentric, its God more horizontal than vertical, its piety more psychological than moral, its gospel more self-focused than cross-centered.*

While it is correct that a born-again Christian will find a deeper purpose for living than a non-Christian, to suggest this is the essence of the gospel is false. Jesus did not die on the cross so you can be happy, healthy, and wealthy. He died to pay your personal penalty for sin and to keep you from going to hell.

In my 2008 book, *Getting the Gospel Wrong: The Evangelical Crisis No One is Talking About*, I exposed several false gospels that were plaguing the church in the early 2000s. The promulgation of erroneous gospels did not slow down, so the publisher released a revised edition of my book in 2013. A third edition exposing even more attacks on the clarity and accuracy of the Gospel came out in 2024. The following sections encapsulate some of the main ideas from that book as further evidence the church is falling away evangelistically.

The Performance Gospel

Ronald Reagan once quipped, "They say hard work never killed anyone, but I figure: why take the chance?" Notwithstanding this humorous one-liner, Reagan was known for being a hard worker. We live in a culture where diligence and effort are rewarded, and they should be. But when it comes to what the world needs most, no amount of hard work will ever bring forgiveness and eternal life. Salvation is a free gift that can only be received by faith. Chuck Swindoll rightly asserts, "A theology that rests its salvation on one ounce of human performance is not good news; it is bad information. It is *heresy*. It is antithetical to the true message that lit the spark to the Reformation: *Sola fide*—faith alone" (emphasis original).

Mankind's proclivity for earning eternal salvation by works is nothing new. It has been a recurring heresy since the early days of the church. Yet, the degree to which a performance-oriented gospel has infiltrated mainstream, evangelical churches in these last days is more evidence of apostasy. It is not just Roman Catholicism or Arminian-leaning protestant churches that are teaching works-based salvation. Mainstream evangelical churches who should know better have jumped on the good works bandwagon as well. Popular evangelical preacher, John Piper, states, "There is no doubt that Jesus saw some measure of real, lived-out obedience to the will of God as necessary for final salvation." Another renowned evangelical pastor, John MacArthur wrote, "The life we live, not the words we speak, determines our eternal destiny." This quote from John MacArthur appeared in the first edition of his book, *Hard to Believe,* in which he explains how salvation requires much more than simply believing the Gospel. It was so controversial, that the publisher deleted the statement from later printings of the book.

The church's acceptance of relativism and moral laxity, which we discussed in Chapter Five, has created fertile ground for those who are inclined to emphasize works as part of the gospel. The trend in today's American culture to accept and embrace all forms of deviant behavior with no apparent standards of morality seems to have reenergized works-based gospel models. Some well-intentioned evangelicals attempt to stem the tide of immorality by placing additional requirements on those who wish to gain eternal life.

For example, John MacArthur writes, "Shocking forms of open immorality have become commonplace among professing Christians." He laments the church contains Christians "whose behavior often is indistinguishable from the rebellion of the unregenerate," which, in his view, indicates they "are tragically deceived" into thinking they are saved when they are not. According to MacArthur one reason this is the case is the church's failure to emphasize up-front conditions, such as full surrender to Christ's authority, as a necessary component of saving faith. He writes, "The promise of eternal life *without surrender to divine authority* feeds the wretchedness of the unregenerate heart" (emphasis added). In other words, to address the problem of sin in the church, MacArthur and other Calvinists who share his viewpoint have turned salvation into a bilateral contract rather than the unilateral gift it is.

If a person *really* wants to be saved, they say, he must "bring something to the table." He cannot merely accept salvation as a free gift; it must cost him something. MacArthur insists salvation requires "a person's *willful obedience in turning from sin* to follow the Lord Jesus Christ" (emphasis added). He adds, "The gospel call to faith presupposes that sinners must *repent of their sin* and *yield to Christ's authority*" (emphasis added). In the same controversial section of the original release of *Hard to Believe,* MacArthur states, "Don't believe anyone who says it's easy to become a Christian. Salvation for sinners cost God His own Son; it cost God's Son His life, *and it'll cost you the same thing.* ...[Salvation] comes from a life lived in obedience and service to Christ..." (emphasis added). In other words, according to MacArthur, Jesus did not really pay it all, as the old hymn says. He paid part of our sin debt, and we must pay the rest on our own.

Obeying, turning from sin, following Christ, and yielding to His authority are all works that relate to the believer's progressive sanctification; they are *not* conditions for the believer's justification. By adding works to faith as a condition of receiving eternal life, MacArthur has relegated salvation to a *quid pro quo*. You must give (or give up) something to get something. This notion is completely foreign to Scripture. Salvation is a free gift. As

Augustus Toplady wrote in the 18th century:

Not the labor of my hands
Can fulfill Thy law's demands;
Could my zeal no respite know,
Could my tears forever flow,
All could never sin erase,
Thou must save, and save by grace.
Nothing in my hands I bring,
Simply to Thy cross I cling;
Naked, come to Thee for dress,
Helpless, look to Thee for grace:
Foul, I to the fountain fly,
Wash me, Savior, or I die.

His lyrics reflect the clear teaching of Scripture. "For by grace you have been saved through faith, and that not of yourselves; it is the gift of God, not of works, lest anyone should boast" (Ephesians 2:8–9). "Therefore, as through one man's offense judgment came to all men, resulting in condemnation, even so through one Man's righteous act the free gift came to all men, resulting in justification of life" (Romans 5:18). Grace and works simply do not mix when it comes to receiving eternal life. "And if by grace, then it is no longer of works; otherwise grace is no longer grace. But if it is of works, it is no longer grace; otherwise work is no longer work" (Romans 11:6).

The Puzzling Gospel

Earlier, I referenced the words of one of my former professors, Howard Hendricks, who said, "A mist in the pulpit becomes a fog in the pew." The fog of confusion surrounding salvation in these last days results from hazy, unclear, and puzzling gospel presentations echoing from church pulpits. They may be clever or trendy, but they are not accurate. They are so far from biblical truth, if these false gospels had a cold, the Bible would never catch it!

Many salvation messages are puzzling because they invoke generic phrases like "come to Jesus," "give your life to Him," "invite Him into your heart," or "commit to Christ," which are vague and unhelpful in the absence of sufficient clarifying explanations. What does "commit your life to Jesus," mean, precisely? A friend and long-time colleague of mine, Charlie Bing, writes,

> *Clear communication is an art. When it comes to telling the Gospel it is an art worth refining. We must work to tell the Gospel as clearly as possible. Not always will we succeed. But isn't it a wonderful fact of life that God can still use us in spite of the misplaced approaches and methods that we use? We know, however, that He can accomplish more through us according to how clear and biblical our message and our methods are. And that means that we are clear in our motives, in our Gospel content, in our statement of the condition for salvation, and in our invitation to believe. Given all that is at stake, we want to share the Good News as clearly as possible in a way that is pleasing to God, not just convenient to men.*

Thankfully, God can hit a home run with a crooked stick. Even though we often use unbiblical terminology when sharing the Gospel, the Holy Spirit uses our flawed words to bring conviction to the lost. Yet, this does not mean we should reach for that crooked bat when we step up to the evangelism plate. The fact that the pure Gospel has become more and more clouded with colloquialisms and hazy verbiage is another sign of the times.

The Purpose Gospel

One of the chief characteristics of what I call the "purpose gospel" is a notable downplaying of the notion of sin. Sin is at best redefined and at worst absent from the discussion altogether. When it is discussed, personal responsibility and guilt are often overlooked. Commenting on this tendency, D. A. Carson laments, "[In] our efforts to make Jesus appear relevant we have cast the human dilemma in merely contemporary categories, taking our cues from the perceived needs of our day." It is difficult to fathom how one can present the Gospel without addressing the sinfulness of mankind. As Colin Smith has pointed out, "We cannot have a gospel without sin any more than we can have a gospel without Jesus. If we replace the message of sin and atonement with a message of fulfillment and satisfaction in Jesus, we are preaching a different gospel."

Yet this is precisely the approach of the purpose gospel. John Portmann, a religion and philosophy professor at the University of Virginia, compiled a collection of essays promoting sin as a healthy aspect of life. Although Portmann could scarcely be considered an evangelical, his book, entitled, *In Defense of Sin*, nevertheless speaks to the prevailing view of sin in the church today. Portmann compares moralists who see sin as a corrupting influence on society to a wide-eyed *Chicken Little* who mistakenly thought the sky was falling. He writes, "Quite a few people have gone on record over the course of the last two thousand years as feeling frightened by the moral decay they perceived around them. If the sky is indeed falling, it is taking a long time to reach the ground. The world keeps turning."

For Portmann, and others like him, the Ten Commandments should be considered merely "good ideas," not "eternal verities." He states:

> *It seems that sins, like radioactive substances, have half-lives, some of which last longer than others. The most lethal chemicals require the most time to lose their sting, and the same is true of sin. Those sins with the longest half-lives will take the most time to recede from our consciousness. The biggest sins are those targeted in the Ten Commandments.*

He is convinced sin is not nearly as bad as it has been made out to be. "Sin wouldn't frustrate us," he writes, "if it didn't stand in the way of something we really would like to do." Given the softening influences of sin in the present age, Portmann concludes, "If the sky does one day fall, it will likely land on a world surprised by sin."

Not unlike Portmann, many evangelicals focus on the softer side of Jesus, who, as Portmann is quick to point out, cautions against casting the first stone. But such a selective appeal to the teachings of Christ in Scripture makes no attempt to reconcile other statements of Christ such as, "If your right eye causes you to sin, pluck it out and cast it from you; for it is more profitable for you that one of your members perish, than for your whole body to be cast into hell" (Matthew 5:29); or "Therefore I said to you that you will die in your sins; for if you do not believe that I am He, you will die in your sins" (John 8:24); or "And I say to you, My friends, do not be afraid of those who kill the body, and after that have no more that they can do. But I will show you whom you should fear: Fear Him who, after He has killed, has power to cast into hell; yes, I say to you, fear Him" (Luke 12:4–5)!

Most evangelicals who espouse the purpose gospel do not eviscerate sin completely the way Portmann does. Instead, perhaps recognizing that the wholesale abandonment of the doctrine of sin would be viewed as a complete departure from orthodoxy, they redefine it. Colin Smith observes, "For most people in our society, the word *sin* has been emptied of its true meaning and filled with another meaning that renders it harmless." But it is no less damaging to the true Gospel to redefine sin than it is to leave it out altogether. Sin is mankind's greatest predicament. Sin is not an inconvenience or temporal hindrance to fulfillment and purpose in life. It is not a mere weakness or limitation; it is a part of every individual's very composition. Mankind is by nature sinful, and that sinfulness is what condemns men to hell. As Mark Dever points out, "People need to grasp not only the theoretical concept of evil and wrong, but also the fact that *they* are evil and wrong." Apart from an accurate awareness of sin, there can be no salvation, for "without sin, what need is there of a Savior?" asks Dever.

The Prosperity Gospel

The American evangelical movement known variously as *Prosperity Theology, Word of Faith, Health and Wealth,* and *Name-It-and-Claim-It,* has its origins in the first half of the last century. Its proponents usually refer to E. W. Kenyon (1867–1948) as the patriarch of the movement. Kenyon was a New England Bible teacher whose teaching greatly influenced several later prosperity preachers such as Kenneth Hagin, Kenneth Copeland, Benny Hinn, Paul Crouch, Frederick K. C. Price, and Charles Capps. The prosperity gospel connects salvation with the promise of earthly blessings such as wealth and good health. Even though it has been around for a while, in these last of the last days, it is surging.

A *TIME* magazine article suggests disciples of the prosperity gospel are on the rise. David Van Biema and Jeff Chu, in their September 18, 2006, article entitled, "Does God Want You to Be Rich?" write,

> *Does God want you to be rich? A growing number of Protestant evangelists raise a joyful Yes!... It is one of the New Testament's hardest teachings, yet generations of church-goers have understood that being Christian, on some level, means being ready to sacrifice—money, autonomy or even their lives. But for a growing number of Christians ... the question is better restated, "Why not gain the whole world plus my soul?" For several decades, a philosophy has been percolating in the ten million-strong Pentecostal wing of Christianity that seems to turn the Gospel's passage on its head: certainly, it allows, Christians should keep one eye on heaven. But the new good news is that God doesn't want us to wait.... Its emphasis is on God's promised generosity in this life and the ability of believers to claim it for themselves.*

Van Biema and Chu captured well the essence of this false gospel. This erroneous teaching has gained traction in recent years through popular evangelical leaders like T. D. Jakes, Joel Osteen, Joyce Meyer, Creflo Dollar, Kirbyjon Caldwell, and others.

The Pluralistic Gospel

Pluralism "maintains that the major world religions provide independent salvific access to the divine Reality," according to Dennis L. Okholm and Timothy R. Phillips in their work, *Four Views on Salvation in a Pluralistic World*. It describes a view about the relationship between religious worldviews which may be characterized as "an egalitarian and democratized perspective that sees a rough parity among religions concerning truth and soteriological effectiveness," as Harold A. Netland and Keith E. Johnson describe it in their article, "Why Is Religious Pluralism Fun—and Dangerous?" In essence, pluralism teaches all religions are equally valid pathways to heaven. In the evangelical church, pluralism is often referred to as *inclusivism*.

This false gospel eschews the exclusivity of Christ as the only object of saving faith. The Bible unambiguously says otherwise. "Jesus said to him, 'I am the way, the truth, and the life. No one comes to the Father except through Me'" (John 14:6). "Nor is there salvation in any other, for there is no other name under heaven given among men by which we must be saved" (Acts 4:12). "For there is one God and one Mediator between God and men, the Man Christ Jesus" (1 Timothy 2:5). One of the most popular evangelicals in America today has publicly espoused an inclusivist view of the gospel.

During an appearance on CNN's "Larry King Live" on June 20, 2005, Joel Osteen was given multiple opportunities to affirm that faith in Christ is the only means of salvation, yet he steadfastly refused to do so. After a lengthy discussion regarding the salvation of Muslims, Jews, and even atheists in which he failed to articulate the Gospel, Osteen responded in seeming exasperation, "You know what, I'm going to let someone—I'm going to let God be the judge of who goes to heaven and hell. I'm not going to go around telling everybody else—if they don't want to believe that that's going to be their choice." To his credit, Osteen later apologized publicly to his congregation for being "unclear on the very thing in which I have dedicated my life [i.e., the Gospel]," but such an apology before a hometown crowd does not undo the damage done before a television audience of millions.

As discussed in Chapter Three, when the church discards the Bible as its only standard, it is left with no stake in the ground to which to tether its beliefs. Joel Osteen should have been able to answer quite easily the question of who goes to hell and who does not. The Bible certainly makes it clear. When the church departs from the Bible, the Gospel is not far behind.

The Pretend Gospel

As we draw closer to the end of the age, a strange new false gospel has reared its ugly head. The onset of artificial intelligence (AI), which is becoming more and more pervasive in every facet of our lives, brings with it pretend gospels that not only are doctrinally aberrant, but also completely fabricated with no connection to the Bible whatsoever. It is one thing to mishandle Scripture using faulty hermeneutics and arrive at an inaccurate salvation message, or to twist the Scriptures intentionally for personal gain. It is quite another, however, to manufacture a false gospel out of thin air.

Advancements in technology are approaching at what seems like warp-speed pace. According to one group of experts in an article for *The Atlantic,* entitled, "How Fast Is Technology Accelerating,"

> *Technology moves faster than our imaginations can keep up with. We invent one breakthrough technology today and then tomorrow's inventors transform it into another we never imagined possible. This has always been true, but it's happening faster than ever—and accelerating—which makes it hard to know what the world will look like when we get older.*

Instead of turning to the self-revelation of mankind in Scripture for the answer to man's sin problem, people are flocking to large language model AI systems like ChatGPT.

Yuval Noah Harari made a shocking claim during a June 2023 interview on AI and the future of humanity with journalist Pedro Pinto in Lisbon, Portugal. According to Harari, "The printing press printed as many copies of the Bible as Gutenberg instructed it, but it did not create a single new page. It had no ideas of its own about the Bible. Is it good, is it bad, how to interpret this, how to interpret that. AI can create new ideas. [It] can even write a new Bible." This "new Bible" AI promises to create comes with a new gospel—a *pretend* gospel that will save no one from his sins.

According to a story in *The Independent* by Vishwam Sankaran, a Berlin-based tech collective has developed a chatbot resembling Jesus Christ, which already has thousands of teen followers seeking advice and guidance. They are calling it *AI Jesus*. This is precisely what the real Jesus warned us about. "Take heed that no one deceives you. For many will come in My name, saying, 'I am the Christ,' and will deceive many" (Matthew 24:4–5). Like the other false gospels addressed in this chapter, the pretend gospel is a dead-end street. No man-made technology will ever be able to supersede God's plan of the ages, according to which He sent His only Son to die in our place on the cross so that we can have eternal life.

In the next chapter, we will delve into an arena that occupied many years of my life: academia. The degree to which Christian institutions of higher learning, like colleges and seminaries, are falling away from sound doctrine, is another indication we are living in the last of the last days.

8

FALLING AWAY ACADEMICALLY

... Knowledge puffs up, but love edifies. (1 Corinthians 8:1)

* * *

There is a humorous tale that illustrates the dangers of academia. Having spent many years of my life in that arena I can relate to this fable. It seems the Devil was wandering through the science building at a large university late one night when he happened upon the lab of a hard-working professor. "Could I interest you in a deal?" the Devil asked. "Suppose I arrange things so that for the next ten years all your research is highly successful. You publish ground-breaking papers and achieve great renown in the academic community. Top students clamber to work in your lab, Harvard and Yale fight to hire you, and you are right at the top of the list for the Nobel Prize. But at the end of the ten years your wife will be miserable, your kids will hardly recognize you, and you will not have a friend in the world. What would you say to that?" The professor thought for a moment and then gave the Devil a very skeptical look. "Come on now! What's the catch?!"

Sometimes academicians can be too smart for their own good. Consumed by their research and studies, they neglect some of life's most important priorities and become disconnected from reality. It is as if they cannot see the forest for the trees. Someone asked, what is the difference between academia and macadamia? Nothing, they are both nuts. That is probably a bit harsh, but when it comes to Christian academics, there is certainly no shortage of professors and institutions that have fallen away from sound biblical teaching.

For more than one hundred years, higher education has been drifting further and further away from such bedrock principles as absolutism and empiricism. It started in the 19th century, gained momentum in the 20th century, and by the 21st century, any hope of a revival was all but lost. Institutions such as Harvard, Yale, and Princeton, which once heralded the Gospel and taught the Scriptures, are now beachheads for belittling and attacking God's Word. The days of institutions like these producing men like B.B. Warfield, J. Gresham Machen, Cornelius van Til, or Woodrow Kroll are long gone. In this chapter, we will examine ways in which Christian higher education has departed from biblical orthodoxy.

Liberalism Isn't Just for Politics

When most Christians hear the word "liberal," they think of far-left politics and public figures like Nancy Pelosi or Gavin Newsome. The term has a different nuance in theological circles. In fact, a theological liberal may be conservative politically, though not always. In the arena of theology, a liberal is someone who denies key fundamental Christian beliefs such as the inerrancy of Scripture, the virgin birth, or the deity of Christ. Churches and schools that have formalized these false beliefs into their core values are known as liberal institutions. A friend of mine once called a popular seminary in Texas to inquire about their Doctor of Philosophy program. When he asked the director of the program if the school believes in the inerrancy of Scripture, he was told flatly, "No." When my friend pushed a little further, seeking to clarify the school's definition of inerrancy, the director responded curtly, "Listen, no matter how you define inerrancy, we do not believe in it."

There was a time when the highest degree an individual could earn at an

American institution was a Doctor of Theology (Th.D.). Yet, as science and reason began to eclipse faith as the basis for beliefs in this postmodern age, Th.Ds. gave way to Ph.Ds., reflecting our culture's preference for worldly philosophy over biblical theology. Even conservative seminaries and graduate schools, that still hold to the inerrancy of Scripture and other fundamental biblical doctrines, have capitulated to the coercions of culture and adopted the Ph.D. nomenclature.

The ideology reverberating from sermons in today's apostate churches first echoed from lecture halls in college and seminary classrooms. Liberal theological institutions produce liberal pastors, and liberal theology in the pulpit leads to liberal worldviews in the pew. There are many reasons the church is falling away in these last days. We have discussed several of them in the preceding chapters. Apostasy has many friends, but there can be no doubt it has been helped along considerably by liberalism in the academy. The most tangible evidence of this is liberalism's impact on the Gospel, as discussed in the previous chapter. According to H. Richard Niebuhr, himself no friend of conservative theology, God's work of salvation from a liberal theologian's point of view may be summarized as follows: "A God without wrath brought men without sin into a kingdom without judgment through the ministrations of a Christ without a cross."

During my years working in higher education, in addition to my teaching load, I was responsible for various aspects of the school's accreditation. This involved leading committees preparing for site visits from accreditors, chairing accreditation task forces, and overseeing departmental self-assessments to ensure we were complying with accreditation standards. Even in the realm of so-called Christian education, it was clear national accreditation trends were making it difficult for institutions to hold firm to sound doctrine.

At one national accreditation conference I attended, a representative from the Council on Higher Education in America (CHEA), a federal oversight group under the umbrella of the Department of Education, gave a seminar about the changing role of textbooks in the classroom. The CHEA rep said in the not-too-distant future, it was likely CHEA would mandate all schools use only textbooks published within the previous ten years. This would mean books by influential theological giants like Charles Ryrie, Lewis Sperry Chafer, John F. Walvoord, and Alva J. McClain, just to name a few, would be off-limits. I left full-time higher education before discovering if this new mandate became a reality, but I remember thinking at the time how this was yet another example of the Luciferian elite exerting their nefarious influence in this country.

Doctrine is Dead (A Satirical Lament)

This just in from *Reuters News Service*: Doctrine died today. The news of Doctrine's demise, while tragic, was not entirely unanticipated. It had been battling a terminal illness for many years. Doctrine's storied history is well known. From its powerful birth in the Apostolic Age; to its rapid rise to a place of centrality in the Christian life during the early centuries of the church; to its serious injuries and repression throughout the Medieval Period; to its incurable diagnosis during the Enlightenment; and finally, its death in this present pluralistic age.

For a brief time, hope of Doctrine's recovery reemerged during the early 20th century, as inerrantists and Biblicists put forth aggressive treatment programs that appeared to cause Doctrine's disease to enter remission. Such hopes turned out to be premature, however. With the onset of postmodern thinking, Doctrine suffered a rapid decline and finally breathed its last breath just this morning.

Reaction to this news has been swift and fairly consistent. One leading evangelical leader wrote, "While we are saddened by this news, we are glad to know that Doctrine's suffering is finally over. Now we can get on with more important matters like relationship building and loving our brothers." Another pastor commented,

> *Our hearts go out to all of those who loved Doctrine and stood by it until the bitter end. We pray they will gain closure and move forward quickly. We invite them to stop living in the past. Come join the rest*

> *of us in mainstream Evangelical Christianity as we seek to change the world through love, peace, and goodwill, rather than the divisiveness of creedalism.*

Not all Christian leaders have been as diplomatic in their comments. One highly influential Christian personality quipped, "It's about time! Doctrine has had a stranglehold on the thoughts and minds of Christians for far too long. Good riddance!"

The general sentiment across Christendom seems to be one of relief. The climate within Christianity has been characterized by a disdain for doctrinal standards for quite some time. Those who draw lines of theological distinction are perceived as unloving, even hateful or mean, while those who draw circles of inclusion are viewed as more progressive, loving, and open-minded. Anyone who claims his view is "right" based upon biblical Doctrine is charged with trying to force his view on someone else. Indeed, the labels "right" and "wrong" have been replaced in favor of less dogmatic phrases like "opinion" and "bias."

Some, evidently not wanting to appear as though they have entirely shunned Doctrine, have attempted to mask their disinterest in Doctrine by referring to "essentials" versus "non-essentials." There are "essential" beliefs that are always right and on which we must always agree, they say, but on "non-essentials" that are a matter of opinion and not a matter of right or wrong, we must give others the liberty to believe whatever they want.

It is an attractive concept, but supporters of Doctrine are quick to point out that the term Doctrine (from the Greek root word *didaskalia*) means "instruction in truth," and since truth by its very nature is always right and never a matter of opinion (a point vehemently denied by opponents of Doctrine), it is therefore *always* essential. Furthermore, within this essential/non-essential paradigm contrived by postmodernists, it seems as though the list of essential beliefs has grown smaller and smaller to the point that no one can identify what is on it anymore.

In any event, it is likely with Doctrine's passing, this "essential/non-essential" terminology will soon disappear entirely, as it will no longer be needed to placate Doctrine's supporters. Those from the "Can't-We-All-Just-Get-Along" political action committee within evangelicalism already have issued a statement celebrating the dawning of a new day:

> *Finally, once and for all, we can put an end to the judgmentalism, hatred, and arrogance of Doctrine's disciples who insist right belief is important. Such an archaic philosophy has been on life support for many years, and we are heartened that we can now move definitively beyond it to happier days of fellowship, joy, affirmation, and acceptance of all people regardless of their beliefs.*

Side note: I tried to join this committee once, but they would not accept me because of my beliefs.

One final addendum to this story. An obscure and little-known Christian leader, who goes only by his first name "Paul," has cautioned that such a celebratory response to the death of Doctrine is typical of those whose "consciences have been seared with a hot iron" and whose "itching ears" desire to hear only what makes them feel good. He goes on to point out that Doctrine is necessary for proper behavior and Christians would do well to "hold fast to sound Doctrine," for in so doing it will protect and preserve all who follow it.

It remains to be seen what effect the laying to rest of Doctrine will have on the church, but if this "Paul" is correct, it can only lead to great unpleasantness. "Take heed to yourself and to the doctrine. Continue in them, for in doing this you will save both yourself and those who hear you" (1 Timothy 4:16).

Nothing New Under the Sun

When you read Solomon's treatise in Ecclesiastes, you might come away with the notion he was the most pessimistic person who ever lived. If that is your takeaway from this fascinating Old Testament book, you have missed Solomon's point entirely. His central theme is that life lived by purely earthly and human standards is futile, but a God-centered life makes sense. Solomon points out that even though every human endeavor lacks ultimate value *on earth,* or as he calls it "under the sun," we should live life in the fear of God (i.e., with the proper recognition of Him) and enjoy life to the fullest as a gift from God. This can only be done if we have a God-centered perspective.

Those with a relationship with God can understand and see all is vanity under the sun. "Vanity of vanities," says the Preacher; "Vanity of vanities, all is vanity." What profit has a man from all his labor in which he toils under the sun" (Ecclesiastes 1:2–3)? Considering the meaninglessness of life apart from God, Solomon says people should have a healthy reverence for God. "Let us hear the conclusion of the whole matter: fear God and keep His commandments, for this is man's all. For God will bring every work into judgment, including every secret thing, whether good or evil" (Ecclesiastes 12:13–14). In other words, there is a God, and you are not Him.

Solomon was the wisest man who ever lived. "Thus Solomon's wisdom excelled the wisdom of all the men of the East and all the wisdom of Egypt" (1 Kings 4:30). "I communed with my heart, saying, 'Look, I have attained greatness, and have gained more wisdom than all who were before me in Jerusalem. My heart has understood great wisdom and knowledge'" (Ecclesiastes 1:16). He concluded there is nothing new under the sun. "That which has been is what will be, that which is done is what will be done, and there is nothing new under the sun" (Ecclesiastes 1:9). Academicians love to write books and enlighten the world with their findings. Unless God is at the center of one's academic pursuits, however, it is all vanity. Solomon said, "And further, my son, be admonished by these. Of making many books there is no end, and much study is wearisome to the flesh" (Ecclesiastes 12:12)

I could not help but think of Solomon's words when I first came across N.T. Wright and his so-called "new perspective on Paul." N.T. Wright is an Anglican bishop and respected scholar at Oxford University in England. In 2007, I heard him speak in person at the 59th Annual Meeting of the *Evangelical Theological Society* (ETS) in San Diego, CA. ETS is the foremost group of "Christian" academics in the world, and their Annual Meeting is like their Super Bowl. Only those with certain academic credentials (master's degree or higher) can join the organization, and thousands attend the ETS Annual Meeting, which is held in a different U.S. city each year. I let my membership lapse several years ago as I saw ETS drifting dramatically away from biblical orthodoxy.

Like scientists making ground-breaking discoveries in a laboratory, some theologians strive to uncover new theological interpretations of the Bible. To borrow the words of Festus, much learning is making them mad (Acts 26:24)! Paul reminds us, "Knowledge puffs up" (1 Corinthians 8:1). When I earned my Ph.D. in Systematic Theology, I thought it stood for "Doctor of Philosophy." Watching the way many of my colleagues wear their credentials on their sleeves, I cannot help but wonder if it really stands for "Piling it Higher and Deeper!" A certain intellectual elitism has found its way into Christian higher education in these last days, and it smacks of the arrogance common in secular university settings.

N.T. Wright has become enormously popular in these great last days of apostasy. He first gained traction in the academic arena by suggesting the church had misunderstood the Apostle Paul's teaching on justification. Thankfully, we have Wright to correct a two-thousand-year error in the church! Wright's influence has reached beyond the academic world, where the question of how many angels can dance on the head of a pin generates enough enthusiasm to fill a multi-day conference, to the laity. Sadly, his books and writings have captured the hearts and minds of Christians throughout the American church.

Whenever someone challenges long-standing biblical doctrines, we should remember the words of Solomon: "There is nothing new under the sun." Wright's book, *What Saint Paul Really Said*, suggests justification by faith has nothing to do with a person's right standing before God. According to him, Paul does *not* deny that human works play a role in individual justification. This is an absurd statement given the plain teaching of God's Word. Paul's view could not be clearer. It does not take a Ph.D. to understand what Paul says.

"Knowing that a man is not justified by the works of the law but by faith

> *in Jesus Christ, even we have believed in Christ Jesus, that we might be justified by faith in Christ and not by the works of the law; for by the works of the law no flesh shall be justified."* (Galatians 2:16)

> *"But that no one is justified by the law in the sight of God is evident, for "the just shall live by faith."* (Galatians 3:11)

> *"For if Abraham was justified by works, he has something to boast about, but not before God. For what does the Scripture say? 'Abraham believed God, and it was accounted to him for righteousness.' Now to him who works, the wages are not counted as grace but as debt. But to him who does not work but believes on Him who justifies the ungodly, his faith is accounted for righteousness."* (Romans 4:2–5)

Faith alone in Christ alone is the only thing that can justify a lost and sinful person before a holy God. "Therefore, having been justified by faith, we have peace with God through our Lord Jesus Christ" (Romans 5:1).

Phil Johnson, in his article, "What's Wrong with Wright: Examining the New Perspective on Paul," warns, "[T]he position Wright lays out in *What Saint Paul Really Said* is not an evangelical position at all. It's a faulty and dangerous reinterpretation of Paul, and it misunderstands Scripture in a way that fatally undermines the doctrine of justification by faith and the principle of *sola fide*." Johnson points out Wright's claim that the church has misunderstood justification by faith throughout church history is "a pretty audacious claim." Audacious is putting it mildly. The fact that foundational truths of Christianity are being challenged and that such challenges are given credibility in the American church today is a sign of apostasy if there ever was one.

What Does God Know and When Did He Know It?

Another example of academic apostasy in recent years is the development of an aberrant theological viewpoint referred to as *open theism*. My colleague and academic mentor, Dr. Mike Stallard, once told me open theism represents the most serious departure from orthodoxy in the modern church. In a 2001 article entitled, "An Open View of God...Does He Change?" Stallard writes, "The last fifteen years or so have seen the development of new theological formulations on many fronts, not the least of which has been the exploration of what appear to be non-traditional ways of looking at God Himself and how He interacts with the created order, especially with human beings." The late Clark Pinnock, John Sanders, and Gregory Boyd are three leading proponents of this false view, though many other pastors and professors have ascribed to it as well.

Open theism is the view that God's foreknowledge is limited. God can only know what is "knowable," and thus He does not know the future until it becomes today. The title of this view stems from the idea that God is "open" to the possibilities of the future and may be willing to change His mind once He learns how we respond. On his website, Dr. John Sanders asks these questions that are at the heart of the open theism issue. (1) Is God open to and influenced by what creatures do? (2) Is the future open or determined? (3) Does God know with certainty what we will do in the future? Even a casual student of Scripture should recognize such questions cut to the heart of the sovereignty of God, and to answer them wrongly amounts to creating God in the image of man.

Just as N.T. Wright suggests the church has been wrong in its understanding of justification by faith for two thousand years, open theists likewise suggest they have uncovered a novel view of God's sovereignty and thus corrected a centuries-old error in the church. The subtitle to Pinnock's book, *The Openness of God: A Biblical Challenge to the Traditional Understanding of God,* makes it clear he and his fellow proponents of open theism are unapologetically challenging the church's traditional understanding of Theology Proper. Open theists suggest the classical view of sovereignty paints a picture of a God who is too distant and unconcerned about His creation. In his book, *The Most Moved Mover,* Pinnock states, "God is certain about some aspects of the future and uncertain about other aspects." He continues, "No being, not even God, can know in advance precisely what free agents will do, even though He may predict it with great accuracy." If those statements do not alarm you, you need to reevaluate what God's Word says.

Open theism is just another attempt on the part of man to reconcile two truths in Scripture that cannot be understood from man's point of view: God's sovereignty and man's free will. We believe God is sovereign and we also believe mankind has free will, not because we can reconcile the two concepts to our human satisfaction, but because the Bible teaches both. Scripture passages that are difficult to reconcile, such as those about sovereignty and free will, are what we call biblical antinomies. The word "antinomy" comes from the Greek prefix *anti,* which means "against," and the Greek word *nomos,* which means "law." Thus, an antinomy is something contrary to natural law, contrary to logic, or contrary to what one would normally think. When the Bible says God is completely sovereign, and yet it also says mankind has free will, this does not make sense to us from our limited, human perspective. It is an *antinomy.* Yet, because the Bible teaches both concepts, we must accept them both as true.

There are other biblical antinomies in Scripture. The Trinity itself is an antinomy. How can God be three but One? The hypostatic union of our Lord is another. How can Jesus be fully God yet fully man? The virgin birth is an antinomy. How can a woman be a virgin yet have a child? We believe these biblical antinomies, not because they make logical sense, but because the Bible says so. We must run everything we believe through the grid of Scripture.

When we overplay God's sovereignty, the way Calvinists do, we make man into completely robotic automatons with no choice whether to accept or reject God's free offer of eternal life. If you are in, you are in. If not, well, good luck! When we overplay man's free will, we turn God into an impotent bystander who is waiting and watching to learn what we will do. This is the view of open theists. Pinnock states, "God, in order to be omniscient, need not know the future in complete detail." Elsewhere, Pinnock asserts, "God is not bound to a script, even his own." If it scares the daylights out of you to think we serve a God who is uncertain, indecisive, and merely a better-than-average predictor, it should!

Open theists highlight biblical passages where God appears to change His mind or seems surprised or grieved by man's actions, but they downplay the wealth of passages about His sovereignty, omniscience, and immutability. Scripture can never contradict itself. The passages in which God is presented as being frustrated, surprised, ignorant, angry, or changing His mind are all examples of anthropomorphisms. An anthropomorphism is a figure of speech in the Bible where human attributes are ascribed to God as a means of helping mankind relate to an infinite God. An eternal God can only interact with His created universe on terms they can understand.

When David prayed, "Into Your hand I commit my spirit..." (Psalm 31:5), he was not suggesting God has literal hands that He must wash before having dinner. When the Bible says, "He shall cover you with His feathers, and under His wings you shall take refuge..." (Psalm 91:4), this does not mean God is a bird who lives in a nest. Anthropomorphisms and zoomorphisms are common throughout Scripture, and they should never be taken as contravening the clear teaching elsewhere in the Bible about God's sovereignty.

What does God know, and when did He know it? He knows everything, He always has, and He always will. We serve an almighty, sovereign God. "But our God is in heaven; He does whatever He pleases" (Psalm 115:3). "For I am the Lord, I do not change..." (Malachi 3:6). "Have you not known? Have you not heard? The everlasting God, the Lord, the Creator of the ends of the earth, neither faints nor is weary. His understanding is unsearchable" (Isaiah 40:28). "Great is our Lord, and mighty in power; His understanding is infinite" (Psalm 147:5). "O Lord, You have searched me and known me. You know my sitting down and my rising up; You understand my thought afar off. You comprehend my path and my lying down, and are acquainted with all my ways. For there is not a word on my tongue, but behold, O

Lord, You know it altogether" (Psalm 139:1–4). To suggest that God is not omniscient, that He does not know everything, flies in the face of the plain teaching of His Word and two thousand years of orthodoxy. Open theism is a troubling sign of apostasy in the church in these last days.

Closing the Gap on the Gap Theory

Another example of academic apostasy in the realm of Christian education is the degree to which old-earth beliefs have become the norm. It is getting harder and harder to find Christian colleges and seminaries that teach the earth is 6,000-8,000 years old and was created in six literal 24-hour days by God. I am not suggesting, of course, that every Christian or Bible teacher who believes the earth is millions of years old is an apostate. Many otherwise solid Bible scholars have adopted an old-earth view of creation because it has been pounded from academic lecterns for more than a hundred years. Indeed, it is the predominant view in the church today. But just because most Christians believe it, does not make it true. Remember what we said about the remnant principle in Chapter Two.

For nearly 1,800 years, the church took the Bible at its word and believed God spoke the world into existence in six literal 24-hour days. Virtually no one in the church believed the earth was millions of years old and mankind evolved from a wet rock. When Charles Darwin came along in the 19th century, this began to change. I covered the influence of Dawin's eugenicist worldview in Chapter Five, so I will not repeat it here except to point out that his teaching was the genesis (no pun intended!) of old-earth beliefs. It is true there are a few pre-Darwin references to an old earth, but Darwin crystallized and popularized this false belief. By the time we get to the dawn of the 20th century, the theory that the earth was millions of years old was widely accepted by most Christians. After all, science had "proven" it. This created tension for conservative Christians who believed the Bible. How could science and the Bible be reconciled? "Perhaps we missed something in God's Word," many Christians began to speculate.

By elevating "science," which was really not science at all but pseudoscience, above Scripture, the church began to postulate ways to fit old-earth beliefs into the Bible. One popular way Christians have done this is through what is called "the gap theory." The late Henry Morris was an American young-earth creationist, Christian apologist, and engineer. He was one of the founders of the *Creation Research Society* and the *Institute for Creation Research.* He is considered by many to be the father of modern creation science. He explains the fallacy of the gap theory as follows.

> *One of the popular devices for trying to accommodate the evolutionary ages of the geologists and astronomers in the creation record of the Bible has been the "gap theory"—also called the "ruin-and-reconstruction" theory.*
>
> *According to this concept, Genesis 1:1 describes the initial creation of the universe. Following this, the standard events of cosmic evolution took place, which eventually produced our solar system about five billion years ago. Then, on the earth, the various geologic ages followed, as identified by their respective assemblages of fossils (trilobites, dinosaurs, etc.).*
>
> *But then occurred a devastating global cataclysm, destroying all life on Earth and leaving a vast fossil graveyard everywhere. This situation is then said to be what is described in Genesis 1:2. "And the earth was without form and void; and darkness was upon the face of the deep." The cataclysm is thought to have occurred as a result of the rebellion of Satan and his angels against their Creator in Heaven, with God then casting them out of Heaven to the earth.*
>
> *Those who advocate the gap theory agree that the six days of the creation week were literal days, but they interpret them only as days of recreation, with God creating again many of the kinds of animals and plants destroyed in the cataclysm.*
>
> *The gap theory was developed mainly for the purpose of accommodating the great ages demanded by evolutionary geologists. This idea was first popularized by a Scottish theologian, Thomas Chalmers, early in the 19th century. In this country, the famous Scofield Study Bible made*

> *it an almost universally accepted teaching among fundamentalists.*
>
> *However, serious conflicts do remain. In fact, there are few, if any, professionally trained geologists and astronomers (to my knowledge there are none) who accept the gap theory. The promoters of this theory have mostly been Bible teachers who hoped they could place these great ages in a gap between the first two verses of Genesis, and thus not have to deal with them at all.*
>
> *With the modem revival of scientific Biblical creationism, many of these teachers have abandoned the gap theory in favor of strict creationism. Most advocates of the gap idea were men of strong Biblical faith, and when they were shown its Biblical fallacies, plus its scientific inadequacies, they were quite willing to reject the evolutionary ages scheme altogether.*

Although proponents of the gap theory point to exegetical and grammatical considerations in the Hebrew text, such assertions are widely disputed and by no means prove there was a gap of time between the first two verses of Genesis 1. According to one scholar, "The gap-theory cannot either be conclusively proved or disproved by the grammatical considerations of [the word 'was" in Genesis 1:2]. Suffice it to say that each side argues for their interpretation of this word on the basis of the context and other grammatical issues. However, the question cannot be settled on the consideration of the meaning of this verb."

The Bible unambiguously teaches death came about after, and because of, sin. "Therefore, just as through one man sin entered the world, and death through sin, and thus death spread to all men, because all sinned" (Romans 5:12). In other words, you cannot have millions of years of death and destruction *before* the creation of mankind. Moreover, Jesus plainly said Adam and Eve were created at the *beginning* of creation. "But from the beginning of the creation, God 'made them male and female'" (Mark 10:6). To place Adam and Eve at the beginning of a second creation, after death was already a reality, violates the clear teaching of God's Word.

My friend, Russ Miller, a leading creation scientist, likes to say, "Science is a Christian's best friend." Contrary to the contentions of Darwinian evolutionists and eugenicists, and notwithstanding the viewpoint of well-intentioned Christians, science proves young-earth creationism. The earth's layers (or, sedimentary strata), which are alleged to have developed slowly over millions of years, were actually formed in a matter of days as a result of a global flood, precisely as described in Genesis 7-8. Evolutionists look at a snapshot of data and assume the earth's processes have been uniform for millions of years. They do not consider the impact of a major, global cataclysm such as the biblical flood. For more research into this subject, I recommend the ground-breaking book, *The Genesis Flood: The Biblical Record and Its Scientific Implications,* by John Whitcomb and Henry Morris. Figure 13 summarizes various false views on the origin of man that have crept into the church as part of the last days apostasy.

Views on the Origin of Mankind

Atheistic Evolution	There is no God. Man formed by chance and evolved by mutation and natural selection.	**Mocks the Bible**
Theistic Evolution	Accepts the theory of evolution but attempts to harmonize it with the teachings of the Bible.	**Marginalizes the Bible**
Day-Age Theory	Rejects literal 6-day creation. Accepts microevolution but rejects macroevolution.	**Mishandles the Bible**
Gap Theory	Accepts literal 6-day creation but capitulates to science regarding the alleged antiquity of the earth.	**Misinterprets the Bible**
Literal Creationism	Accepts literal 6-day creation. God created Adam and Eve from whom every human being since has descended.	**BELEIVES the Bible**

Figure 13

Views such as the gap theory, open theism, and the new perspective on Paul, while advocated by well-meaning Christians, are nevertheless examples of academic apostasy. Unfortunately, what happens in the academy, does not stay in the academy. False teachings that originate from academia trickle down to the church and are embraced by Christians.

In the next chapter, we will examine one final manifestation of apostasy in these last days. Through the mixture of American politics and biblical Christianity, the church is falling away politically.

9

FALLING AWAY POLITICALLY

By me kings reign, and rulers decree justice. By me princes rule, and nobles, all the judges of the earth. (Proverbs 8:15–16)

* * *

The comedian Robin Williams once suggested "politics" is a compound word derived from "poly," meaning "many," and "ticks," meaning "blood-sucking creatures!" I am not normally a fan of political jokes (I have seen too many of them get elected), but that is a good one, and it is probably more accurate than one might think. The depravity of man is on full display in our nation's capital. U.S. politics has become a cesspool of sin, secrets, and sex scandals. It is a shadowy world where pernicious plans emerge as the Luciferian elite huddle in smoke-filled rooms to compare the details of their malevolent machinations. Money, seduction, and power have replaced integrity, honesty, and character as the only currencies accepted inside Washington, D.C. From blackmail to black ops, blackwater to black budgets, BlackRock to the black market, the beltway is a dark, dark place. George Washington warned, "Few men have the virtue to withstand the highest bidder."

Some people wonder whether art imitates life or life imitates art. You can stop wondering. The spy thrillers and political dramas that emanate from

Hollywood are sourced in a reality that begins 2,600 miles away and, like slime through a sewer pipe, oozes west until it shows up on the big screen. Pizzagate, Lewinsky, Epstein, assassinations, affairs, scandals, betrayals, and more all reflect another day at the office for politicians, bureaucrats, and lobbyists. Wendy and I have spent a lot of time in Washington, D.C. We have noticed something. After dark, the rats are sure to come out, scurrying about the streets and metro stations. They are literal *and* metaphorical. Abraham Lincoln forewarned, "America will never be destroyed from the outside. If we falter and lose our freedoms, it will be because we destroyed ourselves."

If you look hard enough within the halls of our government, I am sure you can find a man or woman of faith who stands on principle, loves our country, and truly seeks to do what is right for the right reasons. But pack a lunch, or better yet, several suitcases, because the search will not be easy, and it will take a while. This outlook may sound jaded or too pessimistic to some of you. If so, my guess is you have been watching too much Fox News or Newsmax or some other right-wing news source where debauchery is masked by well-spoken talking heads who tickle our ears with conservative sound bites. For those in the church who value the right/left paradigm more than the right/wrong paradigm, and there are many in that group, all seems well in the "City of Magnificent Intentions," as Dickens called it. Washington, D.C. is a place with "spacious avenues that begin in nothing and lead nowhere," wrote Dickens in 1842. He was referring to the city's infrastructure; the same could be said for its soul.

Given what American politics has become, it is surprising so many Christians hold the U.S. government in such high esteem. Should we not expect more? Demand more? When did the American church become so complacent as to wink and nod at evil as if it were routine? When did we forget that Satan and his earthly co-conspirators love to "masquerade as angels of light" (2 Corinthians 11:14)? My friend and colleague, journalist Leo Hohmann, is spot on when he says, "Mixing good in with evil is a clever tactic to woo the masses and pacify [the conservative] base. Many will be deceived by the bait and switch." This tactic not only works on conservatives, but it also leads Christians astray as well. Indeed, as I am going to suggest in this chapter, the terms "Christian" and "conservative" have become synonyms, and neither means what they used to mean.

"Most Christians have hit the snooze button on their smoke alarm," as Mary Danielsen puts it. We have failed to recognize the "spirit of the Antichrist" is on the rise in these last days (1 John 4:3). Paul refers to Christians as, "sons of light and sons of the day." He adds, "We are not of the night nor of darkness. Therefore let us not sleep, as others do, but let us watch and be sober" (1 Thessalonians 5:5–6). The church in these last days is sound asleep. I do not mean the church is merely dozing off like a freshman in Western Civ 101. I am talking about full-blown REM sleep, dead to the world. Or maybe we should say, dead to spiritual reality and very much alive to the world. The church's somnambulism is nowhere more evident than in its unwitting and unlikely partnership with politics. The Apostle John cautioned, "Beloved, do not believe every spirit, but test the spirits, whether they are of God; because many false prophets have gone out into the world" (1 John 4:1). If we want to heed this warning, we would do well to start our search for false prophets in Washington, D.C.

Christians Are an Easy Mark

The American church today has become indifferent to immorality when it surfaces in our favorite politicians, and this is a significant sign we are falling away. If the Luciferian elite, who are conspiring with Satan to usher in the Beast system, are going to get the United States to jump on board the New World Order train, they are going to need the support of American evangelicals. And Satan's earthly accomplices know this. Most Christians, on the other hand, have no idea what a powerful political pawn the church has become. If Christians, *en masse,* would stand firm in the faith and reject the Satanic agenda, we could stop it overnight. Of course, this will not happen in these great last days of apostasy. Quite the contrary, the church is aiding and abetting the enemy in this endeavor.

One of the biggest lies leading to the church's political apostasy is the perception that the Republican party is the "party of Christians." This is demonstrably false. Carroll Quigley, who died in 1977, was a political science professor who taught at Princeton, Harvard, and for most of his career, Georgetown University. In his 1966 book, *Tragedy & Hope,* he exposed the degree to which the Luciferian agenda has crept into American politics. The book was based on information from the archives of the Council on Foreign Relations (CFR), a key think tank of the Luciferians that serves to advance their agenda. Quigley was the CFR's historian. I cover the CFR in detail in *Spirit of the Antichrist Volume Two.*

As the CFR began to set things in motion, they developed a plan for who would be president, who would be king, who would oversee this sector and that sector, and how they were going to get people to come along and buy into the one-world government that Satan has long coveted. The CFR put together a blueprint, and Quigley revealed it in *Tragedy & Hope.* They got so far down the path they all assumed it was a *fait accompli.* Or at least Carroll Quigley thought so.

Tragedy & Hope amounts to a thirteen-hundred-page, tell-all exposé. It is huge and weighs over eight pounds. I would recommend reading a couple of excellent summaries, sort of *Cliffs Notes* versions. One is by W. Cleon Skousen, *The Naked Capitalist.* The other is *None Dare Call It Conspiracy,* by Gary Allen. Both provide all you need to know about what was exposed and unveiled in *Tragedy & Hope.* Carroll Quigley once said, "I am now quite sure that *Tragedy & Ho*pe was suppressed." When the Luciferian leaders saw he had produced this book, they panicked. This was before the Internet and before widely available information. The Luciferians stole the printing press plates of *Tragedy & Ho*pe from the publisher, then collected and burned as many printed copies as they could. For years the book was not available. It is now back in print. It is hard to suppress the truth for very long.

Here is a salient quote from *Tragedy & Hope*:

> *I know of the operations of this network [talking about the Luciferians] because I've studied it for twenty years and was permitted for two years, in the early 60s, to examine its papers and its secret records. I have no*

> *aversion to it or most of its aims and have for much of my life been close to it and many of its instruments. The Luciferians wish its agenda to remain unknown, but I believe its role in history is significant enough to be made known.*

According to Quigley, the Luciferians' aim is nothing less than to create a "world system of financial control in private hands able to dominate the political system of every country and the economy of the world as a whole. Individual freedom of choice will be controlled within very narrow alternatives by the fact that everyone will be numbered from birth." These things do not just happen. Someone is pulling the strings.

Quigley continues, "We will be followed as a number through educational training, required military or other public service, tax contributions, health and medical requirements, and through final retirement and death. This has all been part of the plan." As it relates to the controlled right/left paradigm in American politics, Quigley said, "The argument that the two parties should represent opposed ideals and policies, one on the right and the other on the left, is a foolish idea. Instead, the two parties should be almost identical so that the American people can 'throw the rascals out' at any election." As I mentioned in *Spirit of the Antichrist Volume One,* when political change occurs, there are never any extensive or long-lasting shifts in policy. Sure, a few things may change that do not impact the Luciferians' overall plan. They must throw conservatives a bone now and then to make us think our vote matters. But nothing significant ever changes.

No one party can fool all the people all the time; that is why we have two parties. In 1924, G. K. Chesterton famously pointed out, "The whole modern world has divided itself into Conservatives and Progressives. The business of Progressives is to go on making mistakes. The business of Conservatives is to prevent mistakes from being corrected." The Republican Party and Democratic Party are both under the control of very powerful and extremely evil people. Those with the courage to look behind the curtain will soon find our so-called democracy is really a Luciferian kakistocracy. The English rock band, *The Who,* put it well.

I'll tip my hat to the new constitution
Take a bow for the new revolution
Smile and grin at the change all around me
And the world looks just the same
And history ain't changed
'Cause the banners, they are flown in the next war
Meet the new boss same as the old boss

Many naïve Christians think all it would take to change the direction of this country would be to have a Republican in the White House, a Republican-controlled Congress, a Republican-controlled Senate, and a majority of Republican-appointed Supreme Court Justices. Surely then we can put a stop to those evil Democrats, right? It is all their fault, those dirty Democrats. Christians who hold that viewpoint are not only deceived, but they also have short memories.

There have been multiple times when Republicans have controlled every branch of government at the same time. In the recent past there was the Gingrich revolution, then the Tea Party revolution. In President Trump's two terms, there were times when the Republicans controlled both houses of Congress. Yet our society is still looking more and more like Sodom and Gomorrah. This is because the right/left paradigm in our U.S. political system is contrived. In America, the Luciferians provide an illusion every four years to string us along until they are ready to enter the end game. "Oh, I don't like these people. They are communists or socialists. I will throw them out." Sadly, the country keeps marching in the same direction, like lemmings off a cliff, and the church is very much a part of the parade. Christians, it seems, are an easy mark.

Evil is the New Good

The lesser-of-two-evils paradigm has become entrenched in the church in these last days. Few Christians like to talk about, or even notice, the *evil* in the two lessers. It is just taken for granted. "Yes. I am voting for evil. What is the problem with that?" The problem is evil is not a matter of degree. There is no place where the Bible tells us to choose the "least evil" option. Evil is evil. Whenever you hear someone use the phrase "the lesser of two evils," quickly remind them of this point. You will likely hear something like this in response. "There are no perfect candidates." Certainly, that is true, but should we not look for a candidate who openly embraces a biblical worldview and holds firm on the most basic, rudimentary moral issues?

I have never understood the popular notion among many Christians that spiritual wisdom is an optional commodity for those in government office. "We're not electing a pastor; we're electing a president!" the saying goes, usually with a confident crescendo, as if the cleverness of the quip itself settles the issue. The widespread idea that we should, or even can, segregate worldly wisdom and spiritual wisdom is bizarre, and it is thoroughly unbiblical. Solomon dispels this notion quite handily. Personifying godly wisdom, he writes,

> *"I, wisdom, dwell with prudence, and find out knowledge and discretion. The fear of the Lord is to hate evil; pride and arrogance and the evil way and the perverse mouth I hate. Counsel is mine, and sound wisdom; I am understanding, I have strength. By me kings reign, and rulers decree justice. By me princes rule, and nobles, all the judges of the earth. I love those who love me, and those who seek me diligently will find me." (Proverbs 8:12–17)*

If this passage teaches us anything, it is that no one, not kings, princes, nobles, or any government leader, can succeed if they try to do so apart from God. So, why are Christians so quick to discount spiritual wisdom when selecting our next Republican marionette?

The underlying flaw with the "Jesus-is-not-on-the-ballot-so-I-will-just-accept-whoever-the-Republicans-give-me" argument is that it assumes our choice in an election is limited to two candidates. This is precisely what Quigley warned us about. The Luciferians want us to stay fixated on the false right/left paradigm. As long as we choose Coke or Pepsi, they can still advance their evil agenda. What is lost on the church is we are swallowing dangerous high fructose corn syrup either way. The lesser of two evils approach offers only two options: (A) a bad choice; and (B) a worse choice.

Satan's co-conspirators are quite comfortable with us choosing what we perceive to be the "lesser" of two evils, so long as one of their evil candidates wins the election. Ralph Waldo Emerson said, "The louder he talked of his honor, the faster we counted our spoons." The louder conservative, mainstream media outlets extol the virtues of a Republican candidate, the faster Christians ought to dig into that candidate's past. For many conservatives, especially conservative Christians, there is only one candidate worthy of their vote. His or her name is, "Not A. Democrat." As long as the candidate is *not* Hillary, *not* Obama, *not* Biden, or *not* Harris, that candidate is acceptable, regardless of his or her views on serious moral issues.

For example, if the Republican candidate is in favor of killing fewer innocent babies in the womb than the Democratic candidate, Christians are comfortable voting for the Republican. After all, killing a few innocent babies is less evil than killing a lot of innocent babies, right? It grieves me that more Christians do not understand the ridiculousness of such a viewpoint, and I am quite sure it grieves the Lord as well. It shows just how deceived the church has become when evil becomes the new good.

The Overton Window Needs Cleaning

One outgrowth of the lesser-of-two-evils concept is it allows politicians, most of whom are controlled by a higher, more sinister, force hiding in the shadows, to keep moving American culture further and further away from its moral foundations. Few politicians today stand on principle. They make their decisions based on perceived public opinion. No matter how "Christian" you think your favorite Republican politician is, if he or she even owns a Bible, chances are it is buried beneath the latest public opinion polls. Remember what we talked about in Chapter Three. According to Barna, a startling 82% of Americans say they "embrace a few biblical principles but generally believe and behave in ways that are distinct from biblical teaching." Do we really think our politicians are in the group of 18% of Americans who view the Bible as their only standard for beliefs, attitudes, and practices?

The *Overton window* is named after the American policy analyst Joseph Overton who proposed that an idea's political viability depends mainly on whether it falls within a range of acceptability by the mainstream public. Legislation has nothing to do with a politician's principles or moral convictions; it is all about perception. According to Overton, the window delineates the range of policies a politician can recommend or support without appearing too extreme to gain or keep public office given the political climate at that time.

When the Luciferians want to shape public thought, they intentionally, patiently, and gradually move the window. For example, they do not lead with, "We'd like to cut off your child's body parts." Instead, they roll out wokeism and the gender surrender movement, which I expose in *Spirit of the Antichrist Volume Two*. What once was *right* has now become *far right*. What once was *liberal* has now become *progressive*. What once was *unthinkable* has become *acceptable*. That is how the Overton window works. Instead of seeing politics through the panes of the Overton window, Christians need to replace the glass—or at least clean it. If the American church keeps espousing a lesser-of-two-evils worldview, the Overton window will keep moving to the left.

Christian Nationalism, Horses, and Sandwiches

As Christians get drawn into politics and continue to believe there are only two choices in an election, the American church is experiencing an upsurge in Christian nationalism. While not new, this disturbing movement has reached a feverish pitch in recent years. What is Christian nationalism? To begin with, we should point out that labels do not always reflect the meaning of their component parts. For example, I like horses, and I like sandwiches, but that does not mean I like horse sandwiches. Similarly, I am a Christian and I am a nationalist. But I am most definitely not a "Christian nationalist."

Like most movements and labels, Christian nationalism has differing nuances depending on who you ask. In a December 29, 2020, journal article published in the periodical, *Sociology of Religion*, academicians define Christian nationalism as follows. "By this we mean a pervasive ideology constituted by identities, values, and historical narratives that center on preserving or 'restoring' the preeminence of an identitarian and embattled form of Christianity in American civic life." Wikipedia puts the cookies on a lower shelf and defines it this way: "Christian nationalism is a form of religious nationalism that focuses on promoting the Christian views of its followers, in order to achieve prominence or dominance in political and social life." While Wikipedia is not exactly the standard-bearer for definitions, it does reflect common perceptions in our culture.

The Christian nationalism movement has captured the attention of politicians, pundits, and the public alike. Will Carless, in a March 7, 2024, article for *USA Today*, writes,

> *Suddenly, it seems, the term "Christian nationalism" is everywhere. News reports about a rising conservative think tank express concerns about its ties to the movement. A high-profile documentary asks whether a new wave of believers will wash away democracy in America. And Donald Trump... is increasingly embracing the narrative that he has been chosen by God — that only he can save America from Satan.*

References to God, Christianity, and morality resonate with the American evangelical church. Yet, typical of Satan's *modus operandi,* Christian nationalism mixes truth with error. While it is true God's fingerprints are all over the founding and history of this country, it does not follow that Christians should revolt and create a theocracy. The only theocracy Christians should be heralding is the one Christ will bring at His triumphant return. Christian nationalism goes well beyond simply exerting a Christian influence on American culture, something all American Christians should strive to do. It represents an overt, and sometimes covert, agenda of which most Christians are completely unaware.

Christian nationalism essentially takes the questionable perspective of American exceptionalism which I critiqued in *Spirit of the Antichrist Volume One* and adds evangelicalism's stamp of approval. Yet, it is more than a mere ideology; it is a movement. And this movement has been co-opted by the Luciferian elite as they strive to usher in the New World Order. Many of its advocates within government and the church are unwitting pawns in the game. Remember what I said earlier. The global elite need the church on their side if they are going to bring down America. The allure of Christian nationalism has captured most conservative Christians. It is hard to resist, especially after four years of far-left, radical politics under President Biden. The pendulum is swinging forcefully to the right, and Christians are pushing it. We need a hero, and Donald Trump has stepped into that role. Whether he was conscripted by nefarious kingmakers or joined the movement willingly is an open question.

Christians today are speaking of a new "Golden Age" for America. The term is pervasive on social media, the Internet, and from America's pulpits. On January 26, 2025, a tweet purporting to be from President Trump's son, Eric Trump, circulated on social media. It said, "Any and all who dare to defy the American Golden Age, heed this warning: You WILL lose. Tow [sic] the line, or we WILL run you down! The gloves are off, and we're not playing around this time. For now, it's tariffs, but trust me: We can, and will, do SO MUCH WORSE." The tweet is of questionable provenance, and is likely a fake, but it nevertheless reflects the attitude of the Christian nationalist movement. Who would not want to be part of a "golden age" that "makes America great again?" However, be very careful. As Shakespeare reminded us, "Not all that glitters is gold."

Turning Point USA (TPUSA) has become a leading voice in the Christian nationalism movement. It is a grassroots organization led by Charlie Kirk whose mission is "to identify, educate, and organize the next generation of Americans to live in freedom!" More than any other organization today, TPUSA illustrates the conflation of church and politics. Kirk speaks in pulpits and on Christian campuses across the country, often accompanied by well-known elected officials. Marjorie Taylor Greene, a U.S. Representative from Georgia, said at a TPUSA event in 2022, "We need to be the party of nationalism. I am a Christian and I say it proudly, we should be Christian nationalists." Another congresswoman, Lauren Boebert from my home state of Colorado, said, "The church is supposed to direct the government." Mike Johnson, the current speaker of the House of Representatives, hangs a flag associated with the New Apostolic Reformation, a Christian nationalist movement, outside his office.

Kevin DeYoung, a Calvinist pastor who misses the mark when it comes to the Gospel, hits the bullseye in his critique of Christian nationalism. In his November 28, 2022, review of Stephen Wolfe's *The Case for Christian Nationalism*, DeYoung writes,

> *The message—that ethnicities shouldn't mix, that heretics can be killed, that violent revolution is already justified, and that what our nation needs is a charismatic Caesar-like leader to raise our consciousness and galvanize the will of the people—may bear resemblance to certain blood-and-soil nationalisms of the 19th and 20th centuries, but it's not a nationalism that honors and represents the name of Christ.*

The Christian nationalism that has emerged in these last days seeks to thrust Christianity on the government by force. Yet, Jesus told Pilate, "My kingdom is not of this world. If My kingdom were of this world, My servants would fight, so that I should not be delivered to the Jews; but now My kingdom is not from here" (John 18:36). Patrick Schreiner is correct when he states, "We advocate for the end of abortion, but we don't kill doctors who perform abortions. We can march and protest, but we don't form mobs of destruction. We work to elect candidates of integrity and conviction, but we don't harass public officials at town halls or school board meetings."

Christian nationalism has as part of its lineage the errors of Dominion Theology, a teaching popularized by R. J. Rushdoony in the 1960s and 1970s. Dominionists, as they are called, seek to institute a nation governed by Christians and impose the Old Testament law on society. Matt Slick elaborates,

> *Dominion theology is the teaching that Christians are to take dominion over all areas of the secular realm: media, government, schools, arts, etc. It is also known as Christian reconstructionism and is often associated with theonomy – the rule of God in society. There are varieties of dominion theology. Some assert that all governments should be replaced with Old Testament law. Others advocate a blending of secular and sacred systems. Whatever the case, Dominion theology urges Christians to take their "rightful" place in all areas of society all over the world. Once this is accomplished, and the world is converted to Christianity, Jesus will return.*

This false teaching is essentially a repackaged form of postmillennialism, the view that once Christians get the world cleaned up, Christ will return at the end of the millennium to bring a climax to the Kingdom age. This view is also known as *Reconstructionism* and *Theonomic Ethics,* and other well-known advocates of this view include Gary North and Greg Bahnsen. One can readily see the similarities between dominion theology and Christian nationalism. Indeed, the nuances of "dominion" and "reconstruction" more aptly describe the movement than "nationalism." It goes well beyond mere patriotic support of government and instead advocates for a complete dismantling and rebuilding of it.

Project 2025 embodies the reconstructionist ideology embedded within the Christian nationalism movement. It is a powerful political initiative organized by *The Heritage Foundation*; a highly influential conservative think tank founded in 1973. The project aims to promote conservative and right-wing policies to reshape the federal government of the United States and consolidate executive power under the leadership of Donald Trump. Although President Trump has at times embraced Project 2025, and at other times distanced himself from it, Nik Popli points out in a January 24, 2025, article for *TIME,* "nearly two-thirds of the executive actions Trump has issued so far mirror or partially mirror proposals from the 900-page document, ranging from sweeping deregulation measures to aggressive immigration reform."

In the months leading up to the 2024 presidential election, Project 2025 received mostly fringe coverage in the media. It is linked to *The Statement on Christian Nationalism* manifesto "which seeks to implement a Scripture-based system of gov't whereby Christ-ordained 'civil magistrates' exercise authority over the American public," according to Jennifer Cohn in a July 7, 2024, article for the *Bucks County Beacon.* Notwithstanding the enthusiastic support many conservative Christians have shown for Project 2025, especially because part of its stated goal is "to take down the Deep State and return the government to the people," it is a dangerous mechanism being used to undermine the constitutional freedoms on which this country is founded. Whenever someone offers to rescue you from the frying pan, beware the fire.

The ideological fingerprints of Curtis Yarvin also appear conspicuously on this proposal to reshape America. Yarvin is the influential anti-democratic founder of a political movement known as neo-reactionism, or the Dark Enlightenment, popular in certain tech circles. He proposes installing an American monarch who would dissolve elite academic institutions and media outlets within the first few months of his reign. Yarvin wants to abolish the U.S. Constitution and refers to those who foolishly maintain a grip on the foundational document of our country as, "rightists." In his March 2024 newsletter, Yarvin stated, "Whether 'rightists' understand this or not (generally, not), the only rational telos of 'rightism' is the restoration of a stable, responsible, and accountable monarchy in which the destabilizing energies that create 'leftism' do not even exist. In this context, 'rightism' and 'leftism' both will only remain as academic and historical tropes—like Catharism or Lollardy."

In other words, Yarvin envisions a day when elected officials in our democratic republic become clichés relegated to the past, like Christian sects from the Middle Ages. Why do I bring up Curtis Yarvin? Only because Vice President J.D. Vance and technocrat Peter Thiel, both of whom yield powerful influence within President Trump's orbit, are two of his more famous disciples. Some have referred to Yarvin, Vance, and Thiel as "The Neo-reactionary Dream Team." According to journalist Melissa Ryan,

> *J.D. Vance's rhetoric will sound familiar to anyone who read Yarvin's work. Vance has cited Yarvin as an influence, but the connection runs deeper. Both Yarvin and Vance have the support and backing of Peter Thiel, an early Trump supporter in 2016 who gave a primetime speech at the 2016 convention. If Yarvin informed Vance's thinking, Thiel fueled his political ambitions by funding a Super PAC for Vance's 2022 Senate run. Without Thiel's financial backing, it's hard to imagine Vance would be in the Senate, much less the Republican nominee for Vice President.*

It is hard to overstate the significance of Yarvin and Thiel on J.D. Vance. And let us not forget, Vance is a heartbeat away from the presidency.

"Curtis Yarvin wants American democracy toppled, and he has some pretty prominent Republican fans," writes Andrew Prokop in an October 24, 2022, article for *Vox*. Prokop continues,

> *[Yarvin] stands out among right-wing commentators for being probably the single person who's spent the most time gaming out how, exactly, the U.S. government could be toppled and replaced — "rebooted" or "reset," as he likes to say — with a monarch, CEO, or dictator at the helm. Yarvin argues that a creative and visionary leader — a "startup guy," like, he says, Napoleon or Lenin was — should seize absolute power, dismantle the old regime, and build something new in its place.*

If that does not send chills down your spine, you really are asleep at the wheel. Let me summarize it for you. Donald Trump, whom many Christians naively view as a "Cyrus," or in some cases, a "savior" sent by God to rescue America, has surrounded himself with anti-democratic technocrats who want to abolish the constitution and install a king to rule America. Anyone have a problem with that? The future Antichrist is probably drafting his resumé for the position as we speak.

As with most things associated with the Luciferian agenda, it is seldom about what it is about. Aside from the biblical problems associated with

Christan nationalism, the fact is the movement is not organic to begin with. There is a much more sinister scheme at play. Just as the Nazis enlisted the help of pastors and Christian leaders in 1930s Germany, Satan's agents embedded within the U.S. government are rallying the Christian masses to help them usher in a new "golden age." It is much easier for the enemy to get his subjects to come along enthusiastically and cheerfully rather than at gunpoint.

As conservative Christians cheer the executive orders and sweeping initiatives being rolled out by Donald Trump in the early days of his second term, I cannot help but wonder whether anyone is paying attention to the real agenda. On January 23, 2025, President Trump spoke to a meeting of the World Economic Forum via remote live feed. He said, "We entered a new golden age of America this week," while hyping his Project Stargate plan to make America the "world capital of AI and crypto." The response to Trump's push for a new golden age reminds me of the group of women in George Orwell's *1984*, who cried out over something trivial while oblivious to their real plight. "Why was it that they could never shout like that about anything that mattered?" wondered Winston. He added, "Until they become conscious, they will never rebel."

Journalist Leo Hohmann is certainly conscious of what is happening. He writes,

> *[President Trump] said Stargate's plan to blanket America with new data centers, needed to power the next generation of AI capabilities, is going to require the U.S. to double its capacity to generate electric power.*
>
> *"We're going to get it done rapidly," Trump said.*
>
> *To speed up the process of getting the AI data centers built, Trump said he will use an emergency declaration to get new power-generation plants built adjacent to the new data-collection centers, which are needed to power the next phase of AI.*
>
> *He announced Stargate at the White House Tuesday, his first full day in office, while flanked by tech oligarchs Larry Ellison of Oracle and Sam Altman of OpenAI, and Softbank CEO Masayoshi Son. Ellison*

> *explained how AI would be used to propel forward a new generation of mRNA "vaccines" against countless diseases, including cancer, failing to mention that these injections are actually gene-therapy, not vaccines. But if he can get Trump's FDA to classify them as vaccines, Ellison knows that he will avoid all legal liability for the harm they will likely do to untold millions of Americans. We know this from the first round of mRNA injections that occurred during the Covid scare.*
>
> *The key takeaway from Trump's speech, and indeed his first three days in office, is "Emergency, Emergency, Emergency." This one word allows him to bypass the legislative branch of government and maximize his executive power. We are seeing government by emergency declaration play out before our very eyes. And the history of nations governing in this manner is very dark, indeed.*
>
> *While declaring an emergency might seem good and necessary for some things, like the border crisis created by Trump's predecessor, building data-collection centers that will likely be weaponized against the American people at some point is a dangerous stretch. AI is the most dangerous global trend currently in existence, and Trump is going full bore into a risky venture with private-industry billionaires who do not have the interests of we the people at heart.*

"The Party told you to reject the evidence of your eyes and ears. It was their final, most essential command," wrote Orwell. Could it be the "golden age" everyone is talking about is providing the infrastructure for, and setting the stage for, the coming full-spectrum planetary control grid spoken of in Revelation? The Trump administration is surrounded by a who's who of technocrats like Elon Musk, Peter Thiel, Sam Altman, and Mark Zuckerberg, and if the church does not wake up, we may all be eating horse sandwiches before long.

Why NAR is DOA

An expression of Christian nationalism that has made its way into the theological public square is known as the New Apostolic Reformation (NAR). As we discussed in Chapter Eight, whenever the word "new" is attached to a theological trend it should cause the church to pause and reflect. NAR is a network of Pentecostal and charismatic leaders who believe God has appointed modern-day apostles and prophets, and given them special power to work miracles, transform the church, establish God's Kingdom on earth, and hasten the return of Jesus Christ. C. Peter Wagner, whom we discussed in Chapter Six, was the founder of NAR.

Douglas Geivett and Holly Pivec provide a helpful summary and critique of the NAR movement.

> *A dangerous set of teachings is shaping America's worship songs, ministries, and political engagement. This new movement is influencing many churches and individual Christians, often without their realization.*
>
> *The New Apostolic Reformation movement (NAR) is a popular, fast-growing movement of Christians who claim God is giving new revelation through new apostles and prophets. They say they are giving strategies the church requires for all Christians to learn to work miracles—such as prophesying, healing the sick, and raising the dead—and "bring heaven to earth." This movement is called the New Apostolic Reformation because its leaders teach that a new reformation—much like the Protestant Reformation but even more significant—is underway.*
>
> *This reformation is bringing authoritative, governing apostles back to the church. All other church leaders, including pastors and elders, must "align" with them (a euphemism meaning they must submit to them). Those who follow the apostles will play a pivotal role in the unfolding of God's end-time plans for the world. Those who don't will sit on the sidelines as mere spectators.*

The rise of Christian nationalism in the church has given new life to NAR in recent years, especially with the election of Donald Trump to his first term in 2016. His defeat of Hillary Clinton was predicted by several NAR prophets and catapulted the movement back into the spotlight. His reelection in 2024, despite multiple assassination attempts, felony convictions, and the mischaracterization of the events of January 6, 2021, as an "insurrection," has added even more steam to the NAR resurgence.

When evaluated through the lens of sound biblical teaching, NAR is DOA—dead on arrival. The suggestion that God is issuing new revelation outside of Scripture through selected latter-day prophets flies in the face of the sufficiency of the Scriptures. The Bible says, "as His divine power has given to us all things that pertain to life and godliness, through the knowledge of Him who called us by glory and virtue" (2 Peter 1:3). We have all we need in the Bible. We do not need self-proclaimed prophets telling us to storm the White House and take back our country. God has already given the church our marching orders. We are to share the Gospel and eagerly await His return (Matthew 28:18-20; Philippians 3:20).

The Seven Mountain Mandate: A Dangerous Ascent

One more aspect of the political apostasy gripping the church in these last days is the so-called Seven Mountain Mandate, sometimes called the Seven Mountains of Dominionism. Rupert Taylor in a November 16, 2024, article entitled, "The Conservative Christian Seven Mountain Mandate," explains, "The concept of Christian Dominionism is woven into the fabric of the Seven Mountain Mandate. This says that God's Word, as expressed through the Bible, gives Christians the authority to take over the world. Some very powerful Americans, including Donald Trump, find this theology attractive." The Seven Mountain Mandate claims there are seven aspects of society that Christians must dominate before Christ will return. These are: family, religion, education, media, arts and entertainment, business, and government.

The Bible passage often cited in support of the notion that American

Christianity must conquer these "mountains" to usher in the messianic Kingdom comes from the Old Testament book of Isaiah. "Now it shall come to pass in the latter days that the mountain of the LORD's house shall be established on the top of the mountains, and shall be exalted above the hills; and all nations shall flow to it" (Isaiah 2:2). This amounts to quintessential proof-texting, the practice of taking a passage wildly out of context. Isaiah meant Israel, not the church, would be the most highly exalted on the earth during Messiah's eschatological earthly reign. The church is never mentioned in the Old Testament.

I mentioned TPUSA founder, Charlie Kirk, earlier. He is right in the middle of the Seven Mountain Mandate agenda. Jack Jenkins, in a January 7, 2025, article entitled, "Who is Charlie Kirk, the new Faith-Focused Enforcer of Trumpism?" writes,

> *Kirk founded Turning Point USA as a conservative student organization in 2012 after serving as a Senate campaign aide and dropping out of a junior college in his native Illinois. The organization now has 800 chapters on U.S. college campuses and claims to have more than a quarter million members, according to the TPUSA website.*
>
> *But in November 2019, Kirk made a pivot to faith: He co-founded the "Falkirk Center" at Liberty University with the evangelical Christian school's then-president, Jerry Falwell Jr. Kirk promoted the organization as a defender of "Judeo-Christian" beliefs until Falwell's career became mired in scandal, prompting Kirk to leave the project in March 2021.*
>
> *Undeterred, Kirk went on to forge a relationship with Pastor Rob McCoy, head of Godspeak Calvary Chapel of Thousand Oaks, in California, and together they founded Turning Point Faith. The effort reaches out to pastors nationwide to encourage them to embrace political messages as a church growth strategy, an initiative that has doubled as an engine for turning out the pastors' congregations for conservative candidates.*
>
> *The political messages Kirk and his allies espouse have also come to include constant defense of Trump as well as Christian nationalism.*

In a speech to the Conservative Political Action Conference (CPAC) on February 27, 2020, Charlie Kirk, said, "Finally we have a president that understands the seven mountains of cultural influence."

Kirk's journey is an interesting one, and it illustrates just how much the Christian nationalist movement has merged with, or been co-opted by, the Republican party. Lauren McKeithen explains.

> *In 2018, Charlie Kirk, a right-wing provocateur who founded the conservative activist group Turning Point USA, strongly criticized the evangelical political movement he now helps lead. Known then for primarily his work mobilizing college-age Republicans, Kirk described Jesus as tolerant and welcoming and denounced Christians' "sanctimonious approach" to homosexuality and other issues. He argued politics should be advanced through a "secular worldview" and slammed attempts by the evangelical right, starting in the 1970s, to "impose" their version of morality "through government policy."*
>
> *Kirk told the conservative commentator Dave Rubin in 2018, "We do have a separation of church and state, and we should support that." Kirk, now 30, has since reversed his position. It's a transformation that, according to political and religious scholars, embodies and reinforces a growing embrace of Christian nationalist thinking within the Republican Party in the era of Donald Trump. "There is no separation of church and state," Kirk said on his podcast in 2022. "It's a fabrication. It's a fiction. It's not in the Constitution. It's made up by secular humanists."*
>
> *Today, Kirk and Turning Point are dominant forces in the Republican Party and MAGA movement, working directly with the Trump campaign on voter outreach while reaching millions of listeners through Kirk's daily radio show and podcast. Along the way, Kirk has become one of the nation's most prominent voices calling on Christians to view conservative political activism as central to Jesus' calling for their lives.*

In a 2020 interview with podcaster Lucas Miles, Kirk said, "I've been a

Christian basically my whole life." He went on to say he first prayed to become a Christian when he was in fifth grade, explaining he "said the words," though it was several years before he understood what salvation truly meant. If this is true, and we have no reason not to take Charlie Kirk at his word, it is strange that his meteoric rise to prominence in the church only began recently. He has a long track record as a conservative voice in America, especially with college students, but his platform within the church seems to have originated about the same time the Christian nationalism resurgence was beginning.

The list of mainstream Christian leaders and politicians who have united under the Seven Mountain Mandate banner is long. Rodney Kennedy, in a September 29, 2022, article for *Baptist News Global,* claims, "Prominent Christian leaders who support such fringe movements as Seven Mountains Dominionism include David Barton, James Dobson, John Hagee, Bill Johnson, Lance Wallnau, and Paula White. Notable politicians who have embraced it include Michele Bachmann, Sam Brownback, Marjorie Greene Taylor, Lauren Boebert, Ted Cruz, Newt Gingrich, Mike Huckabee, Charlie Kirk, Sarah Palin, and Rick Perry." This list is by no means comprehensive, and undoubtedly some of the individuals swept up in the Seven Mountains Mandate are simply God-fearing, patriotic Americans, unaware of the heretical theology and questionable agenda of the movement. Regardless, traveling up the mountains of Christian nationalism is a dangerous ascent.

In the final chapter, we will review and summarize the many examples of the great last days apostasy we have covered in this book and suggest where the American church should go from here.

10

WHERE DOES THE CHURCH GO FROM HERE?

Your word is a lamp to my feet and a light to my path. (Psalm 119:105)

The entirety of Your word is truth, and every one of Your righteous judgments endures forever. (Psalm 119:160)

* * *

Robert James Fitzsimmons was a famous British-born boxer from the late 19th century. He spent his professional career fighting in Australia. Fitzsimmons gained notoriety as boxing's first three-division world champion. He won the Middleweight, Heavyweight, and Light Heavyweight titles, in that order. Michael Spinks was the first Light Heavyweight World Champion who went on to win the Heavyweight title, and Fitzsimmons was the first Middleweight Champion to win the Heavyweight belt. But Fitzsimmons is the only Heavyweight Champion to drop down and win the Light Heavyweight title.

Fitzsimmons had a professional record of 66 wins (59 by knockout), eight losses, four draws, 19 no-contests, and two no-decisions. One of his claims to fame is his appearance in *The Guinness Book of World Records* as the lightest heavyweight champion ever, weighing just 167 pounds when he won the title. Fitzsimmons never let his size, nor the size of his opponent, worry him. He once quipped, "The bigger they are, the harder they fall!" That saying became a common idiom to indicate the more powerful or successful someone is, the more noteworthy it is when they fail. This principle applies to individuals as well as institutions. For instance, when a small mom-and-pop shop goes out of business, it scarcely makes the local newspaper. But when a nationwide retail chain closes its doors, it is the lead story on CNN and Fox News.

The church is a divine institution, chosen by God in this present age to proclaim the Gospel to a lost and dying world. The church has been center stage in God's plan of the ages for nearly 2,000 years. There is no Plan B. If the church fails, it is disastrous. Sadly, as we have seen in the preceding chapters, the church has indeed failed, and "great is its fall," to borrow the words of Jesus (Matthew 7:27). The apostasy of the church, while tragic, is predicted in God's Word and constitutes a significant sign of the times as we await the Rapture. "For the time will come when they will not endure sound doctrine, but according to their own desires, because they have itching ears, they will heap up for themselves teachers; and they will turn their ears away from the truth, and be turned aside to fables" (2 Timothy 4:3–4).

Where does the church go from here? How should remnant Christians respond to the apostasy engulfing the church? Before answering those questions, let us review the manifestations of apostasy we discussed in the previous chapters.

The Evidence of Apostasy

We started with a look at biblical apostasy. Most Christians these days, and I dare say most pastors, exhibit a startling amount of ignorance when it comes to Bible knowledge. Theologian Michael Vlach cites biblical illiteracy as one of the most important issues facing the evangelical church in our day. George Barna's assessment is similar, "The Christian body in America is immersed in a crisis of biblical illiteracy." According to David R. Nienhuis,

Professor of New Testament at Seattle Pacific University,

> *For well over twenty years now, Christian leaders have been lamenting the loss of general biblical literacy in America. No doubt you have read some of the same dire statistics that I have. Study after study demonstrates how nearly everyone in our land owns a Bible (more than one, in fact) but few ever take the time to read it, much less study it closely. Indeed, while the Exploring Religious America Survey of 2002 reports that over 84 percent of Americans consider the Bible to be "very" or "somewhat important" in helping them make decisions in life, recent Gallup polls tell us that only half can name even one of the four Gospels, only a third are able to identify the individual who delivered the Sermon on the Mount, and most aren't even able to identify Genesis as the Bible's opening text.*
>
> *Upon hearing these figures (and many more are readily available), some among us may be tempted to seek odd solace in the recognition that our culture is increasingly post-Christian. Perhaps these general population studies are misplaced in holding secular people to Christian standards. Much to our embarrassment, however, it has become increasingly clear that the situation is really no better among confessing Christians, even those who claim to hold the Bible in high regard. Again, numerous studies are available for those seeking further reason to be depressed.*

My experience in Christian academia validates Nienhuis' findings. Christians today are shamefully ignorant when it comes to the most basic Bible facts.

During my years teaching at a Bible college, we were required to test incoming students on their knowledge of the Bible. The instrument we used was called the Bible Content Test (BCT). The BCT contained one hundred very basic questions like,

- *Who wrote the first four books of the New Testament?*

- *Who delivered the Sermon on the Mount?*
- *Who spent three days in the belly of a great fish?*
- *Who was thrown into the lion's den?*

Upon graduation, we tested the students again to track how much they had learned about the Bible during their time at the school. It helped us assess our effectiveness as teachers. Keep in mind, as a Bible college we attracted *Christian* students, many of whom planned to go on to seminary after completing their undergraduate degree. As the Assistant Academic Dean and Director of Baccalaureate Programs, I was keenly interested in the results of these tests each semester.

During my five years at the school, the average score among incoming freshmen was 30-35%! That was the *average* score, which means many students did even worse. My six children, most of whom were not even teenagers yet, could have scored much better. Thankfully, by the time the students graduated, most were scoring in the 80-90% range, a metric our Dean was quite proud of, especially given where the students had started. Nevertheless, the fact that incoming students, who represented the best and brightest of Christians—those who were preparing for vocational ministry—exhibited such biblical illiteracy, is a clear indication of biblical apostasy in the church.

Once you recognize just how little Christians in America know about the Bible, the other manifestations of apostasy in the American church are not so surprising. Eschatological views within the church are wildly off the mark. Replacement theology, sensationalist date-setting, and widespread disinterest in Bible prophecy are all key indicators of eschatological apostasy. Moral decay in American Christianity is rampant, so much so that the prevalence of immorality in the church matches its pervasiveness in the world. Most American churches today resemble social clubs. Worldly principles have impacted church music, counseling programs, and many other aspects of church ministry. Christian parents are subcontracting out the education of their children to godless government-controlled schools. The social apostasy in the church is undeniable.

The church's evangelistic enterprise in these last days continues to diverge from the clear, accurate, and urgent Gospel message. Works-based models remain the church's favorite false gospel, with never-ending variations emerging with increasing frequency. Within the arena of Christian higher education, biblical orthodoxy left the station a long time ago, leaving in its wake a glut of heretofore unheard-of heretical teachings. Without question, there is an epidemic of academic apostasy in the American church.

Political apostasy also has reached new heights. Most Christians care more about political parties than precious prenatal children. The Overton window has become an alfresco veranda where windows of moral discernment are not just wide open; they are non-existent. Rather than expecting more from their elected representatives, Christians today are comfortable choosing Evil over Evil-er. Political movements with tyrannical agendas have donned pseudo-spiritual clothing, adopted Christian-like terminology, and infiltrated the church. Like the children of Hamelin, Christians foolishly follow the delusive enticements of Pied Pipers beckoning them into church/government partnerships such as the New Apostolic Reformation and the Seven Mountain Mandate.

The great last days apostasy is upon us. "Now the Spirit expressly says that in latter times some will depart from the faith, giving heed to deceiving spirits and doctrines of demons" (1 Timothy 4:1). "For the time will come when they will not endure sound doctrine, but according to their own desires, because they have itching ears, they will heap up for themselves teachers; and they will turn their ears away from the truth, and be turned aside to fables" (2 Timothy 4:3–4). The American church has drifted past the point of no return. Most Christians lack the strength and resolve to stand firm. They are falling in line with the world and falling away from the Lord.

Yet, there is a remnant, as we discussed in Chapter Two. For those Christians with the courage to speak out when no one seems to be listening (Acts 18:9-10); for believers who desire to be found "without spot and blameless at our Lord Jesus Christ's appearing" (1 Timothy 6:14); for those who seek refuge in the "hope set before us" (Hebrews 6:18); there is a powerful resource to which we must cling as the "anchor of our souls" in these unsettling times (Hebrews 6:19). That resource is the Word of God.

The Centrality of the Word of God

As I write this closing chapter, people across America, indeed, throughout the world, are preparing to watch Super Bowl LIX. For the third year in a row (and five out of the last six), the Kansas City Chiefs will appear in the Big Game. There is one thing for sure; after so many years of the Chiefs monopolizing NFL news coverage, the only person you will ever hear ask, "Who is Taylor Swift?" is a *Jeopardy* contestant! As I thought about the upcoming Super Bowl—and I better mention the Philadelphia Eagles will be the Chiefs' opponent in the game, lest my friends in the "City of Brotherly Shove" take offense—I thought about the uniqueness of this game we Americans call "football."

In football, there is no game without the *football.* That is kind of the point. The *football* is the *sine qua non* of football. They do not call it, "Face Mask" or "Cleats." You need a *football* to play football. You can have shoulder pads, jerseys, mouth guards, helmets, Taylor Swift, and other ever-present football accouterments, but if there is no *football,* there can be no football game. Can you imagine the absurdity of teams lining up for the kickoff with no *football* on the tee? An imaginary football will not do. Football needs a real *football.*

The *football* is indispensable in so many ways. Without it, the referee has no way to determine if a touchdown is really a touchdown. "Has the ball crossed the goal line?" fans ask. "What ball?" replies the referee. When the chain gang runs onto the field to measure for a first down, what will they measure if there is no *football*? "Was it a catch, or did the receiver bobble the ball?" fans wonder. "What ball?" responds the referee. The Dez Bryant controversy of January 11, 2015, would not have occurred if there was no *football.* Field goals become a serious problem without a *football.* No more "doinks." Or, in the case of the 2018 NFC Wildcard game (another nod to the Eagles), no more "double doinks." And obviously without a football the term *Deflategate* would disappear from the pages of NFL history like a casualty of the Mandela Effect. The Patriots will have to find another way to cheat if football has no *football.*

You can have literally everything else associated with a football game, but without the *football,* your excuse for not mowing the lawn on Sunday afternoon disappears. The *football* is central to football. Here is the point. There is a central, indispensable component of Christianity that has been lost in the American church today. And when the church tries to be the church without this element, it looks as silly as a lineman tackling Pacheco only to discover Mahomes kept the ball on a bootleg.

The centrality of the Scriptures is what makes the church the church. If the Bible is not the foundation for the church, Christians may as well go mow the lawn. You cannot play football without a *football,* and you cannot be a church without the *Bible.* To help remnant Christians recalibrate our lives around the centrality of God's Word, I want us to examine the amazing, life-changing nature of this book. The Bible really is a book like no other.

The Bible Is Inspired.

The Bible changes lives because it is inspired by God, the Creator of the universe. It originates with Him. It is His self-revelation to mankind. The Bible is God's way of saying, "Here I am. Look at Me!" The Apostle Paul tells us, "All Scripture is given by inspiration of God…" (2 Timothy 3:16–17). The word "inspiration" comes from the Greek word *theopneustos* in Greek. This is the only time this word appears in the New Testament. It is a compound word combining *theos* (God) and *pneō* (breathe). Some English Bibles translate it woodenly, "God-breathed." The Bible really is, quite literally, "God's Word."

Inspiration deals with the source of the Bible. Although the Bible has over forty human authors, it has only one divine Author, God. Peter tells us, "knowing this first, that no prophecy of Scripture is of any private interpretation, for prophecy never came by the will of man, but holy men of God spoke as they were moved by the Holy Spirit" (2 Peter 1:20–21). The word "moved" in this passage is the Greek word *pherō,* meaning "to guide, direct, or lead." The word is used by Luke to describe the wind catching the sails of a ship and driving the ship across the sea (cf. Acts 27:17). As the human authors of Scripture wrote, they were carried along by the Holy Spirit so that what they recorded was precisely what God intended to communicate to us.

When Paul said, "All *Scripture* is given by inspiration," he used the word *graphē*, meaning "writings." It is where we get the English word, *graffiti*. It is not just the ideas or concepts of the Bible that are inspired, but the actual words themselves. The word *graphē* is used 51 times in the New Testament, and it is always translated "Scripture." The Bible contains words that come directly from God, and those words change lives. When Christians neglect the Bible, they do so to their own detriment.

The Bible Is Inerrant.

Because the Bible is "God-breathed," it is necessarily errorless, because God is perfect and incapable of being wrong. We call this the inerrancy of Scripture. Psalm 119 is largely a collection of prayers and meditations on the Word of God. This psalm contains a reference to God's Word in every one of the 176 verses except verses 84, 121, and 122. The psalmist used ten Hebrew synonyms for the Word of God. Words like law, judgments, testimonies, commandments, precepts, statutes, and word all convey the perfection of God's Word. "The entirety of Your word is truth, and every one of Your righteous judgments endures forever" (Psalm 119:160). "Your word is very pure; therefore Your servant loves it" (Psalm 119:140). "I know, O LORD, that Your judgments are right…" (Psalm 119:75). "Forever, O Lord, Your word is settled in heaven" (Psalm 119:89). "Therefore all Your precepts concerning all things I consider to be right…" (Psalm 119:128).

The Bible is the living, *written* Word of God. "For the word of God is living and powerful, and sharper than any two-edged sword, piercing even to the division of soul and spirit, and of joints and marrow, and is a discerner of the thoughts and intents of the heart" (Hebrews 4:12). Jesus Christ is the living, *incarnate* Word of God. "In the beginning was the Word, and the

Word was with God, and the Word was God. He was in the beginning with God. …And the Word became flesh and dwelt among us, and we beheld His glory, the glory as of the only begotten of the Father, full of grace and truth" (John 1:1–2, 14). Figure 14 illustrates the correlation between these two living revelations.

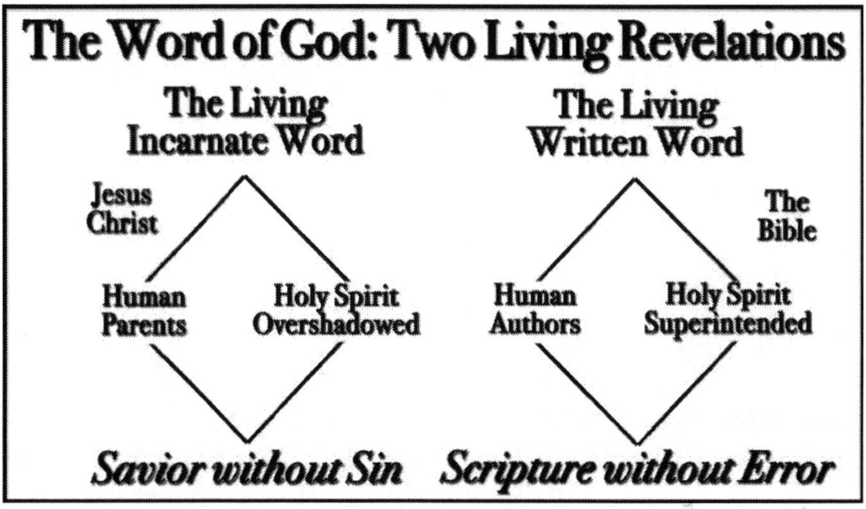

Figure 14

To say the written Word, the Bible, could have errors is tantamount to saying the incarnate Word, Jesus, could be sinful. The Bible is inerrant, and it changes lives.

The Bible Is indestructible.

Another reason the church needs to return to the centrality of God's Word in these last days is its indestructibility. At a time when everything around us is falling apart, the Bible endures forever. Note the last part of the verse I cited above. "The entirety of Your word is truth, and every one of *Your righteous judgments endures forever*" (Psalm 119:160; emphasis added). "Concerning Your testimonies, I have known of old that You have founded them forever"

(Psalm 119:152). I cited Psalm 119:89 earlier as well. Note the first word. "*Forever,* O Lord, Your word is settled in heaven" (Psalm 119:89; emphasis added). "The righteousness of Your testimonies is everlasting; give me understanding, and I shall live" (Psalm 119:144).

Jesus said, "For assuredly, I say to you, till heaven and earth pass away, one jot or one tittle will by no means pass from the law till all is fulfilled" (Matthew 5:18). A "jot" refers to the smallest letter of the Hebrew alphabet, the *yod.* A "tittle" is the tiny stroke of a pen that can change one letter into another letter. For example, in English, we can change a capital P to a capital R with one stroke. Because the Bible contains the very words of God, "not the smallest letter, nor the least stroke of a pen" will disappear (cf. Matthew 5:18, NIV).

The Bible is indestructible. It is the rock on which we stand, and it will be such until the living, incarnate Word, Jesus Christ, the King of Kings and Lord of Lords, returns to take the throne. David said, "My soul, wait silently for God alone, for my expectation is from Him. He only is my rock and my salvation; He is my defense; I shall not be moved. In God is my salvation and my glory; the rock of my strength, and my refuge, is in God. Trust in Him at all times, you people; pour out your heart before Him; God is a refuge for us. Selah" (Psalm 62:5–8). *Selah* is used seventy-one times in Psalms. Most scholars believe it is a musical notation in Hebrew signifying a rest to the singers and instrumentalists who performed the psalms. It inspires the reader to pause, think about, and praise God for what has just been said. Let me encourage you to think about the power of God's indestructible Word today.

The Bible Is Influential.

As far as we know, Mahatma Gandhi never trusted in Jesus Christ as his personal Savior. Even though he was not a Christian, he understood the power of God's Word. Gandhi once leveled a stinging indictment against the church when he said, "You Christians look after a document containing enough dynamite to blow all civilization to pieces, turn the world upside down, and bring peace to a battle-torn planet. But you treat it as though it is nothing more than a piece of literature." The church needs to bring the Word of God back to a place of centrality because it is influential. It changes lives. It cuts to the heart and differentiates that within us that longs for the flesh and that which longs for the spirit (Hebrews 4:12). Howard Hendricks pointed out, "When you read any other book on the planet, *you are doing something to it*. But when you read the Bible, *it is doing something to you*" (emphasis added).

Paul told the Thessalonian Christians the Word of God "effectively works in you who believe" (1 Thessalonians 2:13). The psalmist wrote, "Your word is a lamp to my feet and a light to my path" (Psalm 119:105). "The Word of God gives us strength when we are discouraged. "My soul melts from heaviness; strengthen me according to Your word" (Psalm 119:28). It alerts us to the dangers of sin. "Your word I have hidden in my heart, that I might not sin against You" (Psalm 119:11). It gives us understanding and brings blessing. "I understand more than the ancients, because I keep Your precepts" (Psalm 119:100). "Blessed is the man who walks not in the counsel of the ungodly, nor stands in the path of sinners, nor sits in the seat of the scornful; but his delight is in the law of the Lord, and in His law he meditates day and night" (Psalm 1:1–2).

There are four ways the Bible is influential in the Christian's life. Two of these relate to our beliefs and two relate to our behavior. They are listed in 2 Timothy 3:16-17, which says, "All Scripture is given by inspiration of God, and is profitable for doctrine, for reproof, for correction, for instruction in righteousness, that the man of God may be complete, thoroughly equipped for every good work." According to Paul, the Bible teaches us: (1) What to believe (doctrine); (2) What not to believe (reproof); (3) How to behave (instruction in righteousness); and (4) How not to behave (correction). What more does a person really need to know in life besides these four things? They pretty much cover it all. If you know what to believe and what not to believe, and how to behave and how not to behave, it will take you a long way.

The goal of Bible study is to change lives. The more the church neglects the Bible, the further it will drift from the Lord. God has given us His Word "as a lamp to our feet and a light to our path" (Psalm 119:105). Figure 15 illustrates how God's self-revelation to mankind goes from truth in His mind to changed lives that glorify Him.

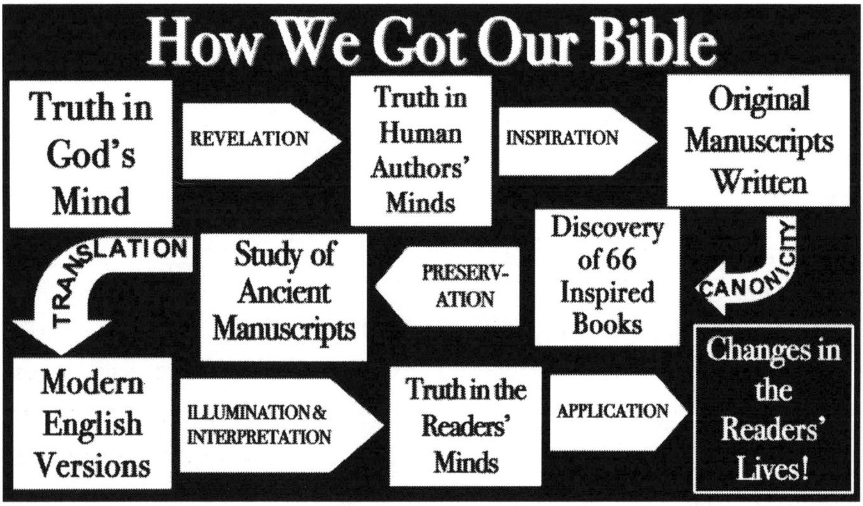

Figure 15

The Anvil or the Hammer?

My first full-time pastorate was at a traditional church on a downtown corner in a midwestern farming community. Founded in the 1840s, by the time I was installed, there had been more pastors of this Baptist church than presidents of the United States. The church had stained-glass windows and a bell tower. When the custodian rang the bell on Sunday mornings, the glorious sound could be heard for what seemed like miles, signifying it was time for worship. I can still remember the smell in the air and the beautiful fall colors as I watched parishioners walking to church from my office window on those mild autumn Sundays.

The traditional sanctuary was adorned with green carpet, brown-cushioned pews, and a shiny brass candelabra resting prominently on the communion table. Only two elderly ladies in the church were trained to play the 19th-century majestic pipe organ. It was used every Sunday, and on the uncommon occasion where neither organist was available, serious consideration was given to canceling services for the day. A church service with no organ music was borderline blasphemy back in that day! A choir loft occupied the space where most churches now have projection screens. I wore a suit and tie to preach, and the only power point I knew of was the one that solicited an occasional "Amen!" from my loyal deacon in the third row.

Much has changed in the American church over the last four decades. I no longer wear suits except for the occasional funeral or wedding, and sometimes not even then. Stained glass windows are rare; belfries are even rarer. I cannot remember the last time I saw or heard a pipe organ. Green carpet and padded pews have been replaced by theater seating and stained concrete floors. One thing that has not changed, however, is the power of God's Word. It is "living and active, and sharper than any two-edged sword" (Hebrews 4:12, NASB). As the remnant waits for the trumpet to sound, we must maintain a firm grip on the Word of God in the midst of the great last days apostasy. "Holding fast the word of life, so that I may rejoice in the day of Christ that I have not run in vain or labored in vain" (Philippians 2:16).

The Bible says, "So then faith comes by hearing, and hearing by the word of God" (Romans 10:17). That means faith for those who are lost and need to be eternally saved, comes by hearing the Word of God, namely, the Gospel. For those who are already saved, the faith needed to grow spiritually mature also comes by hearing the Word of God. Stay in the Word of God. "For the commandment is a lamp, and the law a light; reproofs of instruction are the way of life. (Proverbs 6:23). "Watch, stand fast in the faith, be brave, be strong" (1 Corinthians 16:13).

The Bible is inspired, inerrant, indestructible, and influential. John Clifford said it beautifully in his beloved poem:

Last eve I paused beside the blacksmith's door,

And heard the anvil ring the vesper chime;
Then looking in, I saw upon the floor,
Old hammers, worn with beating years of time.

"How many anvils have you had," said I,
"To wear and batter all these hammers so?"
"Just one," said he, and then with twinkling eye,
"The anvil wears the hammers out, you know."

And so, I thought, the Anvil of God's Word
For ages skeptic blows have beat upon;
Yet, though the noise of falling blows was heard,
The Anvil is unharmed, 'tis the hammers that are gone.

Too many Christians in the American church are swinging worldly hammers. If we want to be a remnant amid widespread apostasy, we must set the hammers aside and stand on the Anvil of God's Word.

As I mentioned in the Preface, it has been forty years since Brother Billy J. Crosby licensed me to the Gospel ministry, authorizing me to perform weddings, funerals, and other ecclesiastical duties. That framed Certificate of License still hangs on my wall today. Brother Billy's signature on the document has almost disappeared, faded through years of exposure to sunlight from my office window. I considered asking him to re-sign it. But then it occurred to me his influence in my life goes well beyond his endorsement on an official certificate. Far more valuable to me is the enduring truth he imparted from the pulpit Sunday after Sunday during my teenage years: "I believe the Bible is the Word of God."

EPILOGUE: A FEW GOOD FOOLS

Let no one deceive himself. If anyone among you seems to be wise in this age, let him become a fool that he may become wise. (1 Corinthians 3:18)

* * *

It is getting harder and harder to find a good fool these days. My ministry travels have taken me across all fifty U.S. states and several countries, where I have spoken in hundreds of churches, and rarely do I come across a bona fide fool. I had high expectations at a conference in Philadelphia a few years ago. Several hundred Christians packed into an auditorium, and I was on the lookout for a few good fools. As I got up to speak, I thought to myself, "Surely this place must be loaded with them." But if they were there, I could not find them.

Where have all the fools gone? There was a day when churches were chock-full of them, but not anymore. In times past, a quick survey of the cultural landscape would reveal a host of fools who stood out among the crowd. They were unique in their appearance, bold in their beliefs, and persuasive in their influence. Two thousand years ago a band of such fools "turned the world upside down" (Acts 17:6). They were called *Christians.*

Gradually, these once avant-garde fools have become the ensemble of the easily influenced. Rather than resembling a stew pot where the Christian component remains distinct from the other ingredients in the kettle, the church has become a melting pot of compromise and equivocation where most Christians are unwilling or unable to be different. No longer do we see a noticeable contrast between the attitudes and behaviors of Christ-followers and the worldview of the populace.

It occurs to me what the world needs most in these great last days are more fools. The world is filled with people who are "wise in their own eyes" and do not "fear the Lord" (Prov. 3:7). They are a dime a dozen. But such worldly wisdom is useless. "The Lord knows the thoughts of the wise, that they are futile." (1 Corinthians 3:20) What is desperately needed are Christians who are willing to be "fools for Christ's sake" (1 Corinthians 4:10). The world needs more Christians who understand "the message of the cross is foolishness" to the average person, Christians who do not mind the label "fool" because they realize the "foolishness of the message they preach" is precisely what the world needs. The foolishness of the cross is the only hope for a lost and dying world (1 Corinthians 1:18-20). Gregory the Great said, "God first gathered the unlearned, afterwards philosophers, nor has He taught fishermen by orators, but has subdued orators by fishermen."

This foolish message of salvation is simple, clear, and pervasive in Scripture. We are all sinners in need of a Savior. The penalty for sin is eternity in a literal place of torment called hell (Matthew 25:41; Luke 16:23; Revelation 20:11-15). Jesus Christ died for our sins and rose from the dead. He paid a debt He did not owe because we owed a debt we could never pay. In His great love, God has offered each of us forgiveness and eternal life if we will simply receive it by faith (Romans 5:8). Jesus said, "Most assuredly, I say to you, he who believes in Me has everlasting life" (John 6:47). Have you trusted in Jesus Christ, and Him alone, as the only One who can give you eternal life? If not, why not do so today?

If you are already a Christian, be wary of the temptation to fall away in these last days. Christians who blend in with the world, adopt secular thinking, and seek the approval of the masses, have forgotten that the "wisdom of this world is foolishness with God" (1 Corinthians 3:19). Would you rather be a fool in God's eyes or the world's eyes? The Apostle Paul put it well when he wrote, "If anyone among you seems to be wise in this age, let him become a fool that he may become wise" (1 Corinthians 3:18). Do you want to know what we really need if we are truly going to change the world? *Just a few good fools.*

If you need encouragement or if you would like more information about how to have eternal life, please contact me at Info@NotByWorks.org or call me at 1-800-895-1851.

Warmly,

J.B.H.

APPENDIX A: 160+ VERSES PROVING JUSTIFICATION BY FAITH ALONE

There are approximately 160 verses in the New Testament that clearly indicate salvation is based solely upon a person's faith in Jesus Christ as Savior.

Luke 7:48-50; 8:12; 18:42

John 1:7, 12; 2:23; 3:15, 16, 18, 36; 4:39; 4:41, 42; 5:24, 45-47; 6:29, 35, 40, 47; 7:38, 39; 8:24, 29, 30; 9:35-38; 10:24-26; 11:15, 25, 26, 41, 42; 12:36, 46; 13:19; 14:1-6, 17:20, 21; 19:35; 20:29, 31

Acts 3:16; 4:4, 32; 8:12, 37; 9:42; 10:43, 45; 11:17, 21; 13:21, 39; 14:1, 23, 27; 15:7, 9; 16:31; 17:4, 5, 11, 12; 18:8, 27; 19:4; 20:21; 21:25; 26:18

Romans 1:16, 17; 3:22, 25, 26, 27, 28, 30; 4:3, 5, 9, 11, 13, 16, 23, 24; 5:1, 2; 9:30, 32, 33; 10:4, 6, 9, 10; 11:20, 30-32; 15:13

1 Corinthians 1:21

2 Corinthians 4:4

Galatians 2:16, 20; 3:2, 5, 6, 7, 8, 9, 11, 14, 22, 24, 26; 5:5

Ephesians 1:13, 19; 2:8; 3:17

Philippians 1:29; 3:9

1 Thessalonians 1:7; 2:10; 4:14

2 Thessalonians 1:10; 2:12, 13; 3:2

1 Timothy 1:16; 3:16; 4:3, 10

2 Timothy 1:12; 3:15

Hebrews 4:2, 3; 6:12; 10:39; 11:6, 7, 31

James 2:23

1 Peter 1:21; 2:6, 7

1 John 5:1, 5, 10, 13

Jude 5

APPENDIX B: SEQUENTIAL ORDER OF END TIMES EVENTS

1. **The Rapture of the church** (1 Thess. 4:13-18; 1 Cor. 15:51-58; 2 Thess. 2:1-12; John 14:1-3)
2. **The Judgment Seat of Christ in heaven for all church-age believers** (1 Cor. 3:10-15; Rom. 14:10; 2 Cor. 5:10)
3. **The Marriage of the Lamb** (Rev. 19:7)
4. **Formation of a western alliance, probably led by the future Antichrist, that invades Egypt** (Dan. 11:40-43)
5. **Battle of Gog & Magog** (Ezek. 38-39). This battle unfolds as follows: [a] Formation of a Northern alliance against Israel (Ezek. 38); [b] Invasion of Israel by this Northern alliance (Ezek. 38:16); [c] The Western alliance protests (Dan. 11:44); [d] God supernaturally intervenes allowing the Western alliance to defeat the Northern alliance (Ezek. 38:21-39:7); [e] This gives the Antichrist world notoriety and paves the way for his reign of terror (Dan. 9:27)
6. **Unveiling of the Antichrist** (2 Thess. 2:3)
7. **The Antichrist signs a peace treaty with Israel** (Dan. 9:27; 1 Thess. 5:3). This constitutes the official commencement of Daniel's 70th Week (Matt. 24-25; Rev. 6-18). Daniel's 70th Week is also called The Great Day of the Lord's Wrath (Zeph. 1:15); Time of Jacob's Trouble (Jer. 30:7); The Tribulation (Matt. 24); Day of the Lord (many OT passages).
8. **The Seal Judgments begin** (Rev. 6).
9. **The ministry of the 144,000 worldwide witnesses begins** (Rev. 7, 14; cf. Matt. 24:14; 13:47-50).

10. **The ministry of the two special witnesses** begins (Rev. 11).
11. **The Antichrist kills the two witnesses** (Rev. 11).
12. **The two witnesses are resurrected** (Rev. 11).
13. **The Antichrist's reign of terror intensifies**. He sets himself up as God and demands worship (Dan. 9:27; Rev. 13; Matt. 24:15). This event is called the abomination of desolation.
14. **The trumpet judgments begin** (Rev. 8-9).
15. **The False Prophet, second in command to the Antichrist, takes on an increased role** (Rev. 13).
16. **The False Prophet controls commerce** (Rev. 13).
17. **There is severe persecution of Jews and all believers** (Rev. 12-13).
18. **The fall of geographic, political and ecclesiastical Babylon** (Rev. 18)
19. **The bowl judgments begin** (Rev. 15-16).
20. **As the Antichrist proceeds with his program, nations from the east (the Orient) will unite and attempt to stop him**. (Rev. 16:12-16).
21. The armies from the East and West will face off in a series of battles in an area around the mountains of Megiddo north of Palestine. **This campaign is called Armageddon** (Rev. 16:14; 19:17).
22. Climaxing the campaign of Armageddon, **Christ will return to judge the nations and establish His Kingdom** (Zech. 14:4; Matt. 25; Rev. 19:11-21).
23. **The Antichrist and False Prophet are cast into the Lake of Fire** (Rev. 19:17-21)
24. **Christ will judge the world** to see who may enter the Messianic Kingdom (Matt. 25:31-46).
25. **The Marriage Supper of the Lamb** takes place at the inauguration of the Messianic Kingdom (Rev. Rev. 19:9; Matt. 8:11).
26. **The millennial reign of Christ over the earthly Kingdom** (Rev. 20:1-6)
27. **The binding of Satan during the millennial reign** (Rev. 20:1-6)
28. **The loosing of Satan at the end of the millennium** (Rev. 20:7-10)

29. **One final battle between Satan and God called Gog and Magog (not the same as Ezek. 38-39) at the end of the millennium** (Rev. 20).
30. **The Great White Throne judgment of all unbelievers** (Rev. 20:11-15)
31. **The final destruction of Satan, the Antichrist, the False Prophet and all unbelievers** (Rev. 20:15)
32. **The destruction of the old heaven and old earth and the recreation of heaven and earth in sinless perfection** (Rev. 21)
33. **The Everlasting reign of Christ over the New Heaven and New Earth** (Rev. 21)

APPENDIX C: NON-NEGOTIABLES WHEN CHOOSING A LOCAL CHURCH

There are many factors to consider when choosing a local church. Here are a few that are non-negotiable.

1. The church should be **theologically conservative**. Meaning they hold to the inerrancy of Scripture, the deity of Christ, the doctrine of the Trinity, and other historic standards of Christian orthodoxy.
2. The church should preach a **clear, accurate, and urgent Gospel message**. Meaning they teach eternal salvation can never be attained by one's own efforts at moral improvement; through a promise or pledge to do better; through making a commitment of some kind to God; by turning from sin; through a willingness to stop sinning or improve one's behavior; nor through any other effort that relegates eternal salvation to some type of two-way contract or agreement between God and man. When it comes to eternal salvation, Jesus paid it all. It is nothing in our hands we bring, simply to the cross we cling! There is one giver: God. And one receiver: man. We receive the free gift of eternal salvation, fully paid for by the blood of Christ, by trusting Him and Him alone as the only one who can forgive our sin and save us from sin's penalty, namely, eternity in hell. **I would stay away from any church that espouses a Calvinistic view of salvation**.
3. The church should be **solidly dispensational**. Meaning they hold to a consistent literal, grammatical, and historical interpretation of

Scripture; they recognize the distinction between God's program for Israel and His program for the Church (i.e., they do not hold to replacement theology or covenant theology); they believe in the pre-tribulational Rapture of the church (i.e., the Rapture will occur prior to Daniel's 70th Week); and they are premillennial (Christ will return to earth to rule and reign for 1,000 years from Jerusalem).

4. The church should **teach the whole counsel of God**. Meaning they do not ignore the roughly 16% of the Bible that deals with unfulfilled end times prophecy. They should teach the Bible expositionally in context without spiritualizing or allegorizing the text.
5. The church should hold to a **young earth view of creation**. Meaning God spoke the world into existence in six, literal, 24-hour days, and the universe is roughly 6,000-8,000 years old.
6. The church should **exude grace** in all its practices and teachings. Meaning it is not legalistic.
7. The church should be **willing to take a stand against government** tyranny. Meaning if the government forbids churches from gathering in person to worship the Lord, or places other types of unbiblical restrictions on the church, the church will not comply.

BIBLIOGRAPHY

Adana, Kor. "What Is the Lutheran Church's Position on Homosexuality –..." Christian.net, March 3, 2024. https://christian.net/theology-and-spirituality/what-is-the-lutheran-churchs-position-on-homosexuality/#currentstanceandpoliciesofthelutheranchurchonhomosexuality_1_3

Akers, Alicia Sparks, and Jennifer Berry. "Endorphins: Effects and How to Boost Them." Medical News Today, January 26, 2004. https://www.medicalnewstoday.com/articles/320839.

Akin, Jon, and Nate Akin. *Concerns about Elevation Church.* Accessed January 21, 2025. https://baptist21.com/blog-posts/2014/concerns-about-elevation-church/.

Alcorn, Randy. "Does the Word 'Evangelical' Mean Anything Anymore?" Eternal Perspective Ministries, July 15, 2011. https://www.epm.org/resources/2011/Jul/15/does-word-evangelical-mean-anything-anymore/.

Alcorn, Randy. "The Doctrinal Crisis in American Evangelical Churches: What Can We Do?" Eternal Perspective Ministries, September 30, 2022. https://www.epm.org/resources/2022/Sep/30/doctrinal-crisis-evangelical-churches/.

"All Stanley Kubrick Movies Ranked." Rotten Tomatoes All Stanley Kubrick Movies Ranked Comments. Accessed January 4, 2025. https://editorial.rottentomatoes.com/guide/all-stanley-kubrick-movies-ranked/.

Allen, Gary. *None Dare Call It Conspiracy*. Seal Beach, CA: Concord Press, 1971.

American Film Institute. Accessed January 4, 2025. https://www.afi.com/.

Anders, Caroline. "US Records Highest Number of Abortions in a Decade, despite Bans." Yahoo! News, March 20, 2024. https://www.yahoo.com/news/us-records-highest-number-abortions-174317331.html.

"Andy Stanley Defends His Controversial LGBTQ Conference, Critics Respond: 'Anti-Christian.'" CBN, October 3, 2023. https://cbn.com/news/us/andy-stanley-defends-his-controversial-lgbtq-conference-critics-respond-anti-christian.

"Andy Stanley Speaks out from Pulpit after Controversial LGBTQ Conference, Critics Respond: 'Anti-Christian.'" Faithwire, October 2, 2023. https://www.faithwire.com/2023/10/02/andy-stanley-speaks-out-from-pulpit-after-controversial-lgbtq-conference-critics-respond-anti-christian/.

"Antisemitic Conspiracy Theories Abound around Russian Assault on Ukraine." ADL, March 3, 2022. https://www.adl.org/resources/article/antisemitic-conspiracy-theories-abound-around-russian-assault-ukraine.

Armstrong, John H. *The Compromised Church: The Cresent Evangelical Crisis*. Wheaton, Ill: Crossway Books, 1998.

Arndt, William, Frederick W. Danker, Walter Bauer, and F. Wilbur Gingrich. *A Greek-English Lexicon of the New Testament and Other Early Christian Literature*. Chicago: University of Chicago Press, 2000.

Atkinson, Grant. "Lutheran Church Has Drag Queen Take to the Pulpit during Sunday Service, Read Book to Kids." The Western Journal, December 18, 2021. https://www.westernjournal.com/lutheran-church-drag-queen-t

ake-pulpit-sunday-service-read-book-kids/.

Bailey, Chelsea. "'A Better Church Is Possible:' Methodists Celebrate as the Church Embraces the LGBTQ." CNN, May 5, 2024. https://www.cnn.com/2024/05/05/us/united-methodist-church-embraces-lgbtq-reaj/index.html
.

Barna, George. "Worldview Determines Views on Abortion - Arizona Christian University." Arizona Christian University - Transforming Culture With Truth, October 11, 2021. https://www.arizonachristian.edu/2021/10/11/worldview-determines-views-on-abortion/.

Barnhouse, Donald Grey. *Man's Ruin*. Grand Rapids, MI: Eerdmans Publishing Company, 1952.

Basham, Megan. *Shepherds for Sale: How Evangelical Leaders Traded the Truth for a Leftist Agenda*. New York, NY: Broadside Books, an imprint of HarperCollinsPublishers, 2024.

Bell, Rob, and David Vanderveen. *The Love Wins Companion: A Study Guide for Those Who Want to Go Deeper*. New York, NY: HarperOne, 2011.

Bell, Rob. *Love Wins For Teens: If God Threw a Party, Would Everyone Be Invited? Would You?* New York: Harper, 2013.

Bell, Rob. *Love Wins: A Book about Heaven, hell, and the Fate of Every Person Who Ever Lived*. New York: HarperOne, 2012.

Benjamin L. Corey. "BLC." Benjamin L. Corey, October 5, 2019. https://www.benjaminlcorey.com/.

Berding, Kenneth. "Dramatic Drop in Bible Reading: Why?" The Good Book Blog - Biola University Blogs, March 15, 2023. https://www.biola.ed

u/blogs/good-book-blog/2023/dramatic-drop-in-bible-reading-why.

Berding, Kenneth. "The Crisis of Biblical Illiteracy." Biola Magazine - Biola University Blogs, May 29, 2014. https://www.biola.edu/blogs/biola-magazine/2014/the-crisis-of-biblical-illiteracy.

Berkhof, Louis. *Systematic Theology*. 2nd ed. Grand Rapids, MI: Eerdmans, 1941.

Bernardi, Nicolò F, Erwan Codrons, Rita di Leo, Matteo Vandoni, Filippo Cavallaro, Giuseppe Vita, and Luciano Bernardi. "Increase in Synchronization of Autonomic Rhythms between Individuals When Listening to Music." Frontiers in physiology, October 17, 2017. https://pmc.ncbi.nlm.nih.gov/articles/PMC5651050/.

Bilek, Jennifer. "JB Pritzker, Jennifer Pritzker, & Synthetic Sex Identities." Tablet Magazine, June 14, 2022. https://www.tabletmag.com/sections/news/articles/billionaire-family-pushing-synthetic-sex-identities-ssi-pritzkers.

Bing, Charles C. "How to Share the Gospel Clearly." *Journal of the Grace Evangelical Society* 7, no. Spring (1994): 58–59.

Boyd, Gregory A. *God of the Possible: A Biblical Introduction to the Open View of God*. Grand Rapids, MI: Baker Books, 2011.

Bullinger, Ethelbert W. *A Critical Lexicon and Concordance to the English and Greek New Testament*. London: Longmans, Green, and Co., 1908.

Burns, Ray. "Bethel's False Gospel and Other Issues (Exploring the Worship Music Debate #3)." Onward in the Faith, June 13, 2024. https://onwardinthefaith.com/bethels-false-gospel-and-other-issues-exploring-the-worship-music-debate-3/.

Carless, Will. "As Trump Support Merges with Christian Nationalism, Experts Warn of Extremist Risks." USA Today, March 7, 2024. https://www.usatoday.com/story/news/investigations/2024/03/07/trump-christian-nationalism-extremist-threat/72869355007/.

Carlton, Genevieve. "Legendary Pastors Who Fell from Grace." Ranker, July 3, 2024. https://www.ranker.com/list/pastors-that-fell-from-grace/genevieve-carlton.

Carson, D. A. *Telling the Truth: Evangelizing Postmoderns.* Grand Rapids, Mich: Zondervan, 2010.

Carson, D. A. *The Gagging of God: Christianity Confronts Pluralism.* Michigan: Zondervan Publishing House, 1996.

Carter, Joe. "What Christians Should Know about the Enneagram." The Gospel Coalition, August 8, 2018. https://www.thegospelcoalition.org/article/the-faqs-what-christians-should-know-about-the-enneagram/.

Chafer, Lewis Sperry. *Salvation.* New York, NY: C.C. Cook, 1917.

"Charles Taze Russell." Wikiwand. Accessed January 13, 2025. https://www.wikiwand.com/en/articles/Charles_Taze_Russell.

Chavez, Nicole. "Antisemitic Incidents in the US Reached Record High Last Year, up 140% from 2022, Adl Says." CNN, April 16, 2024. https://www.cnn.com/2024/04/16/us/adl-antisemtism-2023-audit-reaj/index.html.

Chesterton, G. K. *Illustrated London News,* April 19, 1924.

Chesterton, G. K. *The Three Apologies of G. K. Chesterton: Heretics, Orthodoxy, & the Everlasting Man.* Bristol, United Kingdom: Mockingbird Press, 2018.

Clifford, John. "The Anvil of God's Word." *Poems about the Bible*. Accessed January 29, 2025. https://www.wholesomewords.org/poetry/biblepoems/anvil.html.

Cohn, Jennifer. "Shocking Online Manifesto Reveals Project 2025's Link to a Coordinated 'Christian Nationalism Project.'" Bucks County Beacon, July 10, 2024. https://buckscountybeacon.com/2024/03/shocking-online-manifesto-reveals-project-2025s-link-to-a-coordinated-christian-nationalism-project/.

Constable, Thomas L. "Tom Constables Expository Notes." Plano Bible Chapel. Accessed February 25, 2022. https://planobiblechapel.org/soniclight/.

Corey, Chad. "Austin Church Hosts Sunday Service Drag Show Called 'Drag Me to Church.'" ABC 6 News - kaaltv.com, August 24, 2022. https://www.kaaltv.com/archive/austin-church-hosts-sunday-service-drag-show-called-drag-me-to-church/.

Council on Foreign Relations. Accessed September 3, 2022. https://www.cfr.org/.

Crusading for Moral Authority: Christian nationalism and … Accessed January 27, 2025. https://onlinelibrary.wiley.com/doi/10.1111/socf.12619.

Dever, Mark E. "Communicating Sin in a Postmodern World." Essay. In *Telling the Truth: Evangelizing Postmoderns*, edited by D.A. Carson, 148. Grand Rapids, MI: Zondervan, 2000.

DeYoung, Kevin. "The Rise of Right-Wing WOKEISM." The Gospel Coalition, November 2, 2023. https://www.thegospelcoalition.org/reviews/christian-nationalism-wolfe/.

Dickens, Charles. *American Notes. Https://Www.Gutenberg.Org/Cache/Epub/675/Pg675-Images.Html,* 1842.

Dombovari, Adam. "Press Release: Doomsday Clock Set at 89 Seconds to Midnight, Closest Ever to Human Extinction." Bulletin of the Atomic Scientists, January 28, 2025. https://thebulletin.org/2025/01/press-release-doomsday-clock-set-at-89-seconds-to-midnight-closest-ever-to-human-extinction/.

"The Dominick Nati Show." Domenick Nati, October 4, 2021. https://domenicknati.com/.

"Doomsday Clock." *Bulletin of the Atomic Scientists,* August 28, 2024. https://thebulletin.org/doomsday-clock/.

"Dr. Strangelove." Wikipedia, December 26, 2024. https://en.wikipedia.org/wiki/Dr._Strangelove.

Eakman, B. K. *Walking Targets: How Our Psychologized Classrooms Are Producing a Nation of Sitting Ducks.* Raleigh, NC: Midnight Whistler Pub., 2007.

Ehrman, Bart D. "What Jesus Really Said about Heaven and Hell." *Time,* May 8, 2020. https://time.com/5822598/jesus-really-said-heaven-hell/.

Evans, Tony. *Tony Evans' Book of Illustrations: Stories, Quotes, and Anecdotes from More than 30 Years of Preaching and Public Speaking.* Chicago, IL: Moody Publishers, 2009.

Fee, Gordon D. *1 and 2 Timothy, Titus.* of *New International Biblical Commentary.* Peabody, MA: Hendrickson Publishers, 1988.

Fernando, Ajith. "The Urgency of the Gospel." Essay. In *Telling the Truth:*

Evangelizing Postmoderns, edited by D.A. Carson, 371–83. Grand Rapids, MI: Zondervan, 2000.

"Find an Affirming Church." GayChurch.org, August 20, 2021. https://www.gaychurch.org/find_a_church/.

Fox, Mira. "A Guide to the Most Notable Christian Nationalists Influencing the Nation." *The Forward*, November 7, 2024. https://forward.com/culture/672745/christian-nationalist-guide-influence-trump-election/.

Frazer, Gregg L. *The Religious Beliefs of America's Founders: Reason, Revelation, and Revolution*. Lawrence, KS: University Press of Kansas, 2014.

Fruits, Austin. "The Porn Epidemic: Problem, Consequence, and Hope." Josh.org, September 9, 2022. https://www.josh.org/the-porn-epidemic-problem-consequence-and-hope/.

Geivett, Douglas, and Holly Pivec. "The New Apostolic Reformation, a Threat within the Church?" Patheos.com, December 12, 2022. https://www.patheos.com/blogs/theologicalapologetics/2022/12/the-new-apostolic-reformation-a-threat-within-the-church/.

Goins-Phillips, Tré. "Charlie Kirk Opens up about His Christian Faith." Faithwire, September 11, 2020. https://www.faithwire.com/2020/09/11/charlie-kirk-opens-up-about-his-christian-faith/.

Green, Michael P., ed. *Illustrations for Biblical Preaching*. Grand Rapids, MI: Baker Books, 1989.

Greenblatt, Jonathan A. "The Growing Antisemitism among Young Americans." Time, March 21, 2024. https://time.com/6958957/growing-antisemitism-young-americans/.

Hanegraaff, Hank. *Christianity in crisis: The 21st Century.* Nashville, TN: Thomas Nelson, 2012.

Hardy, Elle. "The Rising Influence of the New Apostolic Reformation." *The New Republic,* November 28, 2023. https://newrepublic.com/article/167499/new-apostolic-reformation-mastriano-christian.

Hill, C.E. "N.T. Wright on Justification." *Ligonier Ministries,* January 23, 2010. https://learn.ligonier.org/articles/nt-wright-justification#user-content-fn-1.

Hindson, Edward E. *The Book of Revelation: Unlocking the Future.* Edited by Mal Couch and Ed Hindson. of Twenty-First Century Biblical Commentary Series. Chattanooga, TN.: Tyndale, 2002.

"Hitler's Letters and Notes Quotes by Adolf Hitler." *Goodreads.* Accessed January 9, 2025. https://www.goodreads.com/work/quotes/3113297-hitler-s-letters-and-notes.

Hixson, J. B. *Getting the Gospel Wrong: The Evangelical Crisis No One Is Talking About.* 3rd Edition. Tacoma, WA: True Grace Books, 2024.

Hixson, J. B. *NBW Book of Theological Charts, Diagrams, and Illustrations.* Falcon, CO: NBW, Inc., 2024.

Hixson, J. B. *The Gospel Unplugged: Good News Plain and Simple.* Falcon, CO: NBW, Inc., 2025.

Hixson, J. B. *The Great Last Days Deception: Exposing Satan's New World Order Agenda.* Falcon, CO: NBW, Inc., 2025.

Hixson, J. B. *Top 10 Reasons Why Some People Go to Hell: And the One Reason No One Ever Has to!* Larkspur, CO: Grace Acres Press, 2020.

Hixson, J. B. *Weekly Words of Life: 52 Devotionals to Warm Your Heart and Strengthen Your Faith*. Falcon, CO: NBW, Inc, 2020.

Hixson, J. B., and Mark Fontecchio. *What Lies Ahead: A Biblical Overview of the End Times.* Falcon, CO: NBW, Inc., 2024.

Hixson, J. B., Rick Whitmire, and Roy B. Zuck, eds. *Freely by His Grace: Classical Grace Theology*. Tacoma, WA: True Grace Books, 2024.

Hixson, J.B. "Not by Works." Not By Works Ministries. https://www.notbyworks.org/.

Hixson, J.B. *Spirit of the Antichrist: The Gathering Cloud of Deception Volume One*. Falcon, CO: Not By Works, Inc, 2022.

Hixson, J.B. *Spirit of the Antichrist: The Gathering Cloud of Deception Volume Two*. Falcon, CO: Not By Works, Inc, 2022.

Hixson, J.B. *Spirit of the False Prophet: Rise of the Global Technocracy*. Falcon, CO: Not By Works, Inc, 2023.

Hohmann, Leo. Trump pushes AI and Stargate in speech to World Economic Forum, January 23, 2025. https://leohohmann.substack.com/p/trump-pushes-ai-and-stargate-in-speech

"How Fast Is Technology Accelerating?" The Atlantic. Accessed January 22, 2025. https://www.theatlantic.com/sponsored/prudential-great-expectations/how-fast-is-technology-accelerating/360/.

"Humanity Is Not That Simple Yuval Noah Harari & Pedro Pinto." YouTube, June 6, 2023. https://www.youtube.com/watch?v=4hIlDiVDww4.

Ice, Thomas. "Why Date-Setting the Rapture Is Wrong - Scholars Crossing."

Liberty University Scholar's Crossing, May 2009. https://digitalcommons.liberty.edu/cgi/viewcontent.cgi?article=1057&context=pretrib_arch.

"Is Hillsong a Biblically Solid Church?" GotQuestions.org, April 2, 2015. https://www.gotquestions.org/Hillsong-Church.html.

Iserbyt, Charlotte. "The Deliberate Dumbing Down of America." Deliberate Dumbing Down. Accessed February 15, 2022. http://deliberatedumbingdown.com/ddd/.

Jackson, Gregg, and Steve Deace. *We Won't Get Fooled Again: Where the Christian Right Went Wrong and How to Make America Right Again.* United States: JAJ, 2011.

Jenkins, Jack. "Who Is Charlie Kirk, the New Faith-Focused Enforcer of Trumpism?" RNS, January 9, 2025. https://religionnews.com/2025/01/07/who-is-charlie-kirk-the-new-faith-focused-enforcer-of-trumpism/.

John Sanders, October 3, 2022. https://drjohnsanders.com/.

Johnson, Phil. "What's Wrong with Wright: Examining the New Perspective on Paul." Ligonier Ministries, January 27, 2010. https://learn.ligonier.org/articles/whats-wrong-wright-examining-new-perspective-paul.

Jones, James Earl. "A Bombardier's Reflection On 'Strangelove.'" *The Wall Street Journal,* November 16, 2004. https://www.wsj.com/articles/SB110055719231074627.

Kennedy, Rodney. "Richard Land Says He Has 'read about' Some Christian Nationalists but He Doesn't Know Any." *Baptist News Global,* September 29, 2022. https://baptistnews.com/article/richard-land-says-he-has-read-about-some-christian-nationalists-but-he-doesnt-know-any/.

Kronenberger, Louis. "The Spirit of the Age." *The American Scholar* 21, no. 1 (1951): 10–20. https://www.jstor.org/stable/41206850.

LaClear, Marc. "Why Date-Setting for the Rapture Always Fails (and What We Can Learn From." Pre, July 1, 2024. https://pretribtruth.com/why-date-setting-for-the-rapture-always-fails-and-what-we-can-learn-from-it/.

"Lauren Daigle Doesn't Know If Homosexuality Is A Sin." YouTube. Accessed January 10, 2025. https://www.youtube.com/watch?v=rXKHm_KPw6o.

"Lauren Daigle Is Now in the Middle of a Political Wrestling Match." RELEVANT, January 25, 2021. https://relevantmagazine.com/culture/music/lauren-daigle-is-now-in-the-middle-of-a-political-arm-wrestling-match/.

"Lauren Daigle on Homosexuality: I Can't Say One Way or the Other If It's a Sin, 'I'm Not God.'" The Christian Post, December 1, 2018. https://www.christianpost.com/news/lauren-daigle-homosexuality-sin-im-not-god.html.

Liddell, Henry George, Robert Scott, Henry Stuart Jones, and Roderick McKenzie. *A Greek-English Lexicon*. Oxford: Clarendon Press, 1996.

"List of Dates Predicted for Apocalyptic Events." Wikiwand. Accessed January 13, 2025. https://www.wikiwand.com/en/articles/List_of_predicted_dates_of_the_end_of_the_world.

Louw, J. P., and Eugene A. Nida. *Greek-English Lexicon of the New Testament: Based on Semantic Domains*. New York: United Bible Societies, 1989.

MacArthur, John F. *Hard to Believe: The High Cost and Infinite Value of Following Jesus*. Nashville, TN: Thomas Nelson, 2006.

MacArthur, John F. *Romans*. Chicago, IL: Moody, 1991.

MacArthur, John F. *The Gospel According to Jesus What Does Jesus Mean When He Says "Follow Me"?* Grand Rapids, MI: Zondervan, 1989.

MacArthur, John. *Faith Works: The Gospel According to the Apostles.* Dallas: Word Pub, 1993.

MacGavran, Donald A. *Understanding church growth.* Grand Rapids , MI: Eerdmans, 1976.

MacInnis, Adam. "Report: 26 Million Americans Stopped Reading the Bible Regularly during COVID-19." Christianity Today, June 27, 2023. https://www.christianitytoday.com/2022/04/state-of-bible-reading-decline-report-26-million/.

Marrs, Jim. *The Rise of the Fourth Reich: The Secret Societies That Threaten to Take over America.* New York: Harper, 2009.

McCall, Ross. "Silent Epidemic: The Church's Problem with Porn:" Josh McDowell Ministry. Accessed January 20, 2025. https://www.cru.org/tt/en/communities/ministries/josh-mcdowell-ministry/silent-epidemic-the-churchs-problem-with-porn.html.

McGee, John Vernon. *Thru the Bible with J. Vernon McGee. vol. 5, 1 corinthians-revelation.* Nashville, Cambridge, Ontario: Thomas Nelson Publishers: Lawson Falle, 1983.

McGraw, Meridith. "Scenes from a Celebration of the Same-Sex Marriage Law at Mar-a-Lago," December 16, 2022. https://www.politico.com/news/2022/12/16/celebration-same-sex-marriage-mar-a-lago-00074441.

McKeithen, Lauren. "Charlie Kirk, Who Once Pushed a 'secular Worldview,' Now Fights to Make America Christian Again." *Beliefnet News*, June 18, 2024. https://www.beliefnet.com/columnists/news/2024/06/charlie-kirk-who-once-pushed-a-secular-worldview-now-fights-to-make-america-christian-again.

Meacham, Jon. "The End of Christian America." Newsweek, April 3, 2009. https://www.newsweek.com/meacham-end-christian-america-77125.

Miller, Paul D. "What Is Christian Nationalism?" Christianity Today, June 27, 2023. https://www.christianitytoday.com/2021/02/what-is-christian-nationalism/.

Miller, Russ. *Creation, Evolution & Science Ministries*. Accessed January 24, 2025. https://creationministries.org/.

Milligan, George, and James Hope Moulton. *The Vocabulary of the Greek Testament*. Peabody, MA: Hendrickson, 1997.

Montgomery, Peter. "Charlie Kirk Teams up with Dominionists and Christian Nationalists in 'Spiritual War.'" *People For*, February 27, 2020. https://www.peoplefor.org/rightwingwatch/post/charlie-kirk-teams-up-with-dominionists-and-christian-nationalists-to-wage-spiritual-war.

Mooney, Britt. "7 Signs We Are in the End Times and Last Days." *Christianity.com*, January 16, 2025. https://www.christianity.com/wiki/slideshows/7-signs-we-are-in-the-end-times.html.

Moore, E. Ray. *Let My Children Go: Why Parents Must Remove their Children from Public Schools Now*. Columbia, SC: Gilead Media, 2002.

Morgan, Robert J. *Nelson's Complete Book of Stories, Illustrations, and Quotes*. Nashville, TN: Thomas Nelson Publishers, 2000.

Morris, Henry M. "Why the Gap Theory Won't Work." *Institute for Creation Research*, November 1, 1997. https://www.icr.org/article/why-gap-theorywont-work/.

Murphy, Caryle. "Most U.S. Christian Groups Grow More Accepting of Homosexuality." *Pew Research Center*, December 18, 2015. https://www.pewresearch.org/short-reads/2015/12/18/most-u-s-christian-groups-grow-more-accepting-of-homosexuality/.

Mwaura, Maina, and Tony Evans. *The Influential Mentor: How the Life and Legacy of Howard Hendricks Equipped and Inspired a Generation of Leaders.* Toronto: Moody Publishers, 2023.

Neely, Mark E. *The Abraham Lincoln Encyclopedia.* New York: Da Capo, 1984.

Nelson, Jeff. "Lauren Daigle Says Some Christians Thought She 'went to the Dark Side' after Appearing on 'Ellen' (Exclusive)." *People.com*, May 18, 2023. https://people.com/music/lauren-daigle-reflects-on-ellen-degeneres-show-controversy-backlash/.

Netland, Harold A., and Keith E. Johnson. "Why Is Religious Pluralism Fun—and Dangerous?" Essay. In *Telling the Truth: Evangelizing Postmoderns*, edited by D.A. Carson, 50 n. 5. Grand Rapids, MI: Zondervan, 2000.

The New King James Version. Nashville: Thomas Nelson, 1982.

Newell, William R. *The Book of Revelation.* Chicago: Moody Press, 1935.

Newman, Alex. *Indoctrinating our Children to Death: Government Schools' War on Faith, Family & Freedom—and How to Stop It.* Pinecrest, FL: Liberty Sentinel Press, 2024.

Niebuhr, H. Richard. *The Kingdom of God in America.* Middletown, Concticut: Wesleyan University Press, 1988.

Nienhuis, David R. "The Problem of Evangelical Biblical Illiteracy." *Modern Reformation*, January 1, 2010. https://www.modernreformation.org/resources/articles/the-problem-of-evangelical-biblical-illiteracy.

North Cook News. Accessed January 21, 2025. https://northcooknews.com/.

Okholm, Dennis L., and Timothy R. Phillips. "Introduction." Essay. In *Four Views on Salvation in a Pluralistic World*, edited by Dennis L. Okholm and Timothy R. Phillips. Grand Rapids, MI: Zondervan, 1995.

Orwell, George. *1984*. Paris: Gallimard, 1972.

Osunsami, Steve, and Sean Keane. "Churches Close their Doors as Fewer Americans Attend," *ABC News*, December 28, 2024. https://apple.news/ABdDO-xgGQTiJdPDqG6RV-A.

Park, Madison. "Timeline: A Look at the Catholic Church's Sex Abuse Scandals." CNN, June 29, 2017. https://www.cnn.com/2017/06/29/world/timeline-catholic-church-sexual-abuse-scandals/index.html.

Patheos. "5 Reasons Christians Are Rejecting the Notion of Hell." *TIME*, August 28, 2014. https://time.com/3207274/5-reasons-christians-are-rejecting-the-notion-of-hell/.

Perloff, James. *The Shadows of Power: The Council on Foreign Relations and the American Decline*. Appleton, WI: Western Islands, 1989.

Perry, Samuel L, Andrew L Whitehead, and Joshua B Grubbs. "Save the Economy, Liberty, and Yourself: Christian Nationalism and Americans' Views on Government Covid-19 Restrictions." *Sociology of Religion*, December 29, 2020. https://pmc.ncbi.nlm.nih.gov/articles/PMC7798614/.

Perry, Ty. "Answering Evangelical Anti-Semitism." *The Friends of Israel Gospel Ministry*, January 14, 2022. https://www.foi.org/2022/01/14/answering-evangelical-anti-semitism/.

Peter Thiel: Bio, LGBT, orientation and more - LGBT stars. Accessed September 19, 2022. https://lgbtstars.org/star/peter-thiel.

Pinnock, Clark H. *The Most Moved Mover*. Carlisle: Paternoster, 2001.

Pinnock, Clark H. *The Openness of God: A Biblical Challenge to the Traditional Understanding of God*. Downers Grove, IL: InterVarsity Press, 1994.

Piper, John. *What Jesus Demands from the World*. Wheaton, IL: Crossway Books, 2006.

Popli, Nik. "Trump's Early Actions Mirror Project 2025." *TIME*, January 24, 2025. https://time.com/7209901/donald-trump-executive-actions-project-2025/.

Portmann, John. *In Defense of Sin*. New York: Palgrave Macmillan, 2003.

Post, Kathryn. "Mennonite Church USA Passes Resolution Committing to LGBTQ Inclusion." *RNS*, June 2, 2022. https://religionnews.com/2022/06/02/mennonite-church-usa-passes-resolution-committing-to-lgbtq-inclusion/.

Price, Lee. "10 Evangelist Preachers Who Fell from Grace." *Listverse*, January 16, 2015. https://listverse.com/2015/01/16/10-evangelist-preachers-who-fell-from-grace/.

Project 2025 | Presidential Transition Project. Accessed January 27, 2025. https://www.project2025.org/.

Prokop, Andrew. "Curtis Yarvin Wants American Democracy Toppled. He Has Some Prominent Republican Fans." *Vox*, October 24, 2022. https://www.vox.com/policy-and-politics/23373795/curtis-yarvin-neoreaction-redpill-moldbug?utm_source=substack&utm_medium=email.

Prokop, Andrew. "The Jerry Falwell Jr. Scandal, Explained." *Vox*, August 25, 2020. https://www.vox.com/2020/8/25/21399954/jerry-falwell-jr-resigns-scandal-liberty.

Quigley, Carroll. *The Anglo-American Establishment: From Rhodes to Cliveden*. Rancho Palos Verdes, CA: GSG & Associates, 1981.

Quigley, Carroll. *Tragedy and Hope: A History of the World in Our Time*. San Diego, CA: Dauphin Publications, 2014.

Radmacher, Earl D. *What the Church is All About: A Biblical and Historical Study*. Chicago, IL: Moody Press, 1978.

"Research - Arizona Christian University." Arizona Christian University - Transforming Culture With Truth. Accessed January 10, 2025. https://www.arizonachristian.edu/culturalresearchcenter/research/.

"Robert Fitzsimmons." *Encyclopædia Britannica*. Accessed January 28, 2025. https://www.britannica.com/biography/Robert-Fitzsimmons.

Roberts, Chad. "How Should Christians React to the Global Surge in Antisemitism?" *Christianity.com*, April 29, 2024. https://www.christianity.com/wiki/christianity-qa/how-should-christians-react-to-the-global-surge-in-antisemitism.html.

Rogers, Kristen, Megan Marples, and Rachel Ramirez. "Doomsday Clock 2024: When Will the World End and How Long Do We Have on Earth?" *CNN*, January 23, 2024. https://www.cnn.com/2024/01/23/world/dooms

day-clock-2024-climate-scn/index.html.

Rohrbough, Brian. "The Culture of Death." *NBW Ministries Podcast,* December 17, 2024. https://notbyworks.org/media/zd4s37y/1093-the-culture-of-death.

Rothkopf, David. *Superclass the Global Power Elite and the World They Are Making*. New York: Farrar, Straus and Giroux, 2009.

Ryan, Melissa. "JD Vance-Peter Thiel-Curtis Yarvin 2024: The Neoreactionary Dream Team." *Bucks County Beacon,* July 22, 2024. https://buckscountybeacon.com/2024/07/jd-vance-peter-thiel-curtis-yarvin-2024-the-neo reactionary-dream-team/.

Ryrie, Charles C. *Basic Theology: A Popular Systematic Guide to Understanding Biblical Truth*. Chicago: Moody Press, 1999.

Ryrie, Charles Caldwell. *Dispensationalism*. Chicago, IL: Moody Publishers, 2007.

Ryrie, Charles Caldwell. *Revelation*. Chicago: Moody Press, 1968.

Sanders, John. *The God Who Risks: A Theology of Providence*. Downers Grove, IL: IVP Academic, 2007.

Sankaran, Vishwam. "Thousands Flock to 'AI Jesus' for Gaming, Relationship Advice." *The Independent,* June 15, 2023. https://www.independent.co.uk/tech/ai-jesus-chatbot-religion-advice-b2358128.html.

Saucy, Robert. "The So-Called Gap Theory." *Aspen Ridge Church,* January 29, 2014. https://www.aspenridgechurch.org/blog/2014-1-29-onwolq7g5uiunqq9ju2wrf4z9q4g8m/.

Schreiner, Patrick. "The Good, the Bad, and the Ugly of Christian Nationalism." *The Gospel Coalition,* April 26, 2023. https://www.thegospelcoalition.org/article/good-bad-ugly-christian-nationalism/.

Schwab, Klaus, and Thierry Malleret. *The Great Narrative*. Cologny/Geneva, Switzerland: Forum Publishing, 2022.

Shakespeare, William. "The Merchant of Venice." 1598.

Shapiro, Ben. *Facts Don't Care about Your Feelings.* Hermosa Beach, CA: Creators Publishing, 2019.

Shortt, Bruce N. *The Harsh Truth about Public Schools.* Vallecito, CA: Chalcedon Foundation, 2004.

Showers, Renald E. *The Most High God: A Commentary on the Book of Daniel.* Bellmawr, NJ: Friends of Israel Gospel Ministry, Inc., 1982.

Skousen, W. Cleon. *The Naked Communist.* Cutchogue, NY: Buccaneer Books, 1958.

Slick, Matt. "What Is Dominion Theology?" *Christian Apologetics & Research Ministry*, December 29, 2024. https://carm.org/carm/what-is-dominion-theology/.

Smietana, Bob. "Churches Continue to Sing Hillsong and Bethel despite Controversies." *Christianity Today*, August 17, 2024. https://www.christianitytoday.com/2023/07/hillsong-bethel-controversy-worship-music-study/.

Smith, Christie. "San Francisco Church Hosts Its First Ever 'Drag Queen Bible Story Hour.'" *NBC Bay Area*, June 19, 2023. https://www.nbcbayarea.com/news/local/san-francisco-drag-queen-bible-story-hour/3254933/.

Smith, Colin S. "The Ambassador's Job Description." Essay. In *Telling the Truth: Evangelizing Postmoderns,* edited by D.A. Carson, 85. Grand Rapids, MI: Zondervan, 2000.

Springmeier, Fritz. *Bloodlines of the Illuminati.* Denver, CO: Pentracks Publications, LLC, 2007.

Stallard, Michael. "'An Open View of God...Does He Change?,'" 2001.

Stallard, Mike. *The Books of First and Second Thessalonians: Looking for Christ's Return.* Chattanooga, TN: AMG Publishers, 2009.

"Stances of Faiths on LGBTQ+ Issues: Evangelical Lutheran Church In..." *Human Rights Campaign.* Accessed January 20, 2025. https://www.hrc.org/resources/stances-of-faiths-on-lgbt-issues-evangelical-lutheran-church-in-america.

Stanley, Andy. "Messages." Messages | *North Point Community Church.* Accessed January 9, 2025. https://northpoint.org/messages/.

Stormer, John A. *None Dare Call It Education.* Florissant, MO: Liberty Bell Press, 1999.

Taylor, Rupert. "The Conservative Christian Seven Mountain Mandate." *Hubpages.com,* November 16, 2024. https://discover.hubpages.com/politics/the-conservative-christian-seven-mountain-mandate.

"Ted Haggard Talks." *Oprah.com,* June 30, 2009. https://www.oprah.com/oprahshow/ted-haggard-and-his-wife-talk-about-the-gay-sex-scandal.

Thomas, Robert L. *New American Standard Hebrew-Aramaic and Greek Dictionaries: Updated Edition.* Anaheim: Foundation Publications, Inc., 1998.

Thomas, Robert L. *Revelation Exegetical Commentary (2-Volume Set)*. Chicago: Moody Publishers, 2016.

Toader, Corneliu, Calin Petru Tataru, Ioan-Alexandru Florian, Razvan-Adrian Covache-Busuioc, Bogdan-Gabriel Bratu, Luca Andrei Glavan, Andrei Bordeianu, David-Ioan Dumitrascu, and Alexandru Vlad Ciurea. "Cognitive Crescendo: How Music Shapes the Brain's Structure and Function." *Brain sciences*, September 29, 2023. https://pmc.ncbi.nlm.nih.gov/articles/PMC10605363/.

"Turning Point USA." *Turning Point USA*. Accessed January 27, 2025. https://www.tpusa.com/.

"Turning Point USA." YouTube. Accessed January 27, 2025. https://www.youtube.com/user/theturningpointusa.

Turtel, Joel. *Public Schools, Public Menace: How Public Schools Lie to Parents and Betray Our Children*. New York: Liberty Books, 2004.

"U.S. Antisemitic Incidents Skyrocketed 360% in Aftermath of Attack in Israel, According to Latest ADL Data." ADL, January 17, 2024. https://www.adl.org/resources/press-release/us-antisemitic-incidents-skyrocketed-360-aftermath-attack-israel-according.

"Unconditional Conference." EMBRACING THE JOURNEY. Accessed January 9, 2025. https://www.embracingthejourney.org/unconditional-conference.html.

Vlach, Michael. "The 9 Most Important Issues Facing the Evangelical Church." *Christian Forums*, May 9, 2006. https://christianforums.net/threads/the-9-most-important-issues-facing-the-evangelical-church.948/.

Walvoord, John F. *The Revelation of Jesus Christ*. Chicago: Moody Press,

1966.

Walvoord, John F., and Roy B. Zuck, eds. *The Bible Knowledge Commentary: An Exposition of the Scriptures*. Wheaton, IL: Victor Books, 1985.

Walvoord. *Daniel: The Key to Prophetic Revelation*. Chicago: Moody Press, 1973.

"Watch Trump's Full Virtual Address to the World Economic Forum." *NBCNews.com*, January 23, 2025. https://www.nbcnews.com/video/watch-trump-s-full-virtual-address-to-the-world-economic-forum-230072389677.

Welch, Craig. "The Rise and Fall of Mars Hill Church." *The Seattle Times*, September 13, 2014. https://www.seattletimes.com/seattle-news/the-rise-and-fall-of-mars-hill-church/.

Wells, David F. "Introduction: The Word in the World." Essay. In *The Compromised Church: The Present Evangelical Crisis*, edited by John H. Armstrong, 31–32. Wheaton, IL: Crossway Books, 1998.

"Which Presbyterian Church Truly Supports Homosexuality?" *Western Church*, August 8, 2024. https://westernchurch.net/churches/which-presbyterian-church-truly-supports-homosexuality/#Which_Presbyterian_Churches_Have_Embraced_LGBTQ_Inclusion.

Whisenant, Edgar C. *88 Reasons Why the Rapture Will Be in 1988*, 1988. https://ia601206.us.archive.org/14/items/ReasonsWhyTheRaptureWillBeIn1988PDF/14080011-88-Reasons-Why-The-Rapture-Will-Be-in-1988.pdf.

Whitcomb, John C., and Henry M. Morris. *The Genesis Flood: The Biblical Record and Its Scientific Implications*. Phillipsburg, NJ: P & R Publishing, 2011.

Whitehead, Andrew L., and Samuel L. Perry. *Taking America Back for God: Christian Nationalism in the United States.* New York, NY: Oxford University Press, 2020.

"Why Do so Many Evangelical Churches Support LGBTQ?" *BibleAsk LIVE,* October 15, 2024. https://bibleask.org/live/why-do-so-many-evangelical-churches-support-lgbtq/.

Wilson, Jr., Robert Evans. "The Most Powerful Motivator." *Psychology Today,* September 23, 2009. https://www.psychologytoday.com/us/blog/the-main-ingredient/200909/the-most-powerful-motivator.

Wolf, Naomi. *The End of America Letter of Warning to a Young Patriot.* White River Junction, VT: Chelsea Green Publishing, 2021.

Woods, Mark. "Intolerable Cruelty? How Evangelicals Are Rethinking the Doctrine of Hell." *Christian Today,* April 1, 2018. https://www.christiantoday.com/article/intolerable-cruelty-how-evangelicals-are-rethinking-the-doctrine-of-hellexecute1/86826.htm.

Wright, N. T. *What Saint Paul Really Said: Was Paul of Tarsus the Real Founder of Christianity?* Grand Rapids, MI: William B. Eerdmans Publishing Company, 2014.

Zauzmer, Julie. "Antisemitic Beliefs Spreading Among Evangelical Christians in America." *The Independent,* August 23, 2019. https://www.independent.co.uk/news/world/americas/antisemitism-evangelical-christian-bible-trump-us-a9077016.html.

Zylstra, Sarah Eekhoff. "More Women Sue Bill Gothard and IBLP, Alleging Sexual Abuse." *Christianity Today,* July 15, 2020. https://www.christianitytoday.com/2016/01/more-women-sue-bill-gothard-iblp-alleging-sexual-abuse/.

About the Author

Dr. J. B. Hixson is the founder and president of Not By Works Ministries. An author, pastor, and national conference speaker, Dr. Hixson has written fourteen books and contributed to many theological journals and other Christian publications. He earned his B.A. from *Houston Baptist University*: Th.M. from *Dallas Theological Seminary*; and Ph.D. from *Baptist Bible Seminary*. He has served on the faculties and adjunct faculties of nine colleges and seminaries. When he is not traveling for speaking engagements, he is in the pulpit at Plum Creek Chapel in Sedalia, CO where he serves as the Lead Pastor. J. B. and his wife Wendy have been married for thirty-two years and have six children and one granddaughter. For more information about Dr. Hixson, or to schedule a speaking engagement, please visit www.NotByWorks.org or download the free NBW Ministries app from the App Store or Google Play Store.

Also by J.B. Hixson

J. B. Hixson is the author of fourteen books and hundreds of articles in theological journals, magazines, newspapers, blogs, and newsletters. To purchase books, streaming video, and other resources by Dr. Hixson, please visit NotByWorks.org/Store.

Spirit of the Antichrist: The Gathering Cloud of Deception Volume One

Is the stage being set for the tyrannical rule of the Antichrist? Volume One unveils the Luciferian Conspiracy. Satan and his earthly co-conspirators are deceiving the world as they roll out the New World Order. His accomplices are exposed as they pull the strings of world affairs and build an empire cloaked in deception. Realities you never knew existed are revealed in this riveting book. Sometimes lies are hidden in plain sight.

Spirit of the Antichrist: The Gathering Cloud of Deception Volume Two

Volume Two delves further into the dark realm of the Luciferians as the spirit of the Antichrist escalates in these last days. The world is on the verge of a great Satanic reset that will bring with it full spectrum planetary surveillance and control. Transhumanism, perversion, paranormal activity, Christian persecution, and more are on the rise as the powerful globalists get closer and closer to their end game. Hold on tight! The information in Volume Two is not for the fainthearted.

Spirit of the False Prophet: Rise of the Global Technocracy

The the first two volumes in the Spirit of the Antichrist series exposed various ways Satan's accomplices are pulling the strings of world affairs and building an empire cloaked in deception, setting the stage for the arrival of the Antichrist. *Spirit of the False Prophet* continues the investigation into the Luciferian Conspiracy by digging deeper into the role of the Antichrist's henchman, the False Prophet. How will AI, biometric surveillance, digital currency, and a global ID system pave the way for the coming global technocracy and the mark of the Beast?

The Great Last Days Deception: Exposing Satan's New World Order Agenda

Satan's lies have swept the globe and continue to dominate the headlines of our time. These falsehoods serve to advance his agenda in very direct ways. Even many Christians have become unwitting and unknowing captives of Satan's global deceptive scheme. We live in a frightening world of lies and hidden agendas. It is a world of spiritual realities, cosmic battles, unseen enemies, and demonic principalities. It is imperative that we "examine everything carefully" and "hold fast to that which is good" (1 Thessalonians 5:21). When we wake up to the world as it really is, it can be terrifying. Yet, wake up we must if we are to survive this *Great Last Days Deception*.

What Lies Ahead: A Biblical Overview of the End Times

"One immediately noticeable quality of this book that strikes the reader is its rare combination of clarity, readability, thoroughness, and doctrinal soundness. Every major aspect of eschatology is explained in simple, practical, and understandable terms, backed by an abundance of Scripture references and thoughtful interaction. While the subject of eschatology may intimidate some believers, there are thirty charts and diagrams that clarify and simplify the subjects being discussed. I highly recommend this book if you're looking for an affordable, easy-to-understand yet thorough overview of Bible prophecy that explains why God's prophetic revelation is so relevant and needed for Christians today. Maranatha!" -Tom Stegall, Duluth Bible Church

Getting the Gospel Wrong: The Evangelical Crisis No One Is Talking About (3rd Edition)

"J. B. Hixson's book is not only the most readable, the clearest, and most concise book on what the gospel is and is not that I have read, it continues to serve as a reference work to which I return again and again. … Hixson accomplishes a rare feat in today's theological world: he is both sharply analytical and interesting. If you want one book on the subject of the gospel which says it all and says it well, this is it!" -Dr. Mike Halsey, Pastor, Hangar Bible Fellowship

The Gospel Unplugged: Good News Plain and Simple
"'The difference between the right word and the nearly right word,' said Mark Twain, 'is the difference between lightning and a lightning bug.' In *The Gospel Unplugged,* using clear biblical content, clever, original illustrations, and refreshing certainty, Dr. Hixson reveals the difference between the gospel and the nearly right gospel, between grace and nearly grace. The distinction is important because the consequences are eternal. Thanks, Dr. Hixson, for writing a necessary book for our pluralistic culture." -Timothy K. Christian, DMin, ThD., Professor of Theology, Mid-America Baptist Theological Seminary

Weekly Words of Life: 52 Devotionals to Warm your Heart and Strengthen your Faith
These short, inspirational devotionals will rekindle your love for God's Word. Readers agree, *Weekly Words of Life* is:

"Heartwarming!"
"Creative!"
"Encouraging!"

Freely By His Grace: Classical Grace Theology

Why is God's grace so amazing and important? *Freely by His Grace* provides a comprehensive survey of the many biblical facets and themes related to God's grace. It has 17 chapters plus indexes (over 500 pages) by 14 different authors presenting a classical Free Grace view. Topics covered include: the definition of Free Grace theology, the biblical theme of God's grace, the meaning of the gospel of grace, 1 Corinthians 15, Lordship Salvation, discipleship, the nature of saving faith, repentance, regeneration and the order of salvation, eternal security, assurance of salvation, sin, practical sanctification, rewards and the judgment seat of Christ, dispensationalism and its link to Free Grace, missions, evangelism, and disciplemaking.

Top 10 Reasons Some People Go to Hell: And the One Reason No One Ever Has To!

"Of all of the doctrines revealed in the Bible, the doctrine of salvation is certainly the most important since a correct understanding and response to this doctrine determines where a soul spends eternity, heaven or hell. Yet, despite its importance, the evangelical church seems to be growing progressively inaccurate and even apathetic concerning how the great salvation truths of Scripture are communicated to the lost. That is why I am delighted with this new volume written by my friend Dr. J.B. Hixson not only arguing for the simplicity of the gospel but holding forth it's truth in light of perpetual misunderstandings of it. I am always delighted to endorse Dr. Hixson's work since he is one of the few scholars who correctly understands the true grace position of Scripture and has the right theology necessary to rightly divide the Word of God on this critically important topic."

–Dr. Andy Woods, Pastor, Sugar Land Bible Church; President, Chafer Theological Seminary

NBW Chart Book

The *NBW Book of Theological Charts, Diagrams, & Illustrations* contains over 100 of Dr. Hixson's most requested full-color charts from his conferences and lectures across the country. These are easily duplicated on a color printer for use in your own teaching/preaching ministry.

The NBW Ministries App

Download the free NBW Ministries app from the App Store or Google Play Store and keep up with our ministry. Access our video content, speaking schedule, live streams, Prayer Board, online store, and more!